HYPNOTHERAPY SCRIPTS

SCRIPTS

A Neo-Ericksonian Approach to Persuasive Healing
Second Edition

HYPNOTHERAPY SCRIPTS

A Neo-Ericksonian Approach to Persuasive Healing
Second Edition

Ronald A. Havens, Ph.D.
and
Catherine Walters, M.A., L.C.S.W.

Routledge
Taylor & Francis Group

LONDON AND NEW YORK

Published by
Routledge
Taylor & Francis Group
711 Third Avenue
New York, NY 10017

Published in Great Britain by
Routledge
Taylor & Francis Group
27 Church Road,
Hove, East Sussex
BN3 2FA

First issued in paperback 2015

Routledge is an imprint of the Taylor and Francis Group, an informa business

© 2002 by Taylor & Francis Group, LLC

ISBN 13: 978-1-138-86961-5 (pbk)
ISBN 13: 978-1-5839-1365-9 (hbk)

Library of Congress Cataloging-in-Publication Data

Catalog record is available from the Library of Congress

**Visit the Taylor & Francis Web site at
http://www.taylorandfrancis.com**

**and the Routledge Web site at
http://www.routledge.com**

*This is still dedicated to
the ones we love.*

CONTENTS

PART I
CONCEPTS AND INSTRUCTIONS

PART II
SCRIPTS

PREFACE
TO SECOND EDITION

Psychotherapy today is at a crossroads, pulled between technology and tradition. On the one hand, forces such as managed care and research on brief behavioral and cognitive therapies lead therapists toward highly structured impersonal techniques directed at precise goals. On the other hand, research on wellness and disease prevention, along with a burgeoning clinical interest in spirituality and diverse forms of cultural wisdom, promote the healing effects of focused awareness and positive expectations, the benefits of rituals and symbols, the power of relationships, and the personal value of "soul."

We are re-creating our book, *Hypnotherapy Scripts*, as a response to these two seemingly diverse modes of thought. The poetic stories and metaphorical communication patterns incorporated into our hypnotic techniques create therapeutic change efficiently and effectively but they also provide a healing relationship within which deeper personal meanings may be explored. Thus, the hypnotic approach we present here allows therapists to incorporate the best of both of these worlds into their practice. It promotes the rapid accomplishment of precise cognitive or behavioral goals while encouraging the development of a deeper appreciation for and sense of self.

This revised edition reflects changes in our own professional work over the past decade as well as suggestions and requests for specific additions from colleagues. Furthermore, it incorporates ideas derived from recent research on wellness and positive psychology as well as recent neurological and psychological research on the role of unconscious processes in everyday life. Taking each of these influences into account, we are adding instructions for creating your own scripts, modifying and eliminating many of our original scripts, adding new scripts, and updating our discussion of the hypnotherapeutic process.

For instance, this edition contains several new induction scripts as well as examples of hypnotherapy scripts for many clinical issues not mentioned in our original text. These issues include divorce, midlife crisis, natural childbirth, parenting, public speaking, the debilitating effects of chemotherapy, fear of medical and dental procedures, recovery from the traumatic effects of natural and manmade disasters, and unfulfilled spiritual longings.

This edition also contains a more detailed presentation regarding the use of direct hypnotherapeutic techniques and a new chapter devoted exclusively to our Diagnostic Trance process. In addition, our list of underlying assumptions now includes the postulate that "Comfort is the primary goal of therapy." Although originally implied throughout this book, we now realize that this concept is so crucial that it deserves special emphasis. Finally, and perhaps most importantly, in an effort to promote the construction of new hypnotherapeutic interventions for each unique problem and personality, we now offer a chapter with detailed instructions for writing your own hypnotherapy sessions.

The chance to write a second edition of our book is a rare and precious opportunity. But the privilege of adding new content to a book we thought was set in stone is nothing compared to the rare and precious opportunity that therapists offer their clients. If revising a book can be a joy, imagine the wonder of revising your life and your Self. That is priceless, and that is why this field is so exciting to us.

One of the things we have not changed in this edition of our book, therefore, is our basic goal. As with the first edition, our goal is to convey the therapeutic potential of hypnosis and provide the straightforward instruction, encouragement, and support needed for all therapists to use it. Obviously, we hope that those who found the first edition of this text to be useful will find this version to be even more valuable. At the same time, however, we also hope that this book will encourage new readers to at least incorporate hypnotic forms of communication into their practices, whether or not they decide to use "hypnosis" *per se*.

A colleague recently asked us, "Is hypnosis psychotherapy?" Given recent research on topics such as automaticity, somatic awareness, priming, expectation, and focused attention, we believe that a better question is, "Why would anyone try to do psychotherapy without it?"

PREFACE
TO FIRST EDITION

This book offers simple and straightforward instructions on how to do hypnotherapy. We maintain that hypnotic trance is a common everyday phenomenon that every student or professional can and should learn to utilize in a therapeutic manner. Anyone who has ever lulled a child to sleep with a bedtime story or used an analogy to convey a new idea already has engaged in virtually the same procedures we employ during hypnotherapy. It is not a strange or exceedingly difficult process.

Our goal is to strip from hypnosis the shroud of secrecy and confusion that you may have encountered already in your efforts to learn more about it. Some authors tell you that there is no such thing as hypnosis, whereas others claim that hypnotherapy is so powerful and complicated that it requires years of study. Some professionals warn that trance is a dangerous foray into the realm of malevolent subconscious forces, whereas others suggest that it is only a matter of good role-playing. What is the dedicated practitioner to think or to do?

Our Neo-Ericksonian approach to hypnotherapy is derived directly from the work of Milton H. Erickson, M.D., a man who is widely recognized as the foremost hypnotherapist of the century. Erickson described hypnosis as a valuable therapeutic tool for enhancing a client's self-awareness and facilitating therapeutic communications. He used it to persuade his clients to assume responsibility for healing themselves and give them the skills they needed to do so. Because Erickson was a consummate therapist as well as a master hypnotist, he was able to use this tool in ways that would be difficult to describe, much less duplicate. On the other hand, the basic tool itself is relatively simple, and learning how to use it to create useful therapeutic intervention is not difficult.

In the following pages we describe this tool called hypnotherapy and discuss what it can and cannot do. We also present specific guidelines for using it in different situations for different purposes. To be more specific, we begin with an overview of the assumptions underlying our approach. Next we provide a summary of the concepts and procedures involved in a typical hypnotherapy session. The remainder of the book consists exclusively of a series of scripts designed to guide your learning about hypnotherapeutic interventions in a step-by-step manner. We offer verbatim examples of trance inductions, metaphorical and direct suggestions for various types of presenting problems, and trance termination procedures. An audiocassette tape recording was developed in conjunction with this book to help you learn how to experience trance and to speak in a trance-inducing manner. Combine the book and the audiocassette and you have the basis for effective hypnotherapy.*

At first you may feel as constricted by our instructions and scripts as an artist working on a paint-by-numbers painting. Eventually, however, you will begin to develop an appreciation for the structure and potentials of this approach and will venture far beyond the guidelines we have provided. At that point you will have became a hypnotherapist.

Hypnotherapy can be an exciting and worthwhile adjunct to any therapeutic practice. Furthermore, when conducted in the Ericksonian manner presented here it can provide clients with a comfortable opportunity to explore and build upon their own unconscious resources. It is not intrusive or authoritarian, and it is not a power trip for the hypnotherapist. It is your chance to give a gift to your clients—the gift of peaceful inner awareness and the ability to relax deeply enough to recognize and use resources that might otherwise be overlooked or misused.

When we began this project, our intention was to produce a conceptual framework and set of guidelines that would make hypnotherapy an accessible and useful tool for counselors and therapists whose backgrounds, clientele, and professional affiliations were as diverse as our own. We felt that if we could produce a truly collaborative integration of our own varied interests and hypnotherapeutic approaches, then perhaps the end product

---

*Now available as an audio CD, for more information visit www.routledgementalhealth.com

would have the broadest possible appeal and utility. Thus, although Catherine was exclusively responsible for constructing the material on habit patterns and Ron developed the chapter on pain management, every other word in the remainder of this book is the product of long hours of discussion, revision, and debate. We leave it to you to determine whether this process accomplished our purpose. Your comments, questions, or suggestions are more than welcome and greatly appreciated.

ACKNOWLEDGMENTS

The authors would like to express their sincere appreciation to those who made this second edition possible and helped shape its contents. First and foremost we must again gratefully acknowledge Milton H. Erickson, M.D., whose inspiration and influence continues to guide us as it did when we wrote the first edition. We can rightfully say that without him, none of this would have been possible.

We also would like to thank the readers of the first edition of *Hypnotherapy Scripts*, whose enthusiastic support and suggestions for additions gave us the impetus to consider taking on this revision project. Then, of course, there are our clients, who continue to stimulate new ideas and teach us what they need and works for them. They have always been our best teachers.

While serving as Acquisitions Editor for Brunner-Routledge, Bernadette Capelle expressed "excitement" about a second edition of our book. Her comments meant a lot to us. George Zimmar, also Acquisitions Editor for Brunner-Routledge, was equally enthusiastic, supportive, tolerant, and helpful. His patience and cooperation when faced with our many questions and requests are a tribute to his professionalism.

Ron would like to offer his special thanks to the University of Illinois at Springfield for granting his request for a sabbatical leave to work on this revision and to his colleagues in the Department of Psychology for leaving him alone long enough to finish it.

We both would like to thank Larry Shiner and Marie Havens for their editorial improvements, senses of humor, and support. And, of course, we continue to be immensely grateful to everyone else we mentioned in the Acknowledgments section of the first edition, including, but not limited to, Elizabeth M. Erickson, Theresa Eytalis, Stephen Gilligan, Carol Lankton, Stephen Lankton, John Miller, Sandy Mollahan, Ernest Rossi, Kay Thompson, and Jeffrey Zieg.

PART I

Concepts and Instructions

1

A NEO-ERICKSONIAN ORIENTATION

The goal of this book is to provide you with the understandings, instructions, and confidence you need to incorporate Neo-Ericksonian forms of communication and persuasion into your practice now. Even if you never actually do "hypnosis" with a patient, this approach offers a way of speaking to people that is captivating, calming, reassuring, inspiring, and therapeutically productive.

This book originally grew out of our experiences as workshop leaders training therapists and physicians in the art of Ericksonian hypnotherapy. We carefully outlined the necessary concepts for them. We compulsively instructed participants in the hypnotherapeutic process. We taught our groups how to devise unique metaphors and anecdotes. In short, we gave them all the basics we thought they would need to become competent hypnotherapists. Yet, when practice sessions began we were faced with something we had not counted on: many participants became tongue-tied and self-conscious. They simply did not know what to say and the more they struggled the less they could do. We soon discovered that our exhortations to "trust your unconscious mind" just did not do the trick. They wanted us to tell them exactly what to say and how to say it. In other words, they wanted a script.

THE EFFECTIVENESS OF SCRIPTS

Our first script was a simple induction script that we incorporated into the practice sessions of our workshops. The Simulation Induction Script in Chapter 4 of this book is a modified version of that original script. The workshop participants not only expressed gratitude for the structure and guidance this script provided to their practice sessions, they also seemed to acquire an effective hypnotic style much more rapidly than they had without it. Furthermore, by the end of the workshop, they demonstrated more confidence in their ability to do hypnotherapy and seemed more comfortable with the idea of actually trying it with their clients.

Although these early impressions were encouraging, we had no objective evidence that they were accurate. Accordingly, we decided to empirically study the impact of using a prepared script on learner confidence. The subjects for our study were thirteen graduate students in psychology and related fields who volunteered to participate in a free one-day workshop and research project on hypnotherapy. The entire morning was spent providing didactic information on trance, trance induction procedures, hypnotherapy, and trance termination. These lectures were followed in the afternoon by a demonstration of trance induction and arm levitation. The participants were then randomly divided into two groups for a practice session. The first group contained seven participants. They were each given a trance induction script, which contained suggestions for an arm levitation (a modified version of the Eye Fixation and Arm Levitation Ratification Induction Script presented in Chapter 4 of this book) and were told to pair up and take turns reading it to each other. The other group of six participants met in a different room and they simply were told to pair up and practice an induction with the goal of obtaining an arm levitation. Using presession and postsession questionnaires with the participants, and postsession rating scales with the hypnotic subjects, we discovered not only that those participants who used the scripts felt more confident, but also their actual success with subjects (measured in terms of trance depth, arm levitation, and learning) was significantly higher. In the group working without scripts, for example, only one subject experienced arm levitation, whereas all subjects in the script group experienced it. (A more detailed account of our method and results is given in Appendix A.)

The results of this simple study confirmed our hypotheses regarding the value of hypnosis scripts as a way to increase practitioner skills and self-confidence. These results also prompted our subsequent decision to provide scripts for every step in the hypnotherapeutic process. The first edition of this book, published in 1989, was the product of that decision. Practitioners responded enthusiastically, and other authors have since followed our example by providing hypnotherapy scripts of their own (e.g., Brickman, 2000; Hammond, 1990; Hunter, 1994).

Although this book contains many hypnotherapy scripts, it also contains the basic concepts that underlie our Neo-Ericksonian approach and explicit instructions for creating your own hypnotherapy scripts. Our intent is to facilitate your development as a hypnotherapist, not merely to provide scripts that you can use. Thus, it is necessary for you to begin with a thorough understanding of the rationale behind the content and structure of our scripts.

The understandings you will need in order to use the scripts presented in this book and create your own are relatively simple and straightforward. The Neo-Ericksonian approach to hypnotherapy is not an arcane practice based on complex theoretical abstractions or mystical notions. The procedures we use and the messages we convey in hypnotherapy and psychotherapy derive from a few basic observations about people, therapy, and the nature of trance itself. These observations are easy to understand, they are consistent with current research, and they can be verified by personal experience.

In the remainder of this chapter we will discuss the eight assumptions about people and therapeutic change that form the foundation for our Neo-Ericksonian psychotherapeutic and hypnotherapeutic approaches. In Chapter 2 we will describe the Diagnostic Trance process, a technique that emerges from and captures the essence of these basic assumptions. An understanding of the rationale and potential utility of the Diagnostic Trance process sets the stage for Chapter 3, where we examine the nature of hypnotic trance and review the basic principles of hypnotherapy.

Our eight fundamental assumptions are derived primarily from the teachings and writings of Milton H. Erickson, M.D. Although we call them assumptions here, we actually think of them as givens or truisms. Each can stand alone as an empirically and observationally verifiable summary of a particular aspect of human functioning and therapeutic change. When these fundamental assumptions and their implications are considered as a whole, they explain the usefulness of a variety of therapeutic techniques, not just the hypnotherapy techniques we present in this book. Thus, no matter what form of therapy you now use, you may find that your approach either may already implicitly recognize or could benefit directly from these observations regarding human functioning.

PAIN IS THE PRIMARY SYMPTOM

Orienting Assumption #1: Pain is what motivates clients to seek therapy.

The common underlying feature of virtually all problems presented by therapy clients is emotional pain and suffering. Whether the presenting complaint is anxiety, depression, problems in a relationship, feelings of inadequacy, or whatever, pain and its consequences are the client's fundamental reason for seeking help.

We began developing this understanding largely as a result of an observation offered by Dr. Erickson during a lecture he gave in San Francisco in 1965. On that occasion he said:

> Every patient that walks into your office is a patient that has some kind of a problem. I think you'd better recognize that problem, that problems of all patients—whether they are pain, anxiety, phobias, insomnia—every one of those problems is a painful thing subjectively to that patient, only you spell the pain sometimes as p-a-i-n, sometimes you spell it p-h-o-b-i-a. Now, they're equally hurtful. And therefore, you ought to recognize the common identity of all of your patients. And your problem is, first of all, to take this human being and give him some form of comfort. And one of the first things you really ought to do is to let the patient discover where he really does have that pain. (cf. Havens, 1985, p. 152)

Because of our involvement in hypnosis, clients suffering from physical pain are often referred to us. As we worked with these individuals along with our traditional therapy clients, the validity and significance of Erickson's remarks became increasingly apparent. It is psychic pain and suffering that motivates people to contact therapists, and therapy involves replacing that suffering with comfort.

We emphasize pain as a central feature of our clients' experience primarily because pain is easier for most people to understand than psychopathology. The experiential qualities, psychological consequences, and interventions required to cope with pain and suffering are relatively simple and easy to grasp in comparison to the complex theoretical systems often associated with many psychiatric disorders. This is true for both clients and therapists.

Mental health professionals, for example, can be so firmly wedded to specific theoretical explanations for particular diagnostic problems that it becomes difficult for them to examine and treat these problems in an objective manner. There is a tendency to impose hypothetical constructs instead of exploring the unique sources of discomfort of each individual. If a client says he or she is depressed, the clinician may immediately begin to look for "learned helplessness" and serotonin deficiencies, or prescribe specific cognitive techniques deemed appropriate for depression. If the same client had instead complained of problems with a spouse or job dissatisfaction, it is possible that the therapist would have focused instead only upon this problem and would have missed the depression. More importantly, in both instances the therapist may have missed the painful source of all of these problems.

When all problems are defined as pain, however, it seems to be easier for most therapists to set aside their own preconceptions and examine and treat each problem from a more unbiased and genuinely inquisitive point of view. The therapist becomes interested in the nature and location of each individual's unique discomfort, rather than trying to fit the client's peripheral symptoms or presenting complaints into a diagnostic category.

Pain also is easier for clients themselves to understand and examine. The negative outcomes of psychiatric labeling are well documented. Defining a problem as psychic pain or emotional discomfort avoids these adverse effects. Clients cooperate more openly in treatment and are less ambivalent about revealing their relevant thoughts and feelings when we refrain from diagnoses and frame their problems only as pain.

When the problems presented to a therapist are construed as various types of pain or suffering, the concepts, goals, and treatments used naturally will tend to be similar to those employed to treat chronic pain. Therefore, it should come as no surprise that the hypnotherapeutic approach presented here is applicable to both physical and psychic pain. The only difference is that the procedures used for physical pain can be much more straightforward because there is less need to avoid ambivalence, resistance, self-conscious biases, and sensitivities.

Thus, there are two reasons for tracing all problems back to an issue of pain. First, our experience suggests that pain is an accurate description of the distress, hurt, and tedium that so often fill a client's life. Second, the metaphor of pain best conveys the perspectives and techniques that are most useful with various psychological and emotional problems and that underlie our hypnotherapeutic approach.

COMFORT IS THE PRIMARY GOAL

Orienting Assumption #2: The primary goal of therapy is the creation of comfort, pleasure, health, success, and happiness, not the elimination of discomfort or pain.

Although pain of one form or another is what brings clients into therapy, the primary goal of therapy is not the elimination of pain. Pain is not the actual problem. The problem is the absence of comfort. Pain, in fact, is a useful warning signal, like the alarms that warn pilots when they are too close to another plane. Pain directs attention toward the location and nature of the thought or behavior that needs to be changed. It illuminates whatever is preventing or interfering with the person's comfort, and it motivates the person to seek help. Thus, pain is a therapeutic ally, something to be utilized rather than something to be attacked and destroyed.

Within this perspective, when a client brings in anxiety or depression, the therapist does not immediately consider ways to eliminate these painful conditions. Instead, the therapist begins to wonder what the client needs to do or to stop doing now and in the future in order to begin feeling comfort and pleasure. Therapy is viewed as a constructive, additive process, not a destructive or confrontational one. The primary goal of therapy, therefore, is to promote the thoughts, feelings, and behaviors required for

each person to experience comfort or pleasure, not to decide how to attack and eliminate pain. As the person begins thinking and behaving in ways that produce comfort
and pleasure, the pain disappears automatically.

The use of pleasure as a source of comfort and healing is not a new concept.
Norman Cousins (1976) helped pave the way for the wellness movement in medicine
by describing his use of humorous movies and TV shows to treat his own serious
illness and the pain that it created. Cousins observed that in addition to promoting
the healing process, "ten minutes of laughter allowed two hours of pain-free sleep."
In support of this idea, Ornstein and Sobel (1989) summarized research on the healing effects of many different types of pleasure, from pleasant tastes, smells, and sights
to pleasurable actions and attitudes. Similarly, Faymonville, Meurisse, and Fissette
(1999) reported on the successful use of the hypnotic remembrance of pleasurable life
experiences as a form of anesthesia in over 1,600 surgical procedures. Their results
indicated that memories of pleasurable experiences can indeed displace awareness of
or concern about physical pain. Finally, Ewin (2001) reported that for many years he
has provided his burn patients with relief from their pain by using hypnosis to help
them find a "laughing place."

By focusing on the patient's pleasure and sense of humor as sources of relief and
healing, the wellness model relies on the healing power that lies within each individual (cf. Seaward, 1999). Within this framework, the healer does not do the
healing, the patient does. Because the goal is to promote health, rather than to attack
illness, the healer motivates and directs patients to use their own inner resources to
establish a healthier way of being.

Along these lines, Erickson once commented, "It is the patient who does the therapy.
The therapist only furnishes the climate, the weather. That's all" (Zeig, 1980, p. 148).
He also defined the therapist as ". . . a needed human source of faith, hope, assistance, and, most importantly, of motivation toward physical and mental health and
well-being" (cf. Havens, 1985, p. 145). Thus, our role is to figure out how to motivate
patients to use their inner resources in ways that promote healthier, more comfortable thoughts and actions. Our goal is to help them discover how to experience well-
being, hope, satisfaction, and happiness.

This also is the goal that Seligman and Csikszentmihalyi (2000) recently proposed
in their call for the development of a "positive psychology." Perhaps taking their cue
from the wellness movement in medicine, these authors note that psychology tradi-
tionally has given "almost exclusive attention to pathology" and has virtually ignored
the factors that "make life worth living." In an effort to correct this disparity, Seligman
and Csikszentmihalyi also served as the guest editors for the January, 2000 issue of
the *American Psychologist*, an issue that consisted entirely of articles investigating the
causes of happiness, excellence, and optimal human functioning. Like those in the
wellness movement, these researchers recognize that by learning how to produce
psychological health, they also are learning how to treat and to prevent psychological

problems. They are identifying behaviors, ideas, and experiences that can displace emotional pain with pleasure. The Neo-Ericksonian approach relies on hypnosis to stimulate such events.

Erickson concentrated his efforts as a therapist and person on redirecting attitudes and behaviors toward positive ways of being (cf. Walters & Havens, 1993). He once commented that "The important thing is to get the patient to do the things that are very, very good for him" (Zeig, 1980, p. 195). He was not particularly interested in problems of the past; he was interested in motivating and enabling people to think and do things now and in the future that were good for them. He emphasized the creative use of existing abilities and an immersion in life-enhancing experiences. He helped his clients and students become more aware of and better able to use the kinds of thoughts, understandings, memories, perceptions, and behaviors that produce well-being. Finally, and perhaps most importantly, Erickson noted that the potentials for positive, comforting experiences already exist within each patient, although they typically exist at an unconscious level outside the range of conscious awareness or experience, where they are often ignored or overlooked.

OUR MULTIPLE MINDS MUST INTERACT

Orienting Assumption #3: People have a conscious mind and an unconscious mind.

If you are at all familiar with the work of Milton H. Erickson, M.D., you will recognize this observation as the cornerstone of his hypnotherapeutic system. In some respects it is unfortunate that he used the term "unconscious mind" because this term has been used by so many other authors and, thus, has many potentially misleading connotations. The "unconscious mind" referred to by Erickson is not the repressed unconscious described by Freud or the rather mystical collective unconscious of Jung. Erickson used the term "unconscious mind" to refer to all of the cognitions, perceptions, and emotions that occur automatically, outside of a person's normal range of awareness. He reserved the term "conscious mind" for the limited range of information that enters the restricted focus of attention of most people in everyday life. A corollary of his observation of this dichotomy is his recognition that people try to rely upon the limited capacities of their conscious mind for direction and support, even though their unconscious mind has more resources and a better sense of reality.

The number of activities our unconscious mind carries out for us is astounding and humbling. Whenever the situation calls for the use of an unconscious memory, ability, or understanding, it seems to appear magically out of nowhere, whether the conscious mind wants it to or not. We reach out and catch a tossed object without giving it a conscious thought. We scratch an itch or straighten our hair without consciously knowing it. Names, dates, concepts, and insights appear in our awareness. Emotional reactions bubble up from nowhere. Without realizing it, we rely upon our unconscious to master the complex skills and provide the many insights and tools we need to cope with everyday life. Walking, talking, driving a car, finding unique solutions to puzzles, suddenly remembering to do something important, sensing the hidden implications of another's movements, and even the ability to ignore distracting sensations and perceptions all depend upon unconscious activities.

Even this brief list of the multitude of activities of the unconscious mind suggests that a conscious/unconscious dichotomy actually is a highly oversimplified conceptual convenience. In daily life we function simultaneously on a variety of levels of perception, cognition, and response. Each of these levels, in turn, operates like an autonomous "minimind." Much as we may like to think that these multiple levels of activity are all monitored and integrated into a coherent set of behaviors over which we have conscious control, this does not appear to be the case. Each individual seems to possess a collection of minds operating in parallel, relatively independent of each other, rather than as a unified gestalt or as a simple conscious/unconscious duet.

Although Erickson generally spoke only in terms of the conscious and unconscious levels of awareness, he clearly recognized that the origins of human behavior are much more diverse than this duality implies. In the 1940s he wrote, "The human personality is characterized by infinite varieties and complexities of development and organization, and it is not a simple limited unitary organization" (Erickson, 1980, Vol. III, Chap. 24, p. 262). At the same time, he indicated that there was not yet sufficient evidence to specify the number or locus of these different origins of human behavior. Thus, although Erickson recognized the limitations of his description of the conscious/unconscious mind as a dichotomy, he employed it heuristically to explain a variety of aspects of human functioning. Over the years, researchers have sought to determine and specify the possible loci of the diverse perceptions and behaviors that Erickson labeled the conscious and unconscious minds.

For example, specification of the multiple origins of human activity was a central theme of the book *The Ghost in the Machine* published in 1967 by Arthur Koestler. Koestler proposed that human behavior can be divided into three distinct categories, each of which can be traced to three distinct layers of the cortex: the archicortex (which mediates behavior in reptiles), the mesocortx (which is more dominant among the lower-order mammals), and the neocortex (which constitutes the higher levels of cortical development and function found in the recent mammals such as primates and Homo sapiens). At the same time, Gazzaniga, Bogen, and Sperry (1967) were beginning to note the different attributes of the right and left cerebral hemispheres, a dichotomy that seemed to account for much of what previously had been described as "unconscious" activity. By 1978, however, Gazzaniga had become disenchanted with this simple dichotomy and was instead suggesting that "our sense of subjective awareness arises out of our dominant hemisphere's unrelenting need to explain actions taken from any one of a multitude of mental systems that dwell within us" (Gazzaniga, 1983, p. 536).

This notion of "a multitude of mental systems" was given further articulation and respectability by Fodor (1983) in his book *The Modularity of the Mind*. Fodor differentiated the various modules or miniminds (which exist as relatively separate cognitive processing systems within the brain) along several different dimensions. For example, he differentiated the vertically organized modules or systems, such as those described by Koestler, from the horizontal divisions described by Gazzaniga. He also specified separate modules for innate versus learned processing systems and for processing systems that are localized versus generalized in their operations. Finally, he noted that some modules are computationally autonomous, whereas others share their resources.

Ornstein (1991) referred to the various modules of the human brain as a "squadron of simpletons," each evolved to respond to different problems and situations. Bownds' (1999) recent description is similar, but a bit more generous. He describes each of us as a "society of minds," a usually cooperative collection of semi-independent selves, only a fraction of which are represented in our conscious operations. Building on Gardner's (1993) notion of multiple intelligences, Bownds speculates that each type of intelligence (music, math/logic, emotion, perception, language, action, interpersonal) represents a separate module and a separate self, with the underlying activities of each being largely unconscious.

The current level of understanding in neuroscience still does not allow us to specify these interactive modules or miniminds exactly. We can hypothesize, however, that such a specification would include at minimum one for each of the senses (i.e., separate visual, auditory, olfactory, gustatory, tactile, and kinesthetic processing systems), and one of each of the different types of information processing centers in the brain (i.e., verbal analytic versus integrative). Then there are the emotional centers, movement coordination centers, sensory integration centers, and centers that are in charge of mapping our environment. The list of separate modules or miniminds probably reads like a catalog of all human talents and abilities, each carried out by a separate system. Each of these miniminds perceives every situation a bit differently, and has different learning histories, skills, and reactions to every event. Although there appears to be some interaction and negotiation between them, there are times when they seem to act quite independently. To complicate matters further, the perceptions, reactions, and responses of each may vary from one time to another in response to variations in the overall physiologic state of the person.

When you interview a client, you interact primarily with that person's conscious mind. This dominant minimind in such interactions usually is the verbal analytic mind. It has the specialized function of providing linguistic labels, verbal differentiations, and categorizations. The conscious mind uses these various labels and categories to derive rules, values, beliefs, and desires about the way things should be or ought not be. From these concepts about how things should be, the conscious mind then constructs a frame of reference, schema, or model of the world. This schema or model of the world, in turn, guides or directs awareness, understanding, and behavior in ways that "should be" useful, correct, and personally productive. Anything that does not fit this schema is ignored or denied. Thus, people are able to perceive, comprehend, discuss, and respond to the world only in ways that are consistent with their conscious frames of reference or schemas.

One of the typical components of the conscious mind's fictionalized view of reality is the mistaken belief that it is responsible for all thoughts and behaviors of the individual. In fact, the primary role of the conscious mind is to invent a story that places itself in the role of the person in charge of everything that the mind/body does. Oddly enough, however, the conscious mind possesses very few skills and is responsible for relatively few actions or creative insights. Its primary activity is creating rationalizations to explain why it did what the unconscious minds actually did. The unconscious aspects of the mind play the major role in the events of everyday life. As Erickson told one of his students, "What you don't realize, Sid, is that most of your life is unconsciously determined" (Rosen, 1982, p. 25). The conscious mind may be able to force attention toward or away from a particular path or stimulus at times, but most decisions and actions appear to be carried out by the unconscious. Nonetheless, the verbal conscious mind usually believes that it is the only source of the decisions, emotional reactions, and responses of that person. A wise therapist recognizes that this conscious sense of being in charge is a delusion and that the explanations of patients for their behavior are myths. The unconscious systems, not the verbal conscious mind, are in charge of most things.

Recent research has supported this observation that a majority of our behavior is carried out by involuntary, nonconscious systems within the brain. After summarizing years of research on subliminal cues, unconscious priming effects, and intentions, Bargh and Chartrand (1999) concluded that ". . . the ability to exercise such conscious, intentional control is actually quite limited." They also concluded that unconsciously activated goals and expectations are often more potent than conscious ones and that most activities of everyday life are determined by unconscious mental processes. Similarly, Wegner and Wheatley (1999) indicated that "the real causes of human action are unconscious" and suggested that conscious "will" is a fiction. Finally, Kirsch and Lynn (1997, 1999) reviewed the research on placebo effects, response expectancies, hypnotic suggestions, and response sets, and concluded that most of what we do is automatic, without any conscious thought or intention. They even proposed that there is some degree of automaticity to all human behavior.

Unconscious automaticity is quite apparent whenever we drive a car or engage in any routine activity. Such behaviors can become so automatic that we go on "autopilot" and end up somewhere other than where we intended, such as when we end up in our driveway instead of at the grocery store where we meant to stop on the way home. But even many of our supposedly conscious or intentional decisions appear to be made for us by the "unconscious" parts of our minds. Libet (1985), for example, determined that supposedly voluntary acts are initiated 350 to 400 milliseconds before we are aware of our "intention" to perform those acts. In other words, there is now a considerable body of evidence leading to the conclusion that the sense we have that we are in charge and making decisions that lead to particular actions appears to be an after-the-fact invention, an illusion.

In order to maintain its delusion of self-importance the conscious mind must account for all internal events and behaviors in ways that make them seem to be coherent or logical results of *its* activity. Thus, the conscious mind constantly takes credit for and finds explanations for the activities of the various miniminds over which it actually has no control at all and of which it is largely unaware. After years of practice, it becomes very good at this. In fact, the conscious mind is able to offer such impressive rationalizations and explanations that even the most skilled therapist may be "taken in" by them.

Accordingly, when talking to clients it is important to remind yourself that there are many thoughts, perceptions, and actions occurring either outside that person's range of conscious awareness or outside that individual's range of conscious control. The multiplicity of miniminds responsible for these events is referred to collectively throughout this text by the term "unconscious mind." Because the unconscious mind consists of the bulk of the miniminds within an individual, it is not surprising that it is much more observant, wise, intelligent, adaptive, and skillful than the conscious mind.

The conscious mind is not entirely impotent, however. The conscious mind can and apparently does influence perceptions and responses in an indirect way because, as Erickson put it, "The unconscious always protects the conscious" (Erickson, Rossi, & Rossi, 1976, p. 13). This means that whenever some perception or information upsets the conscious mind because it suggests that things are not as they "should" be, the unconscious may conveniently distort it or block it out. Similarly, if the conscious mind decides that all awful outcomes must be anticipated in all situations so that they can be avoided, the unconscious will comply. In this way, the conscious mind indirectly directs attention toward goals and events that are compatible with its view of itself and the world, and away from goals and events that are not. Thus, the conscious mind influences what the unconscious mind perceives and does, although indirectly and often to its own detriment.

The relationship between the conscious and unconscious mind is similar to the relationship between the captain of a ship and the crew. The captain (conscious mind) develops charts and maps (schema or frames of reference) that describe the way the world should look and uses these charts to tell the sailors (unconscious miniminds) where to go. The captain also decides what skills the sailors must learn in order to operate the ship. This arrangement works out reasonably well as long as the captain's charts are accurate, the crew has learned the right skills, and close contact and cooperation are maintained between the captain and crew to ensure that events are going smoothly. It also works as long as the crew (the unconscious) does not upset the captain by pointing out things that the captain does not want to see, such as islands that are not on the map.

The conscious mind, like our captain, perceives and responds only to a translated version of the world. Unless reality is consistent with the charts, the conscious mind will become upset and want to ignore it. For example, a person whose conscious schema contains the erroneous belief that he or she is not attractive to anyone may remain completely oblivious and unresponsive to the obvious overtures of an interested party. People ordinarily do not consciously perceive or act upon things that are not allowed by their map or cognitive schema because the unconscious is busy censoring such information for them.

Memories, internal thoughts, images, and expectations are constantly generated by the various miniminds. Any of these may be accepted and acted upon or ignored and misinterpreted by the conscious mind. Whether some perception, memory, intention, or image gets acknowledged and included in its original form or gets distorted or shoved back into the realm of the unconscious is a function of how well it fits into the conscious mind's schema and of how flexible that conscious schema is. Things that conflict too much are rejected.

The conscious mind also may misunderstand or miss much of what occurs inside and outside the person simply because it can pay attention only to a limited number of things at one time. Thus, a person can be so absorbed by a good book that a question from a friend will go unheard or an appointment will be forgotten. Other things go unnoticed because they are so subtle, brief, or remote that they are not perceived consciously. These sources of information are consciously overlooked or ignored simply because they are too minuscule or too far away, not necessarily because they conflict with the conscious charts, but they are noticed by the unconscious. Changes in pupil size of another person, for example, may not be noticed consciously, even though subsequent emotional reactions may indicate that this cue was perceived and reacted to quite intensely on an unconscious level. Likewise, if the conscious mind has difficulty accepting or translating certain thoughts or sensations into verbal representations, they also will go unnoticed, at least consciously. Thus, fleeting sensations or activity in remote areas of the brain or body often will be ignored by the conscious mind, whereas the unconscious is busy scratching the offending itch or adjusting the person's position in the chair.

The thoughts and perceptions of the *unconscious* mind are not constrained by the conscious schema or framework. Like the sailors on our ship, the unconscious miniminds notice icebergs and other dangers, whether they appear on the captain's charts or not. They also notice and produce many things the conscious mind tends to ignore or overlook. The problem faced by the conscious mind is that it must maintain a conscious frame of reference or chart that is both comfortable and useful at the same time not ignoring the skills and important new inputs from these various miniminds.

Navigational errors or even disasters may occur if the conscious captain constantly refuses to use the sailor's skills, accept new information, or change the charts of reality. Not all of what these miniminds do or report is pleasant, accurate, or even useful, and some of it may bring the accuracy of the conscious mind's entire view of reality into question. The problem, therefore, is what information to let through and what to block out, what to use and what to ignore, what to encourage and what to discourage.

In actuality, it is difficult to specify accurately the exact nature of the information allowed in by the conscious from the unconscious because the boundaries between them are neither static nor clear-cut. At times the boundaries between these regions are sealed off, and the uptight conscious personality is kept totally unaware of all unconscious understandings and activities. On other occasions this same individual may drift off into a calm reverie where previously unconscious learnings or ideas are allowed to spring to mind. Sometimes these memories or ideas inspire, sometimes they amuse, and, at times, they startle, confuse, or even terrify the conscious mind. The things that inspire or amuse may be incorporated into the conscious charts or schemas, but the things that cause torment or conflict may precipitate a panicky retreat back into the apparent safety of the conscious frame of reference. By ignoring the unconscious, the conscious mind loses potentially useful information and risks the possibility of a mutiny. Thus, any reaction that produces a blocking off of the unconscious may signal the beginnings of serious psychological, emotional, or adjustment difficulties.

INJURED INTERACTIONS CAUSE PAIN

Orienting Assumption #4: An injured, inadequate, or inappropriate relationship between the conscious and unconscious minds can give rise to a variety of painful emotional, behavioral, and interpersonal problems or symptoms.

Although some problems are a consequence of specific biophysical malfunctions, a majority of the painful difficulties experienced by psychotherapy clients are the result of poor coordination between conscious and unconscious activities. Ideally, the fully functioning individual would have a relatively free flow of material between the conscious and unconscious minds, and the activities of the two would be cooperatively integrated and coordinated (cf. Erickson, Rossi, & Rossi, 1976). The understandings, abilities, and reactions of each minimind would be reviewed and evaluated to determine their overall validity and value to the functioning of the total personality, and these inputs would be integrated into a coherent, adaptive coping pattern.

In this sense, each person is like a large family or entire community populated by specialists who, if allowed to work together, contribute to the smooth and efficient operation of the entire system. But if that group or community is dominated by a misinformed, biased, or narrow-minded leader (the conscious mind), then the end result may be inefficiency, corruption, dissent, or a straightforward revolution. Similarly, the individual who is dominated by a misinformed conscious mind or who has an inadequate, and/or antagonistic relationship between the conscious and unconscious minds may experience unnecessary emotional turmoil, self-defeating patterns of thought, and self-destructive patterns of behavior.

There are clients, of course, whose difficulties and discomforts simply are a result of conscious misinformation or ignorance. When this is the case, counseling may consist of providing new information or correcting misinformation. Such counseling is a straightforward and rewarding process for everyone.

But it is more likely that a majority of your clients are experiencing problems because of a conflict or lack of coordination between their conscious and unconscious minds, not merely because of misinformation. For one reason or another they are unable to operate in the smooth and efficient manner typical of cooperative conscious/unconscious functioning. The relationship between their conscious and unconscious minds has been injured and, as a result, they feel out of control and are unable to take charge of themselves or their lives.

An injured or inadequate conscious/unconscious relationship can produce as much pain as a dislocated elbow or a severed limb. Something is out of place, out of control, or not working properly. The functional integrity of the individual is damaged or threatened in some fashion. As a result, that person's ability to cope comfortably and efficiently is compromised, symptoms develop, and pain or suffering is experienced.

Some injuries are produced by external sources and some are self-imposed. Parents who forbid crying or tease children when they get their feelings hurt may impose a disconnection between conscious awareness and unconscious emotions. Loss of a loved one, physical torture, or sexual abuse also may create conscious/unconscious dissociations.

A self-imposed injury to the conscious/unconscious relationship may be intentional or accidental. When some aspect of the unconscious thinks, perceives, or knows something that the conscious mind cannot tolerate or accept, the conscious mind's reaction may sever all awareness of and communication with it. If, for example, one of the unconscious miniminds notices indications that a friend is lying, that minimind may also notice the conscious mind's discomfort with that information and protect it from further knowledge about it. The conscious mind also may accidentally lose touch with other unconscious sources of information simply because it is unaware of them or unable to utilize them. As mentioned previously, some unconscious events (such as the recognition of pupil dilation in another person or a fleeting thought) may occur so rapidly or subtly that they are overlooked or masked by other events.

Whether intentional, accidental, or from external sources, the end product of an injured conscious/unconscious relationship is either an unwillingness or inability to use unconscious processes appropriately. This means that the person may: (a) lose contact with potentially valuable unconscious resources and information; (b) experience an inability to heed useful unconscious warning signals; (c) misunderstand or misinterpret unconsciously produced events; or (d) inadvertently misuse powerful unconscious abilities in counterproductive ways. Any of these outcomes is painful and produces symptoms that can disable clients to the point where their lives become difficult and unpleasant. From their point of view, something just is not working right.

A few examples may help clarify how malfunctions that occur as a result of inappropriate conscious/unconscious relationships end up producing the symptoms experienced by your clients. Anxiety, for example, typically is the result of fleeting but vivid internal images of things that could happen in the future, such as heart attacks, accidents, insanity, failure, ridicule, or embarrassment. These clients have taught their unconscious to scan the future continuously in an ongoing search for anything and everything that can go wrong. Their generalized anxiety is a consequence of constantly being immersed in the worst-case scenarios obediently produced by their creative unconscious minds. In a similar fashion, panic attacks and phobias usually involve the rapid but intense experience of an unconsciously produced image or thought. They differ from general anxiety only in that these phobia-producing images typically involve a *specific* dreaded outcome.

A fear of enclosed spaces, for example, was unwittingly self-induced by one client who had the remarkable ability to experience vividly all of the sights, sounds, and sensations of the walls of a building caving in on him. Whenever he entered a building, he could hear the support beams snap, see the walls crumble, and feel his body being crushed by them. Furthermore, he could create and experience this entire scenario in only a few seconds and emerge from such thoughts with amnesia for them. All he was left with was an awareness of the remaining intense startle response occurring in his body and a feeling of fear, responses that anyone would experience under similar conditions. After he became aware of the previously unconscious events that were the source of his anxiety, he was able to learn how to use these same imagery abilities in much more pleasant ways.

As is the case with many clients, this man's inappropriate and self-destructive use of unconscious talents began as an appropriate, intentional coping device. Originally, while helping his father renovate old homes, he trained himself to carefully monitor things that could go wrong as they removed pillars and walls. Such monitoring eventually became an overlearned, uncontrolled protective unconscious response of which he was unaware.

Ignored or uncontrolled immersions in unconscious images also can be responsible for depression. Depression, however, often seems to be the result of a continuous review of every previous painful, unpleasant feeling or experience the client has ever had. A chronically depressed, suicidal young woman, for example, discovered that she reviewed and relived every personal failure or trauma in her life over and over again whenever things were not going her way. Even though she no longer meant to do this, it was obvious to her that she originally had used this self-punitive review as a way to justify her intense anger toward herself and her family. When she finally recognized that her own thoughts were responsible for her unpleasant state of mind, she rapidly began learning how to use her unconscious abilities to construct more positive self-affirmations and expectations instead.

Many people have unconscious abilities they are not taught to be aware of or use properly. Sometimes the resulting inadequate conscious/unconscious relationships can produce anxiety, panic, or depression. Sometimes they also can produce an unwarranted fear of one's own unconscious abilities. A twenty-five-year-old woman sought therapy because she was concerned that she was insane. This concern had led to a depressive, self-critical withdrawal from all friends and family several years previously, which then led to three hospitalizations, a suicide attempt, several electroconvulsive treatments, and a variety of psychoactive medications. The sole evidence for her original concern was her discovery that she could imagine herself doing horrible things, such as killing her parents, her spouse, or herself. Her "treatment" consisted merely of instructing her to imagine herself standing on her head in the middle of the street eating a hot dog or doing any of hundreds of other silly things. She was allowed to discover that her unconscious could and would produce any image she could think of, including murder. The simple establishment of an informed and positive relationship with her unconscious abilities reassured her and provided her with an immensely valuable skill, the ability to visualize or imagine virtually anything, including things she enjoyed and wanted to have happen to her.

The results of a poor relationship between the conscious and unconscious minds can be a bit like the results of a poor relationship between an uninformed but haughty tour guide and a knowledgeable, skillful bus driver. The bus driver knows where all of the interesting sights are located, has information about them, and has the skills needed to get there. But the tour guide, being unwilling to admit ignorance or to ask for help, continues to issue directives to the bus driver and to make up information about places that have no significance. Eventually, the guide may force the driver to take an impossible road to nowhere, much to everyone's discomfort. Such often is the case with the conscious mind. It means well, but it takes us down paths we might be well advised to avoid.

INJURIES ELUDE EXAMINATION

Orienting Assumption #5: Clients generally are unable or unwilling to admit, look at, or experience the source of their pain or may fear the perceived consequences of doing so. These attitudes make it difficult to examine or soothe the pain and may perpetuate the symptoms.

Imagine that a man limps into your office and tells you that he feels terrible. When you ask him why he feels so bad, he says he does not know. After a lengthy interview, which reveals nothing, you finally decide to have him relax, close his eyes, and report what comes to mind. He eventually reports a pain in his right leg, so you ask him to be more specific. He indicates that he feels a sharp pain in the heel of his right foot and then remembers that he first felt it when he was walking barefoot in the park. When you ask him to carefully examine his right foot, he discovers a large thorn embedded in the heel. Although he initially is sickened and revolted by the wound, which is becoming infected, you eventually manage to get him calmed down enough so that he can remove the offending thorn.

Further questioning reveals that he always tries to ignore his injuries. He hates the sight of blood, and the thought of being cut terrifies him. He notes that he has had several severe infections over the years, but usually his ignored wounds have healed by themselves.

Now, imagine instead that the original discomfort stemmed from a psychological source of pain. This minor change in the scenario provides a glimpse of the problem frequently faced by the psychotherapist. Clients often do not want to know what is bothering them. In fact, they actively want to not know it.

It is hard enough for people to closely examine physical injuries and defects. We know how the human body is supposed to look, and when it fails to conform to that image we react with panic or disgust. Gaping wounds, infected sores, disfigured bodies, or broken bones create powerful emotional reactions, especially when they happen to us.

Even when the injury belongs to someone else, however, we tend to look away and feel the urge to run from the gruesome scene. But if the injured party is going to receive any help and receive the treatments required for comfort to return, someone has to examine the problem very closely. Paramedics, nurses, and physicians, for example, have to learn to suppress their natural aversions and allow themselves to inspect the damage objectively, decide what can or should be done, and do it. Somehow they have to stay calm and respond to the situation competently.

The same is true when the source of pain is some unpleasant thought, perception, memory, belief, or fear that the client's conscious mind is unable or unwilling to acknowledge or examine. Before anything can be done to correct the problem, the source of the pain must be located and thoroughly inspected.

Almost invariably, therapy clients have a source of emotional pain that they have not faced directly or examined closely. It is difficult to pay attention to any unconscious event that is frightening, confusing, or inconceivable. On the other hand, a decision to ignore something in the hope that it will go away may lead to unpleasant and sometimes severe consequences. Anxiety, depression, alcoholism, and psychosomatic illnesses often reflect a misplaced stoicism, an attempt to overcome pain by ignoring its presence.

This tendency to overlook or deny internal thoughts or experiences because they are distasteful to the conscious mind is perfectly understandable. We all do it to some extent and to some extent it is adaptive. However, therapists must recognize that pain, whether physical or psychic, is an important source of information about how to help the person become more comfortable. It is a signal, a valuable alarm that indicates the nature and location of the problem and provides an indication of the corrective action needed. A consistent refusal to examine painful thoughts and feelings in the mistaken belief that ignoring them will eliminate them eventually results in greater pain and more severe symptoms. As pointed out by Fisch, Weakland, and Segal (1982), it often is the client's attempted solution to a problem that makes the problem worse. An unwillingness or inability to pay close attention to the source of the discomfort is an attempted solution that makes things worse. It prevents the person from discovering what needs to be done to create comfort.

PAIN LEADS TO THE SOURCE

Orienting Assumption #6: Pain is the best guide. It automatically draws attention toward the location of the problem. The therapist must focus on the pain and help the client do so as well.

Pain calls attention to a problem. That is what it is designed to do. If an injury or source of pain is severe, it will override all other stimuli and demand attention. Pain from less dangerous sources of discomfort may recede into the background while attention is captured by something like a fascinating movie. But as soon as the movie gets boring, even those minor aches and pains reappear.

When someone is in pain, his or her unconscious responses will reveal the discomfort. The nature and location of physical pain is revealed by the way that person walks, adjusts his or her position, or unconsciously rubs the affected area. The source of psychological pain is revealed by a client's symptoms, the topics the person avoids, the images that drift through his or her mind, the specific words used to express a thought, or the meanings imposed upon ambiguous stimuli, such as projective tests. These and many other unconscious indications of the existence and source of pain occur whether the conscious mind is aware of that pain or not.

Conscious awareness can be diverted from the experience of pain by a conscious decision to ignore it or an intense external stimulus. But whenever attention ceases to be distracted by external events or the person relaxes and drifts inward, awareness is captured by any existing discomforts and directed straight toward the source of that discomfort. Physical pain seems to be magnified in the quiet darkness of a bedroom because there is nothing else entering awareness. The sites of psychological or emotional pain also are hardest to ignore in those quiet moments, such as the time period just prior to the onset of sleep. Thoughts keep drifting toward those unwanted, unpleasant feelings, worries, or memories.

Even during sleep, pain cannot be avoided. The fitful sleep created by physical pain is mirrored by the disruptive emotion-laden dreams and daydreams of someone in psychic pain. The unconscious is relentless in its efforts to direct attention toward unresolved problems and unattended injuries. It tries to make us aware of our fool-hardy ignorance of the things we are doing or not doing that are responsible for our pain, whether we want it to or not. By focusing upon your client's pain, you enable his or her unconscious to direct you straight to the source of the problem.

AWARENESS PROMOTES HEALING

Orienting Assumption #7: Once the source of pain is identified, clients will reflexively correct or eliminate that problem if they can. People are inherently self-corrective and self-healing.

Both the conscious and unconscious mind attempt to rationally protect the person and do whatever can be done to ensure comfort and survival. Given adequate information, they do an impressive job. When information is suppressed, ignored, or unavailable for inspection, however, the individual cannot develop a coordinated, integrated method of handling the situation.

To use a physical analogy once again, consider the case of a man recovering from a severe lower back injury. When referred for treatment, he could barely walk and was experiencing painful muscle spasms in his back and legs. He also was suicidally depressed. His strategy for dealing with his injury and pain had been to ignore them and attempt to do things the way he had prior to his accident. His struggles to suppress his awareness of pain were exhausting him, and his efforts to do things the way he used to were producing constant irritations and strains on the injured tissues.

Treatment consisted primarily of teaching him how to calmly focus his attention upon the most intense central locus of his pain. This immediately produced both conscious and unconscious changes in his behavior. As long as he paid close attention to the source of his discomfort, he was able to remind himself consciously to avoid certain activities, such as lifting heavy objects. Whenever he started to do something that was too strenuous, the focal point would become slightly more intense as a danger signal to him. Furthermore, simply by paying attention to fluctuations in the intensity of the pain in that focal area, he unconsciously began to alter his gait and other movements in ways that reduced his pain overall and increased his ability to experience pleasure.

By focusing upon the signals produced by an area of discomfort, clients allow all of their conscious and unconscious resources to be brought to bear upon doing things more comfortably. Instead of fighting with their discomfort or overlooking the valuable implications of that discomfort, they can learn to use it as a source of information about how to lead their lives more comfortably and responsibly. This is as true for therapy clients as it is for chronic pain patients.

When therapy clients focus upon their discomfort and discover that the source of their problems is a particular memory, image, desire, belief, behavior, or interpersonal relationship, they usually begin to do something about it immediately if they know what to do and can do it. People gravitate toward comfort if they stop ignoring their discomforts. They may end an unpleasant relationship, alter their lifestyle, change a belief, or revise an expectation. Sometimes they do this consciously and intentionally. On other occasions the changes occur at an unconscious level, seemingly by themselves.

Consider, for example, the case of a woman who sought help because she was becoming terrified of driving. She was unable to remember exactly when or under what circumstance she had first experienced her anxiety, but she did know that it had gotten increasingly worse over the past year. She was taught how to enter a light trance and then was asked to focus her attention upon her fear. As she allowed her experience of that fear to grow in intensity, she was asked to report her thoughts and internal images. She seemed surprised by her realization that her most intense anxiety was somehow connected to one particular place on the highway en route to work and she was unable to find any reason why this particular place should be so fear-inducing. Nonetheless, she was reassuringly told that her unconscious could find a way to cope with this problem and then she was aroused from the trance.

Two weeks later she reported that she was having no difficulties driving at all. When asked to account for the sudden change, she was unable to do so. She just laughed and stated that all she knew was that every day for the past two weeks she had tried to examine that place in the road that seemed to make her nervous. She was curious about why it caused such a reaction. But no matter how many times she reminded herself to look it over carefully, whenever she got to that spot something distracted her. One day it was a song on the radio, the next day a spot on her glasses, and another day a passing car she thought she recognized. Each day she drove by that place without realizing it until it was too late. A year later her phobia still had not returned and she still had not examined the view at that particular place in the road.

As this case illustrates, the unconscious can resolve a problem in a creative manner. This case also demonstrates an important hypnotherapeutic maxim: *The development of an awareness of the nature and location of the source of a discomfort is not the same as providing a theoretical explanation for why that source exists.* From our perspective, it is not necessary to explain why a problem exists in order to change it. The operative concept in our approach is *what* rather than *why.* Even though some clients are able to remember when or why they developed their problems or symptoms, they typically are no longer experiencing them for the same reasons. Frequently they are not experiencing them for any reason at all. They are just old, outmoded, counterproductive habits that once served a purpose but no longer do so.

Furthermore, people are so exquisitely complex that any effort to specify the exact cause of a poor conscious/unconscious relationship usually results only in oversimplified speculations and rationalizations. Different people experience similar problems for different reasons, and many different events typically contribute to the development of any given problem.

Finally, an explanation for why the problem developed in the first place can be relatively useless. Explaining why an injury occurred does not facilitate its treatment or make people feel more comfortable. The important issue is where the injury is, what it looks like, and what can be done to make the person feel good again, not why or how that injury happened.

It also must be emphasized at this point that many therapy clients, and especially therapy clients referred for hypnotherapy, may actually be suffering the effects of an undiagnosed biophysical problem rather than an unexplained psychological problem. Olness and Libbey (1987) found that roughly one out of every five hypnotherapy clients had an underlying physiological basis for their presenting problems. For these people it is critically important to differentiate a physiological source of suffering from a psychological one. Obviously, efforts to impose a psychological explanation and/or treatment could be very detrimental to their well-being. Fortunately, most of these clients seem to know at some level of awareness that their symptoms are biologically based. As a result, when asked to focus their attention upon their pains and deficits and follow them to their central locus, these individuals often can pinpoint the physiological basis for their problems.

This phenomenon is exemplified by the case of a man who was referred with a diagnosis of paranoid schizophrenia. Over the course of the previous three years he had undergone a marked change in personality, become delusional, and experienced visual hallucinations. When asked to focus upon his symptoms while in a light trance state, this man reported that it felt as if his head had been blasted with electricity. He then related this feeling to an incident wherein he was in fact struck by lightning. Although this event had occurred only days before the onset of his early symptoms, neither the client nor any of his physicians or therapists had postulated a causal relationship. A neuropsychological evaluation revealed considerable residual organic impairment consistent with a massive high-voltage electrical discharge over the surface of his cortex. His presenting symptoms of suspicion, grandiosity, confusion, and emotionality abated once he had obtained a realistic description of the nature and location of his problems. After rehabilitation training provided him with alternative coping strategies, he returned to his family and a productive life.

There are numerous other examples of similar incidents in our files. When encouraged to allow their pain and discomforts to direct their attention to the source of their symptoms, clients have been able to locate physical symptoms that have led to the discovery of previously undiagnosed brain tumors and cysts, viral infections, hormone imbalances, allergies, kidney infections, and cardiovascular problems that were the actual cause of their difficulties.

The primary goal and purpose of therapy, therefore, is to enable clients to admit, accurately locate, and precisely examine the source of their pain. Clients with adequate conscious and/or unconscious problem-solving and coping skills automatically engage in the self-healing, self-corrective actions needed to replace suffering with pleasure and comfort. All they require is a clear view of the source of their problem and an opportunity to consider a variety of new ways of thinking or doing that are more pleasant and comfortable. The therapist does not have to do anything other than give these clients the opportunity to engage in the self-healing process. Others may require a bit of help.

ASSISTANCE MAY BE NEEDED

Observation #8: Not all clients can correct their problems without help. Some need to learn new skills or have their attention directed toward new ways of thinking and doing, or be reminded of old skills and understandings before they can do so. It often is best if this learning occurs at an unconscious level.

Mere identification of the circumstances responsible for a client's discomfort does not guarantee that the client has the conscious/unconscious resources needed to alter those circumstances. Some clients require a variety of hints suggesting alternative solutions before they can figure out what to do. Others may be able to figure out what to do but may not have ready access to the previous learnings or abilities needed to carry out their selected solution. At times, therefore, you need to help your clients develop the skills required to find and implement potential solutions to their problems.

On the other hand, it would be presumptuous and disrespectful to assume that anyone is able to determine the right responses or the necessary skills for someone else. The complexity and uniqueness of each person prevents us from knowing the best action another individual can or should take in any given situation. In fact, even the conscious mind of that particular person has such a limited and biased view of the situation that it may be unwise or inappropriate to leave such decisions up to it. In 1962, during a presentation to the San Diego Society of Clinical Hypnosis, Erickson compared this problem to that of helping someone get comfortable in a bed (cf. Erickson, 2001, p. 13). We might invite a person to get into a bed and find the most comfortable position, but it would be presumptuous to tell that person exactly what position is most comfortable. Each individual must determine what position is best.

Hypnotherapy offers a way to motivate change without defining that change. Trance-induced experiences can be used to direct attention toward previous learnings and offer the person an opportunity to reorganize those learnings into a host of new skills and problem-solving strategies. Clients can be taught to view events from a different vantage point, such as a disinterested newspaper reporter, child, or wise sage. They can learn to alter their sensations and perceptions in a myriad of ways: amplifying some, minimizing others, and transforming a few into an entirely different experience. They can be shown how others have solved similar problems. They can be reminded of childhood learning experiences and abilities overlooked or unused for years. In brief, the abilities and understandings of the various unconscious mini-minds can be introduced to each other while new abilities and understandings are developed.

Given the motivation and opportunity, clients use these added unconscious resources automatically in whatever way seems appropriate or productive to them. By helping your clients build new reservoirs of inner resources, you enable them to solve problems in their own unique way, to create their own unique paths to pleasure, without interference from your biases or from their own conscious prejudices and concerns. More importantly, you enable them to learn how to trust, use, and expand their own unconscious capacities to find more pleasure and comfort in the future and, thus, discover how to avoid unnecessary pain and suffering.

CONCLUSION

The Neo-Ericksonian approach to hypnotherapy presented in this book is based upon the proposition that chronic emotional and physical pain are highly comparable, if not identical, experiences. Both stem from a problem or injury. Both signal the existence of that injury and guide attention toward it. Left unchecked, both can result in a myriad of additional problems or symptoms. Both are unpleasant experiences that people are highly motivated to eliminate if at all possible. Most importantly of all, both can be treated or alleviated in a similar manner; that is, by building and utilizing the unconscious self-healing, self-corrective, comforting, and pleasure-seeking resources of each client. Although other therapeutic approaches may accomplish this goal, our Neo-Ericksonian approach is specifically designed to do so.

Given the orienting assumptions presented in the preceding, we begin therapy with the attitude that our clients' pain will provide an avenue to a clear view of the problem. We also assume that this clear view of discomfort will motivate clients to automatically use their creative unconscious energies in an effort to devise a way of responding that is more comfortable, healthy, and useful. This is the basis for the Diagnostic Trance process described in the following chapter. In some cases, this simple trance procedure is all the help people need. Allowed to examine and respond to their discomfort in a relaxed state of mind, they may automatically discover how to become comfortable instead.

We recognize, however, that many people require additional hints and encouragements beyond a Diagnostic Trance before they can develop or utilize solutions to minimize their discomfort. This realization is the basis for the more complex induction and suggestion strategies described in the remainder of the book.

2

CONDUCTING A
DIAGNOSTIC TRANCE

The conceptual orientation presented in the first chapter defined the general goal of our approach to therapy as the identification of the nature or source of emotional pain and its replacement with comfort and pleasure. In this chapter we provide the specific information and instructions you will need in order to use the Diagnostic Trance as your first step toward the possible accomplishment of that goal.

We maintain that the client is in a better position than we are to locate and describe the source of any physical, emotional, or psychological discomfort. We also believe that the client is in a better position than we are to determine how to move toward a more comfortable solution. Accordingly, we almost invariably begin treatment with what we call a Diagnostic Trance.

HOW THE DIAGNOSTIC TRANCE PROCESS WORKS

The Diagnostic Trance process is designed to create change as quickly and efficiently as possible. This technique begins with a request for the client to relax with eyes closed and get as comfortable as possible. Next, the therapist mentions that this relaxed state makes it easier to pay close attention to the problem or uncomfortable symptoms that brought the person into the office in the first place. In fact, it is difficult not to do so. Discomfort calls attention to itself.

As the client relaxes, he or she is then encouraged to allow attention to drift toward the center of that discomfort or problem, let it fill awareness, and examine it carefully. Questions may be asked about the location of the discomfort, its size, shape, color, texture, temperature, weight, and type of pain involved. This type of questioning distances the person from the discomfort and enables attention to become even more focused upon it in a detached manner.

As attention is quietly focused on these internal events, the client begins to develop a mild trance. A trance is simply a state of highly focused attention. This very mild trance state, in turn, allows the client to pay closer attention not only to the problem under consideration, but also to all of the other thoughts, images, and emotional reactions that come to mind while focusing on the problem. Accordingly, at this point the therapist asks the client to simply pay attention to the discomfort, wait patiently to see what other things come to mind, and report whatever bubbles up into awareness. The associative connections revealed by this process often provide new insights to both the therapist and client regarding the origin or nature of the presenting symptoms or problem. The case mentioned in Chapter 1 of the man who previously was diagnosed a paranoid schizophrenic but who turned out to be suffering from the neurological aftereffects of being hit by lightning is a case in point. By paying attention to the symptoms he was able to pinpoint the approximate date of their onset and identify the precipitating event.

Finally, the client is asked to think about the discomfort going away, dissolving, or vanishing and wait patiently to see what images or thoughts come to mind while doing so. Often this produces no results at all, but sometimes the client suddenly becomes immersed in an imagined action or interaction that seems to reduce or eliminate the discomfort entirely. When this happens, therapy is essentially over. The woman mentioned in Chapter 1 whose fear of driving was spontaneously resolved after she realized that her terror was associated with one particular stretch of highway exemplifies this outcome.

The primary source of difficulty for most clients is that they are unable or unwilling to pay close attention to critical or uncomfortable issues for very long or at all. Their conscious attention typically is caught up in an actively defensive or critical analysis of one thing after another. They protectively screen their perceptions, censor and distort their responses, and use all of their conscious effort to maintain the integrity of their current conscious framework. Furthermore, they even have difficulty focusing on pleasant things for more than a few seconds before they are distracted by a new sensation, thought, or image. Left alone, they remain unaware of the source of their pain and possible steps they can take to feel better. That is at least part of the reason why they have been forced to seek help to resolve their problem. They are keeping themselves in the dark, and probably will keep their therapists there as well if allowed to do so.

During the brief Diagnostic Trance process, however, attention is highly focused and restricted to thoughts or sensations that ordinarily are overlooked or denied. The idea is to help the client develop a passive observer state of mind similar to that experienced by the members of an audience enthralled by a symphony or enchanted by a good story. In that state of mind, events are observed and experienced, not censored or altered.

The Diagnostic Trance technique follows logically from the orienting assumptions presented in Chapter 1. If we assume that "pain leads to the source" and "awareness promotes healing," then it makes sense to encourage people to pay attention to their pain. Not only does this enable clients to give therapists a better description of what is going on inside, but it also provides an opportunity for them to reduce the pain by automatically beginning to respond to those internal events in a more comfortable manner.

Thus, there are several reasons for conducting a Diagnostic Trance process. One is to provide the therapist with additional insight into the nature and source of the problem that might not otherwise come to light. Another is to help the client gain this same information. Finally, paying close attention to the discomfort underlying the problem may actually precipitate an automatic internal adjustment that alleviates the discomfort entirely. People are so self-healing that when encouraged to examine what is going on within them a bit more closely, they often spontaneously realize how to begin doing things in ways that feel better.

We call this simple intervention a Diagnostic Trance because the primary goal is to obtain an accurate description of the thoughts, emotions, and memories that may be attached to the discomfort of the client. In our training to become psychotherapists, many of us learned to rely upon two rather limited ways of understanding our clients. Most of us learned to think of people in terms of traditional diagnostic categories and/or focus on the presenting problem as the major source of information about a client. Both diagnostic categories and problem-focused assessments provide a shorthand way of sorting and using information about clients and, as such, perform useful functions. However, we have found that this shorthand way of thinking about clients often prevents a perception of the unique aspects of each problem and may block a therapist's ability to select an individualized approach for each client.

We do not believe that just because clients have similar presenting problems or can be placed into the same diagnostic categories they necessarily are experiencing the same thing for the same reason. Nor do we believe that they should be treated in the same manner. Your clients can experience similar patterns of symptoms for entirely different reasons. A simple phobia, for example, may be most accurately described as a self-induced panic reaction for one client and a natural response to an unconsciously held misunderstanding for another. Thus, no matter what the presenting symptoms, the best way to determine the most accurate description or diagnosis of a problem is to give the client an opportunity to describe everything that comes into awareness when paying attention to the focal point of discomfort.

In order to develop a clear concept of the specific nature and source of each client's problem, therefore, we recommend that you conduct a thorough Diagnostic Trance before you begin therapy. The Diagnostic Trance involves an exploration of the various unconscious images and associations connected to the problem, including unconscious images and associations related to solutions to that problem. The procedures involved are very simple.

Specific scripts for the Diagnostic Trance process are not provided because it is a highly individualized interaction or ongoing conversation between you and your clients about their internal experiences. The exact wording of your instructions and questions is not the critical issue. Just follow the basic steps described in the following, be open-mindedly curious about your clients' inner world, express your optimistic belief that they can use their own unconscious to identify and even resolve this problem, and accept whatever they offer as potentially useful information.

STEP 1: FOCUS ON THE DISCOMFORT

Procedure: First of all, ask your clients to close their eyes, relax for a while, and then concentrate upon the unpleasant sensations or feelings they associate with the presenting complaint.

Uncomfortable feelings and emotions tend to capture attention fully when we pay attention to them at all. In fact, attention tends to be drawn automatically to such sources of pain and discomfort whenever we relax and allow things to happen without interference. Aches and pains that went unnoticed throughout the day suddenly capture attention when we go to bed. When clients relax and simply allow their attention to be drawn into their discomforts, a light to medium trance usually is the end result. In this initial trance clients begin to become accustomed to the rituals of hypnotherapy (e.g., eye closure and relaxation), and they begin to learn to pay attention in a detached sort of way to somewhat uncomfortable internal events. More importantly, with this procedure clients recognize that they are learning how to examine and take charge of themselves instead of avoiding the difficult issues. Learning to recognize and utilize the potentials of one's own previously unconscious thoughts, feelings, and images is a significant part of learning to become fully aware and functioning.

STEP 2: WAIT AND SEE

Procedure: Ask your clients to wait patiently and quietly while observing those unpleasant sensations or feelings and just report whatever thoughts or images suddenly come to mind.

The idea is to help clients observe their discomfort without thinking negatively about it and just allow associated memories or ideas to spring to mind. Tell your clients to report anything they experience and observe them very carefully as they do so. If you notice any changes in expression or indications of a change in their state of mind, then ask them to report what is going on inside.

This simple procedure often reveals a pattern of thinking, a series of images, or even a specific memory that is connected to and responsible for the client's pain and other symptoms. The client may report a voice repeating a particular phrase, a "secret" decision to block out an unwanted bit of information, a seemingly unrelated image, or a previously forgotten incident. If the client seems blocked and unable to come up with anything, ask questions about the discomfort itself, such as its location, size, color, texture, shape, smell, temperature, or solidity. Focusing on these qualities may lead the client to experience additional thoughts and associations.

The relationship of these internal, automatic or unconscious associations to the pain or problems experienced by the client may be obvious to everyone involved or their implications may be very obscure and uninterruptible at the time. Even when the relationship to the problem is not obvious, the resulting images still offer a valuable basis for deciding which metaphors to employ during hypnotherapy. This is discussed in more detail later. However, no matter what comes to the client's mind, always assume that it is relevant or significant.

When this procedure clearly reveals the internal events, activities, or situations responsible for the discomfort, some clients immediately are able to figure out how to prevent further pain. They may at that moment decide to change jobs or majors, break off a relationship, alter their habits, or replace their self-defeating beliefs and attitudes with ideas that are more comfortable.

Therapeutic solutions are not always so intuitively obvious to the individual, however, and the unconscious associations to the pain are not always so easy to understand that they lead to immediate resolutions. The next, and final, step in this Diagnostic Trance procedure, therefore, is designed to facilitate the identification of unconsciously generated solutions and therapeutic recommendations.

STEP 3: IMAGINE THE SOLUTION

Procedure: Ask your clients to find a pleasing thought or image that removes or displaces their unpleasant feelings. If this proves to be too difficult, ask them to clearly imagine how it would feel if the discomforts were gone, if they felt happy and content instead, and then have them wait until their unconscious shows them what to do to make that happen.

Many clients know in precise detail at an unconscious level exactly what they can do to resolve the problem. From the moment they enter your office, these clients know what will help. Most other clients have all of the resources required to figure out what they need to do. All they lack is the opportunity to do so.

Accordingly, we have incorporated an optimistically permissive expectation of self-healing throughout this book, including this opportunity for it to occur spontaneously in the initial Diagnostic Trance process. As indicated previously, we maintain a minimalist philosophy of therapy that postulates that the therapist should never do more than is necessary and should always encourage or allow the client to do most of the work. If a client enters your office with some secret understandings of how to resolve the problem or with the unconscious resources necessary to do so, you might as well use them. This portion of the Diagnostic Trance, therefore, is devoted to discovering whether or not those understandings and resources already exist.

If your client discovers a particular thought or image that does eliminate the uncomfortable feeling (e.g., the fear, depression, or grief) or that emerges when imagining how it would feel to be happy and comfortable, then therapeutic change can be accomplished merely by having the client actually do or think whatever he or she has just imagined. This procedure is similar to the "pseudo-orientation in time" technique described by Erickson (1954a) and the "posthypnotic predetermination" technique presented by Havens (1986). If your client is unable to find a thought or image that is associated with relief from the painful feelings, then the hypnotherapeutic procedures outlined in the following chapters probably will need to be employed.

EXAMPLE OF A DIAGNOSTIC TRANCE

A brief example may help clarify the flow of events in a typical Diagnostic Trance. Here is a summary of the procedure used with a twenty-year-old university student who was referred for treatment because of her long-standing inability to speak in the classroom. This was her first session. She was unable to specify when the problem began and the therapist had no idea what might be going on either.

Therapist: Now I would like you to just close your eyes, sit back and relax for a while. That's right. Let your arms relax, your legs relax, your face relax. Just let your entire body relax as you continue to listen to me and pay attention to your own thoughts and feelings.

You have said that you feel paralyzed and upset whenever you are asked a question during a class or are expected to speak out loud. You also have indicated that you become terrified whenever such things happen to you but you have no idea why or when you began to feel this way.

Now, I know this is not a nice thing to ask, but I think it would be very useful if you could let yourself remember now that terrified feeling and tell me what you notice as you do so. In other words, I would like you to remember that feeling so clearly that you actually begin to feel it right now. Can you do that?

Client: Yes, I think so.

Therapist: Good, and what do you notice when you do so? What do you experience?

Client: I feel scared, really upset.

Therapist: OK. But where do you feel that scared feeling? What part of your body feels scared? Where do you notice it most?

Client: My stomach I guess. And my throat.

Therapist: And what is it you feel in your stomach and throat?

Client: A tight feeling, kind of hot and tight.

Therapist: Good. Now, as you let that hot tightness in your stomach and throat get more and more intense, I would like you to just pay very close attention to those sensations. Pay very close attention to them without trying to think about anything else at all. Just let your mind focus on those sensations while we wait and see what your unconscious mind can tell us that might be useful. Just pay close attention to that terrible hot tightness and tell me whatever thought or image just seems to come into your mind as you do so. Whatever it is that you become aware of as you pay attention to that sensation, I want you to tell me about it. And I'll just wait until you notice something that just seems to pop into your mind out of nowhere. (*long pause*)

Client: That's funny. I just remembered Mary. She sat in back of me in eighth grade. We were best friends. I really liked her. I was talking to her when Mr. Brown screamed at me that day.

Therapist: What day was that?

This young woman went on to describe a traumatic incident that we eventually determined had precipitated her anxiety and led to her inability to speak aloud in class. Evidently, her teacher had yelled so loudly at her for continuing to talk to her friend after he entered the room that he had virtually stopped her in her tracks. She felt frozen with fear and was completely unable to answer any of his subsequent questions about why she was talking and what she was talking about. This inability to speak generated more anger from her teacher and further frightened her. When he then asked her to begin reading out loud the material assigned for that day, she just sat there dumbfounded and embarrassed. Over the next several weeks she became more withdrawn and self-conscious, eventually vowing to never speak in class again. Although this incident eventually led to a poor adjustment to school and probably was singularly responsible for her problems with speaking in a classroom setting, she indicated that she had not thought about it in years and had no idea beforehand that it was the source of her problem.

This example of the Diagnostic Trance illustrates the simplicity and therapeutic benefit of gently directing attention toward the underlying discomfort. The client's own unconscious understandings are allowed to surface while the therapist merely waits and provides the incentive needed to focus upon what otherwise would be avoided.

The next step in this procedure is an attempt to obtain an unconscious recommendation regarding therapy. In the case described in the preceding, the woman was eventually asked to imagine how it would feel to be relieved of that anxiety and to be free to speak in a classroom setting again. She readily identified and described the release of tension from her stomach and throat. She was then asked to hold onto that comfortable feeling and wait while her unconscious considered what she could do to create that feeling and conveyed its solution to her via another internal image. After several seconds she announced that an image had just come to mind of her writing a letter to that teacher to explain the effects of his yelling at her. This, of course, was given to her as her homework assignment.

When she returned the following week she had written and sent a letter to her teacher in hopes of helping him avoid doing the same thing to someone else. He did not respond to her, but she felt much better nonetheless. She subsequently enrolled in a speech class and had no trouble asking questions or giving oral presentations in any of her college classes.

WHY AND WHEN TO USE A DIAGNOSTIC TRANCE

Even if you never use anything else mentioned or described in this text, we strongly encourage you to incorporate this Diagnostic Trance technique into your practice. Use it during the first session with new clients or whenever you are not quite sure what to do next. It is the purest and most respectful intervention you can offer, and perhaps the most beneficial as well.

The Diagnostic Trance process begins with an honest admission that you do not really know either what the exact nature of the problem is or what the best solution might be for that particular person. This acknowledgment is then immediately followed by another truth, that the person does not know these things either, at least not consciously. Finally, the person is assured that his or her unconscious mind certainly does know things that will be useful to resolving the problem and is encouraged to wait patiently for the unconscious to communicate something of value and interest. These comments clearly convey your respect for that person's own unconscious understandings and potentials.

By demonstrating a willingness to rely on that person's unconscious to guide and direct your professional understandings and even your therapeutic interventions, you are telling that person in no uncertain terms just how important and useful the unconscious mind is. If you respect it that much, the client will begin to do so as well, which means that he or she also will develop more self-respect.

By admitting ignorance and enlisting the aid of the client's unconscious, you establish your honesty and enhance that person's self-awareness and self-esteem at the same time. Not only will you increase the likelihood that the client will develop an understanding of the source of the pain, you will also provide an opportunity for that client to develop a solution.

Following our initial description of the Diagnostic Trance process in the first edition of this book, Stanton (1991) published a report on his use of our technique in a school environment. His article presented a detailed description of three cases (one with examination anxiety, one with difficulty making friends, and one who was afraid to speak up in class) that he treated successfully with this approach. In addition, Stanton indicated that of 103 cases where he used this technique, ". . . 70% reported discernible improvement in their handling of the specific problem which had been causing them trouble" (Stanton, 1991, p. 282). This is quite consistent with our own experiences.

In all fairness, we should mention that the inspiration for the Diagnostic Trance process came from a discussion by Erickson (1954b) regarding brief hypnotherapy techniques. His approach consisted of emphatically telling his patients that their unconscious would soon communicate important information regarding their case and then having them sit quietly, sometimes for two hours or more, until something unexpected or apparently meaningless came to mind. He also would enable people to discover what their unconscious was trying to tell them by having them "randomly" underline words in a book, pick up any object in his office that appealed to them, or choose a book from his bookshelf.

Sigmund Freud also reported using a similar technique with his patients early in his career (cf. Corsini, 1978). In 1909 Freud gave a series of lectures at Clark University describing his recent work and thoughts. After indicating that he had given up his attempts to use hypnosis in therapy because he was unable to hypnotize many of his patients, he went on to describe the procedure that he was using instead. Whenever his patients indicated that they did not know anything more about the nature or source of their problem, Freud would assure them that they did know more and that whatever was responsible for their symptoms would suddenly emerge into their awareness when he touched their forehead. It is perhaps unfortunate that he had stopped using hypnosis before he began using this technique.

Additional inspiration for this approach came from the work of Eugene Gendlin (1981). Gendlin instructed his clients to focus their attention inward and to patiently observe what their inner experience was telling them. When a demonstration subject in one of his workshops noted that there was a pain in her chest, for example, Gendlin asked the woman what shape it was, what color, what texture, and so forth. By focusing on these unusual ways of categorizing or describing her inner experience, this woman was able to gain new insights into the problems she was experiencing at the time.

Because the Diagnostic Trance process is simple to use, nonthreatening, respectful, and often the only intervention required, we highly recommend that you always use it prior to any decision to employ the more complex hypnotherapeutic and metaphoric procedures described in the remainder of this book (preferably during the first session). If nothing else, it will encourage you and your clients to "trust the unconscious," an attitude that maximizes the probability of a positive therapeutic outcome.

3

———

ON DOING HYPNOTHERAPY

The previous chapter described how to use a Diagnostic Trance to identify the nature or source of emotional pain and, perhaps, replace it with comfort and pleasure. If a client is unable to experience the mildly focused and relatively calm self-observational state of mind requested during the Diagnostic Trance process or does not develop a clear idea of how to resolve things during that process, then it is appropriate to transition into procedures designed to induce and utilize a more profound state of hypnotic trance. In this chapter we describe the rationale and purpose of the various components of a typical Neo-Ericksonian hypnotherapy session. This information sets the stage for your use of the scripts presented in subsequent chapters.

First we explain why the passively focused attention typical of a trance is an especially valuable therapeutic tool. Then we look at some basic rules you can use to guide your decisions about when and with whom to use trance or hypnotherapy. Next we examine the nature and purpose of each step in the hypnotherapeutic process. Finally, we tell you how to proceed from here in your development as a therapist who is able to use various forms of hypnotic communication, including metaphorical anecdotes, to capture and redirect attention in ways that foster therapeutic change.

HOW TRANCE AND HYPNOTHERAPY WORK

The term trance refers to the daydreamy but highly absorbed state of mind often experienced by people when they meditate, listen to music, attend a long lecture, drive on a freeway at night, undergo a hypnotic induction, or wait patiently in a therapist's waiting room. The only difference between these various types of trance is the mode of induction. Whether elicited by a hypnotist or induced by a long stretch of highway, a trance is a trance.

Trance is a state of steady, passively observant, focused inner awareness. This state is associated with a vivid involvement in imagined events, a shift into a context-free, literal understanding of words or phrases, and a removal of the restrictions ordinarily imposed upon unconscious abilities and responses. Furthermore, this stabilized attention can be focused internally upon thoughts, images, or sensations that ordinarily would be overlooked, ignored, or actively avoided. The hypnotherapy process is designed to take full advantage of all of these characteristics of trance.

People in a hypnotic trance are able to pay closer attention to their own unconscious sources of potential information and guidance. They also are able to more comfortably accept indirect and even direct statements from the therapist that they might otherwise reject. Finally, while in a trance state, clients can experience imagined events with such clarity and relaxed involvement that they undergo many of the same changes in learning, performance, and belief that they would in the actual situation.

Unfortunately, most people do not know how to enter or are not comfortable entering into a deep hypnotic trance at first. Thus, the hypnotherapist must learn how to speak to people in ways that facilitate the development of trance and that reassure them that they can safely remain in that state of mind for an extended period. The trance induction scripts presented in Chapter 4 offer examples of procedures designed to accomplish this.

After the client develops a trance, the hypnotherapist must direct attention in ways that are therapeutically productive. Because the trance state makes it more likely that clients will accept and act on new ideas or be able to access previously unused memories and abilities, direct therapeutic approaches can be used with some clients to resolve matters quickly and efficiently. These approaches are discussed in Chapter 5.

For most clients, however, it is necessary to gently but persuasively guide attention toward the murky or disturbing areas of internal discomfort and potential pleasure with more sophisticated hypnotherapeutic techniques, especially metaphorical anecdotes containing symbolic references. Such indirect approaches or metaphorical hints provide a nudge toward an understanding of the problem and/or its solution, but still rely heavily upon the client's own initiative and resources. The scripts contained in Chapters 6 through 17 offer examples of this metaphorical approach to hypnotherapeutic communication and persuasion.

It should be noted that our approach to hypnotherapy does not depend upon the increased suggestibility commonly associated with hypnosis. *Giving clients the hypnotic suggestion that when they awaken they will no longer feel anxious, depressed, and so forth simply does not work. The notion that hypnosis magically gives the hypnotherapist the power to demand the disappearance of symptoms is a popular misconception that probably stems from faith healing and exorcism or wishful thinking! We strongly urge you to resist any temptation to try to use hypnosis in this unrealistic and unsophisticated manner.* Efforts to use hypnosis in this way not only are largely ineffective, but they also create a great deal of resistance, convince clients that hypnosis cannot help them because it does not work, and perpetuate superstitious beliefs about the nature of hypnosis itself.

PRE-TRANCE CONSIDERATIONS

Here are some basic rules and recommendations for you to consider before you begin to use hypnosis in your practice.

Client-Oriented Issues

1. We recommend that you *do not use* these hypnotherapeutic approaches with people who are psychotic or who demonstrate the symptoms of a borderline personality disorder. These individuals already have a very tenuous degree of control over their conscious experiences, and the use of trance with them can add to their confusion or create anxiety and paranoid ideation. Also, the use of hypnotic techniques with people manifesting borderline personality responses can add to the interpersonal relationship problems frequently encountered by these people in the normal course of events. Erickson did use trance effectively with several individuals suffering from schizophrenia (cf. Zeig, 1985), but because we are not Erickson we prefer to err on the side of caution.

2. Although the hypnotherapeutic process can be used successfully with clients of below-average intelligence, procedures used with these individuals typically need to be more direct, concrete, or straightforward than most of the approaches presented in this textbook. In general, the scripts presented in this volume require at least average intelligence and vocabulary.

3. The hypnotherapeutic procedures presented here can be used effectively with persons suffering from neurologic impairment, as long as the organicity has not resulted in a loss of verbal skills or abstract reasoning abilities. Where abstract reasoning is problematic, direct suggestions and inductions should be used. When verbal skills are impaired, nonverbal approaches not covered in this text are called for.

4. When a client has an external locus of control, and thus believes that the resolution of his or her problems depends entirely upon changes in someone or something else, the initial goal of therapy is merely to precipitate a shift toward an internal locus of control. Hypnotherapy is not effective as long as an individual believes that he or she has no control over or responsibility for his or her own feelings, thoughts, or behaviors. At first, therefore, the Diagnostic Trance procedure and perhaps various metaphors should be used to help the client begin to experience at least a minimal appreciation for the correlations between his or her thoughts, images, feelings, and behaviors and develop an acceptance of personal responsibility for their occurrence.

5. Many habit problems, such as smoking, overeating, and so on are very resistant to change. Only clients who genuinely are committed to change tend to respond to any form of intervention, including hypnosis. With individuals who view hypnosis as a magic cure that will somehow make them cease their habit pattern, the odds are that hypnosis will not work. This failure, in turn, will confirm their conviction that they cannot change. Trance facilitates alterations of habit patterns and makes the change process easier, but it does not and cannot force it to occur. The first order of business, therefore, is to use hypnosis to motivate the person to change, not to try to force such changes. Although this is true for other problems as well, it is especially true for habit problems.

Procedural Issues

1. Although not absolutely necessary, it is best to conduct hypnotherapy in a quiet, comfortable atmosphere with as few distractions as possible. A comfortable recliner may facilitate the process.

2. For most clients, especially during the first several sessions, trance is a tenuous or fragile state. They will "snap out of it" every now and then (in response to particular words, sensations, outside noises, or internal thoughts), at which point they will tend to swallow, shift their position slightly, or even open their eyes. When this happens, simply say, "That's right, you can drift down into trance and back up to the surface quite automatically and then you can drift down again without any effort at all." Then proceed with whatever you were doing previously.

3. Other clients may possess such a highly developed capacity for imaginative involvement, hence a high hypnotic responsiveness, that there may be no need for a hypnotic induction at all. Indeed, their ability to become absorbed in imaginative events actually may be the source of their discomforts. For example, it is possible that they are anxious or depressed simply because they consistently become immersed in anxiety-producing or depressing ideation and are so responsive to these internal events that they suffer profound physiologic consequences. In any event, it is always a good idea to test a client's preinduction responsiveness by having the person close his or her eyes and imagine doing something, such as eating a slice of lemon or remembering something pleasant. If the person is able to imagine it so clearly that it generates an appropriate physiologic response, it is often possible to conduct therapy using the hypnotherapeutic techniques described in the scripts presented later in this book without ever doing an induction or even mentioning hypnosis at all.

4. Whatever the patient experiences or does during the hypnotherapy process must be accepted as appropriate and potentially useful. Never imply or suggest that he or she has done something wrong, unusual, or weird, or that he or she has failed in any way. Even if the client suddenly starts telling you that it is not working, nothing is happening, or

he or she wants to stop, it is fine. Do not become disappointed or argumentative. Just inform the patient that he or she is doing fine, but that it takes some people several sessions to get comfortable with the process.

5. Clients know more about what they need than do their therapists. If a client protests or declines a hypnotherapy session, it usually is wise to abide by his or her wishes.

6. Don't panic! There is no way to predict or control a person's experiences while that person is in a trance. Every individual encounters something different when he or she becomes absorbed by or comes into contact with his or her own inner unconscious thoughts and feelings. At times clients experience some very disturbing material. If someone becomes upset, simply ask what is happening and reassure him or her as the problem is explained to you.

7. If a client falls asleep, just wake him or her up the way you would any sleeping person. Do it gently but firmly. Use a more active or direct approach with that individual during the next session, such as an arm levitation induction, and have him or her assume a less comfortable position, such as sitting up straight or even standing.

8. Clients are their own best therapists. In general, the primary goal of the hypnotherapist is to evoke a trance state within the client with the assumption that the client can use that state as an opportunity to do therapy. Accordingly, we recommend a minimalist approach to hypnotherapy. Do as little as possible and consistently *trust the unconscious.* Do only what is necessary to evoke a trance and then stop doing a trance induction. Do as little as possible to promote therapeutic activity during a trance and then sit with a quiet expectation of success. As a general rule, *it is always better to do too little than too much.* Begin with a simple trance induction and add more elaborate induction comments only if a trance does not develop. Once a trance develops, offer a few direct suggestions, statements, or images to encourage therapeutic activity. If nothing happens, use general and more complex metaphorical anecdotes and implications such as those presented in our scripts.

9. Clients can accomplish a lot between sessions if given the tools to do so. For example, Fromm (1975) instructed her

subjects to simply enter a self-induced trance once a day. After two to three weeks, several of them reported significant emotional and psychological gains from this totally undirected exercise. Erickson's position was that all hypnosis is basically self-hypnosis (cf. Erickson & Rossi, 1977) and, at times, he would simply help his client enter into trance and then let the subject do the work. Thus, the last two scripts presented in Chapter 4 are designed to help clients develop the ability to enter into and utilize trance on their own. We recommend that you help clients master self-hypnotic procedures after one or two hypnotherapy sessions. Some clients seem to find it helpful if the therapist makes a tape recording of their sessions that they can use at home for added practice. Again, this approach recognizes the fact that clients are their own best source of therapeutic material and that ultimately they are responsible for their own trances and their own therapeutic change.

STEPS IN THE HYPNOTHERAPEUTIC PROCESS

A typical hypnotherapeutic trance session consists of the following steps:

Step 1: Transition into Trance
Step 2: Trance Induction
Step 3: Direct Statements or Suggestions Regarding the Source and/or Solution of the Problem
Step 4: Metaphorical or Anecdotal Guidance toward the Source and/or Solution of the Problem
Step 5: Trance Termination
    a. Rehearsal and review
    b. Ratification
    c. Reorientation
    d. Distraction
Step 6: Follow-up Evaluation

This brief summary of the flow of events in a typical hypnotherapy session is the core framework around which the scripts in this book are organized. Accordingly, the purposes and procedures involved in each step must be reviewed before you begin selecting specific scripts upon which to base your hypnotherapeutic efforts.

Step 1: Transition into Trance

The first time a hypnotherapeutic trance is used with a client it is appropriate to initiate the transition from an ordinary conversation into trance work with a comment such as, "I would like to do something a bit different for a few minutes that I think might help. OK?" Or you might simply say, "Now might be a good time to begin working with hypnosis. OK?"

When your client agrees, you should give a behavioral directive (e.g., "Move to this chair." "Close your eyes.") that you will use on all succeeding occasions as your transition into trance. Exactly what directive you provide will depend upon the seating arrangement in your office and what position you believe will be most comfortable for you and your client, but here are a few typical examples:

"Why don't you move over to this chair? It is a recliner and you probably will be more comfortable if you can just sit back, close your eyes, and relax. That's right."

"Just get into a comfortable position there and go ahead and close your eyes as you allow yourself to begin to relax. That's right."

"So sit up straight with your hands resting comfortably in your lap and allow your eyes to close as you take a deep breath and feel your body relaxing more and more completely. That's right!"

Each of these instructions provides a nice transition cue *and* initiates a light trance at the same time. The authors almost invariably have their clients close their eyes right from the beginning of the hypnosis session and then add some comments about relaxation. This immediately eliminates distracting sights in the environment and focuses your client's attention inward upon thoughts and sensations. Usually a light trance quickly develops.

Transition comments and instructions should follow the basic format used in these examples, but it is not necessary for you to say exactly the same thing each time. What is important is that you *ask your client to do the same thing each time*. This provides a clear experiential signal or cue that something different is about to happen. Once your client has experienced a trance following a specific transitional shift into a new position, whenever that client is instructed to assume the same position in the future he or she will tend to re-enter trance again. This phenomenon, probably a result of simple associative learning processes, makes re-entry into trance a simpler, more automatic process on succeeding occasions and eventually may even eliminate the necessity for a formal trance induction.

Step 2: Trance Induction

The purpose of any trance induction procedure is to provide instructions and stimuli that promote entry into the trance state of passively focused inner awareness. Trance is a natural event that every client has experienced many times almost every day of his or her life. Most people, however, do not know how to intentionally allow themselves to shift into this mode of functioning. Thus, it is up to the therapist to provide a situation that first elicits trance and then teaches the client how to stay in that trance while observing internal unconscious events.

In order to help your clients learn how to allow a trance state to develop, you need to be able to say the right things in the right way. The trance induction scripts presented in this book contain comments that will trigger or facilitate trance states in a majority of subjects. Some of the scripts rely upon confusion to create a trance, some use boredom to stimulate a trance, and most include many puns, *non sequiturs*, and other wordplays to propel the person into a less normal, less conscious state of mind. When spoken with the voice tone and voice rhythm you will acquire by working with our practice tape, these scripts can be very compelling.

We have provided several different induction scripts because different individuals and situations call for different approaches. The Induction Selection Criteria presented at the beginning of Chapter 4 will help you decide which induction may be most useful with each of your clients.

Step 3: Direct Statements or Suggestions Regarding the Source and/or Solution of the Problem

Although the Ericksonian and Neo-Ericksonian approaches are well known for their use of metaphors and anecdotes to precipitate therapeutic change, the potential value of straightforward messages and instructions cannot be overlooked. Many clients can benefit greatly from direct statements about the source of their problems or from specific suggestions about what to do to enhance their situation, but most are not willing to actually hear what the therapist is saying. A trance state improves the ability of clients to hear and use such direct messages without defensiveness or resistance.

By a "direct approach" we mean:

1. *Direct statements* of fact or opinion by the therapist that are designed to correct misconceptions or alter a client's self-defeating opinions.
2. *Direct suggestions* of one or more subsequent alterations in awareness or perception that will provide the client with a pleasant experience.
3. *Similes* designed to offer the client a simple and direct way of imaginatively altering sensations, perceptions, reactions, or attitudes.

When a direct approach works it produces change rather quickly. Accordingly, it makes sense to try a direct approach or two before introducing more complex metaphorical anecdotes into the mix. On the other hand, when a direct approach does not work, the client may begin to question the value of the hypnotic process itself. Because these techniques must be used carefully and judiciously, we explain these direct approaches in detail in the following chapter (Chapter 4).

Step 4: Metaphorical and Anecdotal Guidance toward the Source and/or Solution of the Problem

According to Zeig (1980), Erickson used stories or anecdotes to identify the problem, create rapport, suggest potential solutions, enhance motivation, embed directives, foster unconscious learning, lower resistance, establish unconscious response sets, alter expectations, change beliefs, stimulate trust in oneself, and induce and deepen trance states. Haley (1993) suggests that Erickson employed stories as parables to convey ideas that otherwise might have been unacceptable to his patients. Along these lines, Gerrig and Pillow (1998) propose that people are predisposed to believe stories and experience imagined events as real and must actually make an effort to not do so. Thus, when stories are told in a trance-inducing manner that depotentiates the conscious mental sets required to question and disbelieve, it is much more likely that the listener will experientially enter into the events being described or accept the underlying message without reservation.

Erickson told stories or metaphorical anecdotes about himself, his children, his relatives, past patients, people he had observed in ordinary situations, plants, animals, the beliefs and rituals of other cultures, and many other subjects. He told these stories in a way that captured the imagination, focused attention, turned awareness inward, encouraged receptive listening, and communicated messages that changed the way people thought and behaved.

Metaphorical anecdotes are short stories about one topic that actually are intended to be stories about the listener. Thus, for example, Erickson could describe teaching his two sons to enjoy hoeing a garden by having them do it in triangles, circles, and other patterns, and in that way surreptitiously convey the suggestion that his patient find ways to make life more fun as well.

Metaphorical anecdotes are used during hypnotherapy for the same reason that they are used in nontherapeutic settings; that is, because they communicate ideas persuasively, provoke personal conscious and unconscious associations to the subject matter, and stimulate creative thinking. Whether used within a hypnotherapy context or not, virtually all metaphorical anecdotes can trigger a rich assortment of conscious and unconscious associations, any one of which may direct a person's attention toward personal issues, provide a useful insight, or stimulate a new way of responding to various situations. Thus, all of the metaphors presented in this text also could be used with some probability of beneficial effect during an ordinary conversation or nonhypnotic therapy session.

Actually, the metaphorical anecdotes presented in this text incorporate a variety of persuasive rhetorical devices, such as allusions, rhyme, poetic rhythm, and so on. As a result, these metaphorical anecdotes stimulate therapeutic events in several different ways.

On the one hand, the basic content and events of a story may be symbolically or metaphorically descriptive of your client's personality, situation, or problem. This descriptive analogy can lead that client toward a more direct examination and appreciation of an undesirable or counterproductive internal state of affairs than might otherwise be possible. In effect, the basic metaphor says to your client, "Here is what you are doing to yourself!" "Here is the situation you are in!" "Here is how you look to others!" The metaphorical anecdotes presented in this book are designed to do this in an indirect manner that does not threaten the conscious personality or arouse resistance to the message. A metaphor merely plants the seed of an idea at the unconscious level. If that idea is useful, it will grow to fruition over time at a conscious level and result in a consciously experienced change in thoughts, actions and/or reactions.

In addition, the events of a metaphorical anecdote may be prescriptive. In other words, the story told may contain examples of problem-solving strategies, coping skills, or new perspectives that your client could apply to his or her circumstances. It is assumed that many clients will simply recognize at some level the merits of the problem-solving approach offered in this story and use it later as a template or guide to resolve their own problems. Other clients will experience such a vivid involvement in their own imaginary participation in the story that they learn the strategies vicariously.

The chains of association initiated by the characters, events, settings, or words used within each story offer another source of therapeutic benefit. By scattering key words, phrases, incidents, and symbols throughout each metaphor, you can gently guide or direct thinking toward specific topics such as childhood, family, sex, anger, loss, and so on. Again, your client is indirectly encouraged to consider issues that ordinarily might be ignored or avoided.

Finally, clients themselves may invent or project a therapeutic meaning onto any metaphor or anecdote. Because pain continually draws attention toward the source of difficulties, when therapy clients hear an ambiguous message their inner search for meaning almost invariably leads them toward the very things they are trying hardest to avoid, for example, pain, secrets, unpleasant memories, the need for change, and so on. Clients naturally assume there is a reason why their therapist is telling them a particular story and they immediately begin searching for the hidden message or personal relevance. If the metaphor is too obviously descriptive or prescriptive, they may notice the implications right away and reject the message and/or the message bearer. Thus, the less direct or more symbolic and ambiguous the personal relevance of a metaphor, the more a client is forced to rely upon intuition and unconscious insight to decipher the meaning.

Our experience suggests that the *therapeutic significance and impact of self-generated meanings are inherently greater than anything we might have said directly*. Discovered meanings are always more powerful than imposed meanings, and the ambiguity of metaphors makes them an ideal way to promote such discoveries. Therapy begins as soon as the client begins to wonder why the therapist is telling this story and begins trying to decipher a meaning.

The most ambiguous metaphors are called general-purpose metaphors. These metaphors contain ideas and suggestions that are relevant to the full functioning of anyone in the general population, but they have no obvious personal relevance to any specific individual. As such, they allow each client complete freedom to "discover" a personally relevant implication or meaning for himself or herself.

If a general-purpose metaphor fails to elicit significant self-discoveries, however, then it may be necessary to provide a metaphorical message that is somewhat more personally descriptive or straightforwardly prescriptive for that individual. Ideally, this personalization increases the client's sense that what the therapist is saying is specifically directed toward him or her (which, in turn, may increase the motivation to discover and use the hidden meaning), but remains subtle enough to avoid creating reactance or resistance.

There are at least three possible sources of topics for personalizing metaphors. First, you may be able to use the metaphors presented by your clients themselves during a Diagnostic Trance, an ordinary therapy session, or a discussion of their dreams. When one client announced that he felt like he had been run over by a truck, metaphors dealing with driving and animals trying to cross expressways were used during that session. Similarly, when another client reported a dream about swimming, metaphorical anecdotes about the ocean, fish, and other related topics were incorporated into her hypnotherapy.

A second way to signal clients that you are using metaphors personally relevant to them is to select ones that reflect your own metaphorical associations to that particular individual. Focus upon the client's outstanding physical features, behavior, interpersonal style, or whatever characteristics seem to stand out in your mind. Then ask yourself what thoughts or images these features create in your own imagination. Erickson once used a story about an ironwood tree with a broken branch as a metaphor for an elderly gentleman suffering phantom limb pain from an amputated arm (Haley, 1985, pp. 324–325). We have used stories about fluttering birds, a crazed vase, and the process of making maple syrup, to name a few, because some quality of the client conjured up these associations.

The third and perhaps primary source of metaphorical associations is the client's problem itself. This method of selection has an obvious advantage in that metaphors that are related in some symbolic manner to the presenting problem often contain inherent implications for alternative problem-solving strategies. Thus, a person whose presenting problem is that he or she is anxious and high-strung might suggest a metaphor involving a guitar player who finally learned how to play well when she loosened the strings on her guitar.

Logically, the most effective metaphors are derived from all of these sources at once. This enables each metaphor to reflect the client's view of the problem, the therapist's view of the client, and the therapist's suggested solutions to the problem. Such individualization would be expected to maximize the client's interest in and vicarious participation in the metaphor and to enhance the therapeutic impact.

Probably it should be mentioned at this point that we prefer naturalistic metaphors that are based upon actual events or real phenomena rather than fictional or allegorical stories. Our experience suggests that this naturalism gives the metaphor more legitimacy and validity than a made-up tale. It also allows the therapist to tell the story with more conviction, detail, and clarity.

Step 5: Trance Termination

The trance termination process is a multipurpose closing ceremony. First, the person is allowed to review what was learned and rehearse any newfound skills and changes in attitude or behavior that may be useful to him or her in the future. Next, an opportunity is provided to experience something that will validate or ratify the trance as an unusual and potentially important event. Finally, as the client arouses from the trance to an externally focused waking state, distracting comments are made to prevent conscious analysis, rationalizations, or dismissal of the previous trance experiences.

This stage of the hypnotherapy process obviously involves a crucial series of events. Complex as it may seem, however, each of these aspects of the trance termination process is relatively easy to accomplish and can be conducted in much the same manner with every client. As a result, only one trance termination script is provided in this book. Variety or individualization is not particularly necessary or useful during this final termination stage.

For example, the portion of the trance termination script that is designed to promote the review and rehearsal of new learnings is purposefully vague and nonspecific. This enables clients to integrate whatever they have learned, even though it may not be what the therapist thought was being taught. Clients learn what they need, not necessarily what we offer to them. Allowance must be made for their inventiveness and creativity. Thus, the review and rehearsal segment offers clients the opportunity to solidify their unique learnings.

Trance ratification is accomplished most simply by offering suggestions for amnesia about the trance events and for a distortion of the sense of the amount of time spent in a trance. Both amnesia and time distortion are typical consequences of the trance experience anyway, perhaps because the contrast between the relaxed trance state and ordinary waking state is so great that it precipitates state-dependent learning and memory (cf. Rossi, 1986). This effect is magnified by the insertion of distracting or irrelevant comments about some previous topic of conversation or some item in the room immediately following a return to wakeful awareness. Not only do these distracting comments inhibit a critical analysis of the trance process, but they also minimize the transfer of trance memories into conscious awareness and promote the experience of amnesia. By taking advantage of these natural consequences, the therapist can easily demonstrate the unusual nature of the trance experience to the client.

Arousal from a trance also is easily accomplished. A noticeable shift in voice tone and speed into a more conversational style immediately signals the end of the trance process. A waking state orientation is further established by redirecting awareness back toward external stimuli, such as sounds from outside the room, a ticking clock, a source of light, and so on. An indication that the unconscious mind can allow conscious awareness to return to a normal, comfortable, and refreshed feeling reassures the person that the transition into wakefulness will be smooth and automatic. Finally, an expectant pause, a shift in position, and a deep breath by the therapist all imply that this part of the session is over.

People do not get stuck in a trance, although they may be reluctant to leave such a relaxed state and sometimes take their time doing so. Some clients may require a rather direct command to "Wake up now!" but that is rare and such a directive should be used only as a last resort. Many therapeutic understandings can develop during this transition stage, and it is wise to allow clients to take their own time to go through it. In general, we recommend that therapists begin to terminate a trance process at least ten minutes before the desired end of a session. This allows enough time for a transition into wakefulness, a period of reorientation, and either feedback from the client or a general conversation about therapeutic issues.

Step 6: Follow-up Evaluation

Feedback from the client can be obtained after one or two irrelevant or distracting post-trance conversations have occurred. This gives your client a chance to forget those things best forgotten and put some distance between the trance and an analysis or review of it.

Feedback at this point usually is spotty or minimal, but most people are able to remember particular things they enjoyed, things that increased their involvement in the process, or things that disrupted the trance (e.g., outside noises or a particular topic). For feedback regarding the therapeutic benefits of the hypnotherapy process, however, you probably have to be content to wait, watch, and listen. Your client may immediately demonstrate some insights, changes in attitude, alterations in emotional reactivity, or changes in behavior, but usually such changes are not obvious to the client, are not obviously related to the trance, or do not manifest themselves until later. Only the passage of time allows an accurate determination of therapeutic benefit and change. It takes time for new learnings to be integrated into or change the neurophysiologic response patterns of that person.

Clients may or may not attribute whatever changes occur over the course of the next few days or weeks to their hypnotherapeutic experiences. If they do, such attributions may be gracefully acknowledged with an indication that you merely provided an opportunity for them to do whatever was in their own best interests. If they do not see a relationship, however, no effort should be made to point out to them how their changes are related to specific comments or suggestions you gave them during the hypnosis session.

The changes precipitated by hypnotherapy often seem fortuitous, naturalistic, or spontaneous because they typically emerge from and are controlled by the unconscious mind. Clients should be allowed to take credit for them and attribute them to their own unconscious resources. This acceptance of personal responsibility for desirable changes enhances self-esteem, develops an attitude of an internal locus of control, promotes expectations of continued success in the future, and gives people a profound respect for and willingness to rely more fully upon their own unconscious storehouse of understandings and abilities. After all, their welfare is the primary concern, not the perceived power or skill of the therapist. Accordingly, we suggest that you give credit where credit is due—to the client and the various components of the client's own unconscious mind.

GUIDELINES FOR THE USE OF THIS BOOK

Now that you are familiar with the background concepts, format, rationale, and rules of hypnotherapy, we recommend that you do the following:

1. If you have not already listened to the audiotape produced in conjunction with this text and participated in the trance process, now is the time to do so. Take your time learning how to allow yourself to enter into a trance. This experience will give you more information more directly about the nature of trance than any discussion or description of it we could offer. Listen to these two inductions to determine which is the most comfortable or effective for you.

2. After you have experienced a trance (even a brief or a light trance will do), find and begin reading aloud the transcript of that induction. [The transcript for Side A is the

Basic Induction Script presented in the next chapter, Chapter 4, and the transcript for Side B is the Naturalistic Induction Script, also presented in Chapter 4.] At first, try to simulate the voice tone and rhythm of the demonstration. We do not suggest this because we believe that either of these demonstrations is perfect or contains the exact voice tone, rhythm, or style that every hypnotherapist should use. We suggest it because we want you to learn how to speak from within a trance, and we have found that the easiest way to teach therapists how to do this is to have them imitate a session that already is associated with their own entry into trance.

We want you to learn how to speak from within a trance because you must learn how to speak in a manner that is consistent or harmonious with the trance state of mind. When you speak from within a trance, you guarantee that your voice rhythm, tone, volume, and pacing as you read the trance scripts are appropriate for the experience of trance. What you say during hypnotherapy is important, but how you say it is equally important. Our scripts will help you learn what to say, but you also must learn how to say it in a manner that is conducive to trance. The easiest way to accomplish this is to learn how to speak while in a trance. When you speak from within a trance your entire demeanor is consistent with that trance, and the listener virtually is compelled to enter into a trance with you in order to maintain congruity and understand what you are saying.

As you imitate the demonstration by reading the transcript aloud, you automatically will begin to re-enter a trance yourself. As you do so, continue reading the transcript with whatever voice tone, pacing, or volume feels right to you or fits with your relaxed state of mind. Practice your own particular trance style until you are able to reproduce it whenever you wish.

3. While you are practicing your trance style, read the introduction to all of the remaining chapters and review the scripts presented in each. Please note, however, that the scripts themselves are not particularly informative or entertaining when read silently to oneself. In fact, they probably will seem somewhat silly, confusing, or boring to

you. Remember, these scripts were designed to minimize conscious awareness and stimulate unconscious understandings and events during a trance, not to appeal to the conscious mind's critical faculties or aesthetic sensibilities.

Instead of reading these scripts silently to yourself, therefore, we strongly recommend that you and a colleague read them to each other. Take turns reading an induction script, a metaphor script, and the trance termination script to each other. If possible, tape record these practice sessions and review them together.

This procedure serves a dual purpose. It enables you to receive feedback regarding the effectiveness of your trance style as a hypnotherapist and experience the effects of the various aspects of these scripts directly when you serve as the practice subject. Such experiential practice sessions are the single most useful and efficient method of learning hypnotherapy.

If you are unable to find a colleague to practice with, try listening to and participating with your own tape recordings of several induction and suggestion scripts. Although probably not as effective as working with a colleague, this approach can provide more of an appreciation for the content and structure of the scripts and for the effects of voice tone and rhythm than can a straightforward silent reading of them.

4. We recommend that novice hypnotherapists begin practicing within a pain management context if possible. If this is feasible, focus your reading and practice on the material contained in Chapter 7 for a while.

5. Begin learning to conduct hypnotherapy sessions by conducting Diagnostic Trance sessions with appropriate clients. This will help you get used to talking to people with their eyes closed and provide the understanding needed to select appropriate scripts for each client. Postpone further hypnotherapeutic work until at least the next session, however, and use the intervening time to select or create and review the kinds of scripts you intend to use.

6. Conduct a hypnotherapy session with a client based upon the scripts you selected or created after doing a Diagnostic Trance. There is no need to be shy or coy about reading the material if that is what you choose to do. Clients usually

are perfectly comfortable with this approach, especially if you indicate that you prefer to read material specifically designed or selected for that client so that exactly the right words are used throughout. Take your time. Pay attention to the various reactions of the client as you proceed. Study the person carefully so that you can modify your approach in response to his or her reactions. Remember that each session typically requires:

    a. A transition into trance

    b. An induction to create a trance

    c. Perhaps a direct suggestion, statement, or simile to stimulate change

    d. Either a general metaphorical anecdote or a specific diagnostically-based metaphorical anecdote to stimulate therapeutic insights

    e. The trance termination procedure

7. Each session will last approximately thirty to forty minutes depending upon which induction, suggestion, and metaphorical anecdote scripts are used. It usually is not necessary to explain the rationale or nature of the process. Just indicate that you would like to try something that might be of value and interest, and then proceed. Most clients seem to find the experience to be pleasant and interesting, even though it may be unusual and puzzling at first.

8. We would like to emphasize that the materials presented in this book are designed to serve as supplements to other sources of professional training. Mastery of these materials does not qualify anyone to practice hypnotherapy without additional supervision, reading, and training in the field. Relevant workshops are offered on a regular basis to qualified mental health practitioners by various individuals and organizations. Persons who intend to use hypnotherapeutic techniques in their practice should contact the following organizations for more information:

The American Society of Clinical Hypnosis
140 N. Bloomingdale Rd.
Bloomingdale, IL 60108-1017
(630) 980-4740
www.asch.net

*The Society for Clinical and Experimental Hypnosis Central
    Office*
Washington State University, P.O. Box 642114
Pullman, WA 99164-2114
sceh@pullman.com
http://sunsite.utk.edu/IJCEH/scehframe.htm

The Milton H. Erickson Foundation
3606 North 24th Street
Phoenix, AZ 85016
(602) 956-6196
http://www.erickson-foundation.org

9. We also would like to emphasize that the scripts presented
   in this book should be used only by professional psychotherapists or counselors who are qualified to make the
   kinds of observations and judgments necessary to use them
   with clinical sensitivity and acumen. There can be no guarantee
   that a given script will have the desired effect for everyone. Similarly, when used inappropriately or with inappropriate clients, hypnotherapy (like any therapeutic technique)
   could produce undesirable or counterproductive outcomes.
   In the final analysis, the decision to select and utilize all or
   part of a particular hypnotherapy script with a particular
   client is a judgment call that demands the utmost in clinical skill. Although we have found the material contained
   in these scripts to be useful and have published them here
   in the hope that others will find them equally beneficial,
   we cannot predict their impact when used by someone
   else nor can we assume responsibility for it. We suggest
   that you use these procedures with the same degree of
   caution and care that you would any other intervention.
10. Becoming adept at creating your own hypnotherapeutic
    inductions, metaphorical allusions, and hypnotherapeutic
    suggestions requires practice and dedication. Erickson loved
    language, enjoyed playing with the multiple meanings of
    words, and used every rhetorical device available to commu-
    nicate his insights, suggestions, and therapeutic directives.
    He seemed to do this effortlessly later in his life, but he
    spent hours early in his career writing out scripts for up-
    coming sessions, then reducing them from fifty pages to

their essence (cf. Rossi, 1980, Vol. I, p. 489). He recommended this same process to his students, knowing that it would improve their ability to capture attention and express complex ideas in the simplest, most precise and persuasive manner possible. We encourage you to do so as well and offer detailed instructions for writing your own scripts in Chapter 18.

PART II

Scripts

4

TRANCE INDUCTION

Each induction script presented in this chapter has a different format and emphasis. One is designed for clients who have experienced hypnosis before; one is for people who are unable to remember ever having even one common, everyday trance experience; and one never mentions hypnosis or trance at all. The last two scripts are designed to teach clients how to induce trance in themselves.

These scripts also vary in length and complexity. Some are very brief and straightforward, and a few are relatively long. Remember that it is not necessary to continue with a long trance induction once a trance has developed. As soon as the client demonstrates the *muscular relaxation, immobility, reduced breathing rate, slowed heart rate, reduced or eliminated swallow reflex, slowed eye-movements, and quiet receptivity* characteristic of a light trance, it is appropriate to segue out of the trance induction and into the provision of ideas, suggestions, or metaphors designed to lead the client toward therapeutic awareness.

Please keep in mind the fact that these trance inductions can and do work. We have used these procedures successfully with hundreds of clients. Most people are able to learn how to enter into a trance state in only one or two sessions, especially if the therapist has a confident expectation that this will happen. Any concern about or lack of faith in the client's ability to enter into a trance will be conveyed to that person by subtle verbal and nonverbal cues, with negative results. On the other hand, absolute confidence in the subject and in the procedures used will help ensure a positive outcome. The role of confident expectation of therapeutic results is extremely powerful. In fact, it may be more significant than any other element of the hypnotherapeutic process (cf. Erickson, 1985, p. 126).

On those rare occasions when an induction does not seem to help a client relax at all, the client should never be left with the impression that she or he has failed. Relaxation and trance are new and unusual experiences for most people and it may take time for them to adapt to the experience. As long as you maintain a positive expectation of success and reassure the client that she or he is doing well and that she or he eventually will be able to relax completely, that individual is likely to benefit from the process.

Also, please remember that trance is not a stable condition. Clients frequently drift in and out of trance in response to internal and external events. Should conscious arousal occur spontaneously, all you need to do is comment that drifting up and back down is fine. Then continue with whatever was being said prior to the arousal.

We advise you to review each script before you decide to use it. Although carefully worded to avoid problems and elicit the desired trance, these scripts are designed to serve as guidelines, not a substitute for your own creativity and style. Each may be modified or elaborated upon in any manner that seems comfortable to you.

INDUCTION SELECTION CRITERIA

Which type of induction script should you use with a specific client? Here are our recommendations:

Category I.   If your client has never experienced trance before but appears to be reasonably relaxed and cooperative, then use one of the Basic Inductions.

Category II.   If your client is compulsive, rigid, or highly controlled, then use the Confusion Induction.

Category III.   If your client is agitated, fearful, or distractible, then use a Conversational Induction.

Category IV.   If your client is a bit anxious and the room is noisy, then use the Naturalistic Induction.

Category V.   If your client has experienced hypnosis before and that experience was positive, then use the Revivification Induction.

Category VI.   If your client has never experienced a formal hypnosis process but can remember experiencing a trancelike state in some situation (e.g., jogging, meditating, driving), then use the Simulation Induction.

Category VII.   If your client is looking for a demonstration of the power of hypnosis for reassurance or proof that it can and will help, then use the Eye Fixation and Arm Levitation or Eye Closure Ratification Induction.

Category VIII. If your client is an experienced subject who is willing and able to enter trance again, then use one of the Brief Inductions.

Category IX.   If your goal is to help the person learn how to use self-hypnosis and that individual does not have much experience with hypnotic trance, then use the Traditional Self-Hypnosis Training Script. If the person is familiar with hypnotic trance, then use the Rapid Self-Hypnosis Training Script.

OR

If you are most comfortable with or confident in one of the inductions other than the one we have recommended, then use it instead.

Before you begin to use any induction procedure, remember to initiate the process with an appropriate transition comment. Conversational Inductions can be conducted without an obvious transition, but we advise you to use one nonetheless.

Note: The scripts throughout this book are presented in a format that conveys the intended rhythm and phrasing. A pause between each line establishes a rhythmic presentation conducive to trance, gives emphasis to specific words or ideas, and gives the client time to experience internal events relevant to those words and ideas. During the first part of any induction procedure, each line should be spoken in synchrony with the client's exhalations. After the first few lines, however, the pace should be slowed gradually until a rhythm of presentation is reached that seems to be appropriate for or compatible with the relaxed state of trance. Once established, this basic rhythm of presentation can be used throughout the hypnotherapy process. The audiotape recording designed in conjunction with this text provides a demonstration of this alteration in rhythm over time.

CATEGORY IA: BASIC INDUCTION SCRIPT

Applications: For use with cooperative subjects who have not experienced a formal trance induction before. The purpose is to inform them about the process of trance and initiate trance experiences. (This is the script used for the demonstration induction presented on the audiotape cassette "An Orientation to the Trance Experience" that was produced in conjunction with this text.)

That's right!
With your eyes closed
you can begin to relax,
though at first
you may be more aware of some things
than you were before,
the sounds in the room,
the sound of my voice,
sensations in hands or feet,
thoughts and images
that drift into the mind automatically.
Because,
with the eyes closed
it becomes easier and easier,
to become more and more aware
of a variety of things
that otherwise would go overlooked,
or ignored,
thoughts,
feelings,
sensations,
and the alteration
of awareness
as the mind begins to experience
that gradual letting go,
letting go even
of the effort it takes
to be aware
of exactly where
the arms are positioned
or the hands,
or fingers,
and even the effort it takes
to be aware
of which leg
seems to relax more quickly, or completely
than the other

may seem to be
too much effort
to bother making.
But it takes time
to experience that letting go,
your own time,
in your own way,
as you begin to learn
even more than before
about your own ability to relax,
and let go,
and the mind
begins to flow
down
toward that place
of quietness
and calm awareness,
a place
that almost seems
to give off signals
that direct awareness down,
toward it,
into it
more . . .
and more completely,
a place of effortless relaxation
and letting go,
where even the effort it takes
to be aware
of the sound of my voice
or the meaning of my words
may almost seem to be
too much effort
to bother making.
It's so much easier
simply to relax
and allow events to occur

almost by themselves,
a drifting down,
and a drifting back
upward,
toward the surface of wakeful
    awareness
at times,
and that's fine.
It all belongs
to you.
Because you have a conscious mind,
and an unconscious mind,
and that unconscious mind,
the back of the mind,
can continue to hear,
to understand,
and respond,
to those things I might say
without the need for you
to do anything at all.
It's so much easier,
for the conscious mind,
to be able to relax
and enjoy
that drifting down,
into that place
of quiet calmness,
and effortless awareness,
of many different things,
without needing to make an effort
even to remember
exactly how
to make the effort it might take
to tell the exact position
of the entire body,
that seems to float
in time and space—
that free-floating place
of effortless letting go
and allowing events to occur
in their own time,
and in their own way.
That's right. . . .
The unconscious mind

can allow that drifting
to occur,
while the conscious mind
drifts off
someplace else entirely now.
That's right.
In your own time,
in your own way,
aware of events
that occur along the way,
as the unconscious mind
begins to utilize
that opportunity
to alter your experience
and to continue that learning
in whatever way
is the right way
for you.
Learning that feeling
of letting go,
of allowing the unconscious mind
to assume more and more
responsibility
for guiding and directing awareness
as you continue
to explore
your own abilities
and capacities
to learn as you relax,
and enter into that trance
more and more completely,
more and more comfortably,
more and more effortlessly
than before.
That's right.
[Go to a direct approach, metaphorical
anecdote script, or trance termination
procedure.]

CATEGORY IB: ANOTHER BASIC INDUCTION SCRIPT

Application: For use with cooperative subjects who have not experienced a formal trance induction before but who demonstrate a high level of imaginative involvement; for example, they will begin to fall backward if asked, while standing with their eyes closed, to imagine falling backward.

Now,
just closing your eyes . . .
as you sit there
and relaxing,
you can begin to notice
how much easier it is
to pay close attention
to your own sensations,
your own thoughts and images
that move through your mind
as I continue talking,
and I can remind you
of a time, a memory
of quiet comfort
and deep relaxation,
a feeling of safe freedom
and the pleasure of play
where the mind can stay
and enjoy that deep smile
while paying close attention
to the things that I say
and going back to that day,
to that way of being,
to that way of feeling,
that way of allowing
the mind to drift
along with the pleasure
of learning something new,
like how it feels
to drift in dreams,
where the sweet smell of a rose
can pleasure your nose,
and the warmth of the sun
is absorbed by the mind
as you keep on learning
just how it feels
to allow things to happen,

to watch and observe
as your unconscious mind
begins to allow you
to go anywhere at all,
to experience it all,
as you notice
just how easy it can be
to drift down completely
to drift in a trance
where I can say
many different things
and you can learn
many different things
from your own unconscious mind,
your own unconscious abilities,
those things needed
and wanted
by you. . . .
That's right!
[*Go to a direct approach, metaphorical anecdote script, or trance termination procedure.*]

CATEGORY II: CONFUSION INDUCTION SCRIPT

Applications: For use with highly intellectualized or rigidly controlled individuals whose conscious minds would continue to analyze, critique, plan, and so on throughout a basic induction or for whom letting go of control is a concern. This script is not recommended for persons who are suspicious or paranoid.

[The initial part of this script should be presented rather rapidly, with a gradual slowing down into a more typical trance induction rhythm.]

Now,
before we begin,
I should say,
how glad I am
to be working with you today,
instead of a dull-witted mind,
the kind you might find,
in the gutter someplace
arguing with everyone,
mad at the world.
Because when I see them,
they keep shifting around,
scratching itches,
never getting comfortable,
thinking they know it all,
and no one
can tell them what to do,
not even to help them
and they refuse to learn or do
anything that might get them
to climb out of that place
and take care of themselves.
So it is nice to know
that anyone with your intelligence
can easily learn
how to let themselves
drift into trance.
So you can sit there,
in that chair,
here,
while you try,
to be aware,
of the exact meaning
of the words you hear
and of all the changes

that occur there
in your thoughts,
sensations
or awareness
as I speak here.
Or you can forget
about trying
to make all
the unnecessary effort
to pay close attention
to everything that happens
or does not happen
in your experience
as you listen to me
and also to your own thoughts,
or to your sensations
that change over time,
or stay the same,
in an arm or an ear,
and your legs or fingers.
And what about the thoughts,
and the variety of images,
that speak to your mind's eye
as I speak to your mind
to remind you
that what you speak
to yourself
speaks for itself
as you try to search
and find
that things
may seem to be one thing,
but turn out to be another.
Because two and two
are four,

but two can also
mean also
and no two are alike.
It all belongs
to you
and to your own ability
to relax
those two ears too,
and to begin to know,
that you really don't know
what means yes
and what means no, here,
though you may
try to guess
where you're going
to go or not go,
you don't know
that there is no
real way to know
how to let go
while holding on
or to recognize
that there is nothing
you need to try to know,
to do,
or not do,
because everything you do
allows you
to recognize that
you already know that
I can say
many different things
and there is no need
for you to make
the effort it takes
to try to make
the effort
to pay close attention
to each thing I say
or don't say,
because there was a time
when the effort
to train
the mind

to stay on track
was not worth
the trip
that led the mind
back to that time
of peaceful,
calm awareness,
of effortless
letting go,
and knowing,
that you don't need
to try to
hear or even understand
what I might say
later on here today.
because the conscious mind,
can go anywhere it wishes,
while I continue
to talk
and your unconscious mind
continues to hear,
the way you overhear
a conversation
or a radio station
while driving.
You don't even need
to do anything at all.
It all belongs to you,
as you begin to hear,
the way you do,
here and now,
with eyes closed,
comfortable,
that voice or sound,
in the background,
of the mind,
as you listened
to that show,
and it showed you
how to notice
the relaxed
drifting
glow
of a slow,

sound
show
of quiet
calmness
and thoughts,
like dreams,
following themselves
as I spoke,
turning,
spokes in a wheel,
turning,
where we'll be drifting,
effortlessly down a path
into a quiet,
still place,
where words
can remind
your mind
of those things
needed
for you.
[*Go to a direct approach, metaphorical
anecdote script, or trance termination
procedure.*]

CATEGORY III: CONVERSATIONAL INDUCTION SCRIPT

Applications: For use with clients who are anxious about the hypnotic process or who might be reluctant to engage in hypnosis **per se.** *This induction procedure does not mention trance or hypnosis. Instead it focuses upon the development of relaxation and comfortable self-awareness. Obtain the client's permission to help him or her learn how to relax more fully before you begin. Once the client has learned how to relax completely, reorient him or her to wakeful awareness and then obtain permission to conduct a hypnotherapeutic session. This procedure avoids any impression of deceit or trickery and is an honest demonstration of respect for the client's autonomy.*

I know that sometimes
it is difficult
to *relax*
or to learn how
to *relax* more
than you have before.
And so,
as you sit there
with your eyes closed,
and begin to become aware
of your own thoughts,
of your own sensations,
I begin to wonder
if you have ever
had the *pleasure*
of sitting on the bank
of a river,
or on the shore
of a lake or ocean.
Because there is something
very *comforting*
about just sitting there,
listening to the *peaceful* sound
of the waves,
as they move in,
and out,
in a continuous flow,
that just seems to go on and on.
Relaxing in the sun,
feeling the *soothing* warmth,
and just letting the mind drift,
effortlessly,

with that *quiet*, almost silent,
sound,
in the background of awareness.
I'm not even sure
you've ever done that before,
relaxed in that way,
listening to the *peaceful quietness*,
of water washing the shore.
Perhaps it was a waterfall,
or just a silent place
in the center of a woods,
a *happy* memory of *contentment*,
or just a dream . . .
of a place so *comfortable* and *safe*,
that it was *easy*
to allow the body
to *relax*,
everything
to *relax*.
I don't know,
but I do know
that *everyone* has a place
they can go,
a relaxing space
deep down inside
where they can *really let go*
of all their cares and concerns,
and wonder at the wonder
of those waves of relaxation,
at the smooth *heaviness*
of arms and legs
as *relaxation* continues.

Maybe it was the warm *smoothness*
of the soft white sand,
you could hold in your hand
and watch *flow effortlessly*
through your fingers,
the same sand
that flows in an hourglass,
hour after hour,
with nothing to do for a time,
except *let go* and flow,
warm, heavy sand,
listening to the *waves*
of relaxation,
secure inside and out,
while you were sitting there,
by the shore
forgetting to make
the effort it takes
even to try
to be aware
of when
or where
that *relaxation* began
and the *soothing* sounds
or sensations were.
[*Either continue with a different induction or*
awaken the client and discuss his or her
progress in relaxing.]

CATEGORY IV: NATURALISTIC INDUCTION SCRIPT

Application: For anxious subjects and/or a noisy environment. Because of the content of this induction, it should not be used with anyone who is afraid of water.

You're resting in the chair,
with your eyes closed,
and you may notice your eyes,
even wish to open them from time to time,
and that's fine,
because I really wouldn't want you
to not go into a trance too quickly.
So much easier
simply to allow
that feeling in a shoulder, in a hand . . .
to continue as you listen
to the sounds of my voice
the sounds in the room,
the sounds outside the room,
other voices, other rooms,
while you pay close attention
to the changes in an arm, a hand,
and wonder if you are going
to be able to go
into a trance
while your conscious mind
has already begun to drift down
to let go for a time,
allowing the body to relax the mind
to relax with it
without knowing at times
how much more comfortable
you really can become.
And sooner or later
everyone's had the experience
of falling asleep
while watching television,
paying close attention
to the story line
just closing the eyes a moment
to rest quietly,
hearing the music,
listening to the voices
in that comfortably relaxed way,

when a word or a phrase
reminds you of a particular memory,
and you drift,
dream away for a time . . .
come back to the words again,
drift, dream away again . . .
until the words
and the music
become a soothing sound
in the background of the mind
just for a time,
and the unconscious mind
continues to hear
everything of importance to you,
while the conscious mind
may not notice
that you need not listen
to everything I say.
Because you've known all along
how much easier it is
to learn something when you're
          relaxed . . .
though I wouldn't want you
to relax too deeply at first,
so much more important
for you to recognize the small changes,
tiny changes, barely noticeable,
happening in your breathing . . .
in your pulse . . .
in the relaxation of the face,
in a feeling of comfort . . . security.
Because your unconscious will choose
to relax your little finger
before those feelings begin in a thumb,
or perhaps your wrist
will be the handiest place
to begin relaxing,
but the conscious mind can enjoy
being curious about exactly where

those feelings will begin.
If you drop a pebble
into a pool of water
the water flows in ripples on the
     surface,
but just below the surface . . .
just beneath the surface of awareness,
the pebble drifts
down . . .
And as that pebble drifts down,
past the water animals, . . .
drifting down past the water plants,
gently floating down . . .
nothing is disturbed
as it slowly comes to rest
on the bottom of the quiet pool.
Even the surface ripples
become slower and quieter,
and beneath the surface
all is still, calm . . .
And you can recognize your ability
to relax and comfortably reflect
upon your problems in a certain way,
remembering those times
when you were sure things were one
     way
and they turned out
to be something else entirely.
Perhaps as a child,
learning that liberry
is really library,
or telling the difference
between feet and feat,
changing old beliefs,
learning new meanings,
new ways of doing things.
And I wonder if those new feelings,
those hypnotic feelings
will stay the same
or continue to deepen even more
as you try to remember
everything I've said to you
about those TV dreams
and pebbles that drift down,

sometimes more quickly,
sometimes very slowly . . .
[*Go to a direct approach, metaphorical
anecdote script, or trance termination
procedure.*]

CATEGORY V: REVIVIFICATION INDUCTION SCRIPT

Application: For use with clients who have successfully experienced hypnosis before. The goal is to enable the client to re-experience trance by remembering what it was like on that previous occasion.

Now you can continue
to begin to relax,
with your eyes closed,
listening to the sound of my voice,
which allows you
to begin to remember
those other experiences of hypnosis
that you had before,
able to begin to remember
how it felt to listen
to that voice,
speaking to you then,
remembering that sound
and the feeling . . .
as you began
to drift down.
That feeling
in your hands
or legs
or arms,
somewhere that feeling
of relaxation, perhaps,
or what you noticed
as you began to recognize
that deep trance state,
the sensations and images,
the alterations in awareness,
as your conscious mind
became more and more
comfortable
and your unconscious mind,
assumed more and more
responsibility
for guiding and directing
thoughts
and responses.
Remembering
where you were,

in what position,
what you did,
how you felt
as you learned to allow
that trance to continue.
And even now,
as you continue
to re-experience the memory
of that event,
and to allow those feelings
to become a part
of your experience now . . .
I would like you
to have the opportunity
to enjoy allowing
that trance to continue
as you drift deeper
and deeper
and my voice drifts
down with you,
to become a part
of your experience
as you become
more deeply relaxed
and comfortable again
in that trance
and I continue to
talk to you.
[*Go to a direct approach, metaphorical anecdote script, or trance termination procedure.*]

CATEGORY VI: SIMULATION INDUCTION SCRIPT

Application: For use with clients who can remember a nonhypnotic trance experience they have had in a particular situation such as jogging, sitting by the ocean, and so on. Information about this experience should be obtained prior to the induction and incorporated into it where appropriate.

You are sitting there . . .
Your eyes are closed . . .
You are hearing
many different sounds,
including the sound
of my voice,
and I really do not know
how you are aware
of your hands resting there,
or your legs,
or your feet,
but I do know
that some muscles
can feel more relaxed
than others
as you continue listening
to my words
and become more
and more comfortable
becoming more deeply hypnotized,
because you are
breathing in . . .
and breathing out . . .
and you are able
to be aware
of many different sensations . . .
and thoughts . . .
including those thoughts,
images
and sensations
that come to mind
in response to my words.
So, as I continue
to say things to you . . .
and you continue
to be more aware
of some things than others,

it may become easier and easier
for you to begin
to remember
particular things
about your experiences
while (*jogging, reading, or whatever the
person specifically mentioned that has
absorbed attention or created a trance
in the past*).
Because even though
you are sitting
in this room
you can begin to imagine
the experience of (*jogging, reading, and so
on, as in the preceding*),
can you not?
You can return your attention
to that experience
and begin to remember
many different things
about it.
You may be able
to feel (*insert something usually felt in that
situation*).
You may be able
to see (*insert something usually seen in that
situation*).
You may be able
to hear (*insert something usually heard in
that situation*).
In fact,
you may be able to experience
so many different things
that it almost seems as if
you can return to that experience
quite completely.
And even as you continue . . .

to enjoy those feelings
of deep relaxation
and comfortable letting go,
of becoming more and more
a part of that experience,
I can continue
to speak to you now,
and you can allow
my words
to drift through your mind
as your unconscious mind
allows you
to experience those things needed.
[*Go to a direct approach, metaphorical
anecdote script, or trance termination
procedure.*]

CATEGORY VIIA: EYE FIXATION AND ARM LEVITATION
RATIFICATION INDUCTION SCRIPT

Application: For use with clients who expect or are seeking a demonstration of hypnosis or who might benefit from the experience of an unconscious alteration of behavior or sensation. This approach helps to validate hypnosis as a real and potentially influential phenomenon.

[*This induction works better if the client is sitting upright rather than reclining or lying down.*]

The first thing
I would like you to do,
before you continue
to relax
and enter into a trance,
is to place the very tips
of your fingers very lightly
on your thighs,
with your arms in the air,
elbows away from your sides,
as if your arms and hands
were just floating there,
fingers just barely touching the cloth,
so you can just feel the texture.
That's right!
Fingers just barely touching,
and focus your full attention
on those sensations
in the very tips of those fingers,
where they just barely touch,
where that floating continues,
because,
as I talk to you
and you continue to relax,
and to pay close attention,
to those sensations,
would you pick a spot there,
anywhere at all
on that wall there
and begin to stare at that spot there
while I talk to you,
really aware of that spot there
and of how
an interesting thing is beginning to happen
to one of your arms, floating there,

just above your legs,
while you try to concentrate
on looking at that spot,
because everyone knows
how easy it is
to learn something
when you're comfortable.
and sooner or later
everyone has the experience
of learning something new
when they're relaxed,
so go ahead and allow
that comfortable feeling
to continue
with the recognition
that after a while
you also can notice
that your eyes naturally
begin to get tired
of staring at that spot,
and it becomes difficult
to keep holding them there,
or even to keep them open,
and it really would be much easier,
more comfortable to close them,
and you may do that
as staring at that blurry spot
seems to be too much effort
to bother making any more,
but as you let them
very slowly begin to close now,
you can also notice,
as they slowly close,
a light floating feeling
in one hand
or the other, or both,
so that as eyelids feel heavy
and you continue to let them go down,

an arm floats up a bit,
and then a bit more,
floating away from your leg,
because as it feels lighter
the eyes may seem to feel heavier,
but as your heavy eyes continue to close
your light floating arm
moves upward a bit more
as it feels even lighter
than before,
and you can feel it lifts upward,
drifts upward,
almost by itself at times
more and more,
as you continue
bit by bit
to close those heavy eyes,
and your light, lifting arm,
floating up as you drift down
with your eyes,
arm lifting upward at times,
and then back down perhaps,
and then back upward again
an automatic movement upward
as your unconscious mind
lifts that hand, that arm, upward,
one small step at a time,
upward and then a bit more,
like being pulled upward
with a soft string.
It may be difficult
to tell exactly how much
that arm and hand have drifted up,
to tell exactly
what position they are in,
and it may be difficult to tell
when that slow effortless movement
occurs more and more rapidly,
as it drifts up,
lighter and lighter,
higher and higher.
That's right. *[pause for upward movement]*
That's right . . .
And that arm and hand
could continue to drift higher

and get lighter and lighter,
but after a while
you may begin to notice now
that as you allow
your eyes
to close comfortably now
and your mind to relax,
that relaxed heaviness spreads
and that arm
begins to feel heavier too,
as it begins
to move back down
and as you pay close attention to it,
you may begin to notice
how it feels now,
how tired and heavy it is,
as your unconscious mind
reminds your mind,
to pay more and more attention
to how good it feels
to go back down.
And that arm moves down now,
as that heaviness increases,
because it would be so comfortable,
just to allow
that heavy arm
to drift all the way down now
as you drift down
into a comfortable relaxation,
eyes closed, arms relaxed.
That's right,
and drifting down with it,
down into a deep, deep trance,
as your arm relaxes
and the mind relaxes as well,
and you drift deeper and deeper
as I continue to talk,
eyes closed now,
and your arms and hands
feel so comfortable,
your entire body comfortable,
comfortable and relaxed.
That's right.
[*Go to direct suggestion, metaphorical anecdote script, or trance termination procedure.*]

CATEGORY VIIB: EYE CLOSURE RATIFICATION INDUCTION SCRIPT

Application: Like the Eye Fixation and Arm Levitation Ratification Induction, this script is designed to elicit an unconscious pattern of responses to hypnotic suggestions that will ratify or validate hypnosis as a real phenomenon. The purpose is to convince the person at a conscious level that something unusual or different and potentially very useful is happening to his or her state of mind.

[Obviously, the client should leave his or her eyes open for this induction procedure. Stop the induction and move on to a direct approach, metaphorical anecdote, or trance termination if the client's eyes close early in the process.]

As you sit there
and let yourself get comfortable,
you can look at [*pick a point or an object which the subject must look upward slightly to see*].
That's right,
just let your eyes rest up there,
looking at that particular spot,
and continue to relax,
because as you relax
and look at that spot there,
you can begin to notice
any changes that occur here.
You can notice any blurring,
or the difficulty of focusing,
of holding your eyes there,
looking at that one place,
although at first
it may be difficult
to recognize those changes here
as you attempt to try
to be unaware of them
or to keep staring at that spot,
using all of your effort
to hold your eyes there,
but after a while
you can begin to notice
the effort it takes
to try to be unaware

of those changes that occur . . .
just little ones at first,
that slight blurring of vision,
the heavy tiredness in the eyes,
or the way the spot seems to move about,
or changes shape, or color,
and your eyes become more and more tired,
tired and heavy,
a tired heavy feeling
that you have felt before
as you stared at something
and your eyes began to water
and begin to want to close,
to blink closed,
and to want to stay closed,
and rest that tiredness.
That's right,
because everybody knows
how it feels
when the eyes get tired,
as the body relaxes
and the mind relaxes,
so tired and heavy
and the eyes begin to close,
everybody knows,
how much more comfortable it would be
to allow the eyes to close now.
That's right,
because after a while
they have become
so tired and heavy
that they almost seem to close
by themselves.

And your eyes *can close now*,
and as they *close*
you can feel
that heavy, tired relaxation
begin to spread
throughout the entire body,
the arms,
the face,
the legs,
and the mind relaxes as well.
With the eyes closed
the entire body can relax
and you can drift down
into a deep, sound sleep,
a comfortable relaxed trance,
where I can talk to you,
and your unconscious mind
can listen
even as your conscious mind
drifts off
in the same effortless way,
that the eyes drift closed
and relax.
[*If the subject's eyes are closed, go to a direct
approach, metaphorical anecdote, or trance
termination process. If his or her eyes are still
open, continue with the next few sentences.*]
So go ahead now and allow
the eyes to close.
That's right, close your eyes *now*.
and feel the mind relax
as you continue
to drift deeper and deeper
into a relaxed trance
and I continue
to talk to you.
[*Go to a direct approach, metaphorical
anecdote script, or trance termination
procedure.*]

CATEGORY VIII: BRIEF INDUCTION SCRIPTS

Applications: For use with experienced subjects or for the creation of light trances such as those used for diagnostic purposes.

A.

Do you know now
that you are already
beginning to go
now
into a trance
and that as you listen
to me talking
you can continue
to go deeper,
as deeply relaxed
as you need to be
to be able to do
those things for you
that will allow you
to become more
and more

comfortable
in whatever way
is useful for you
now?
(*Pause while relaxation and trance develop.*)
That's right,
you can know
how it feels now
to continue to allow
that trance to grow
as you listen
to the things I might say
along the way.
[*Go to a direct approach, metaphorical
anecdote script, or trance termination
procedure.*]

B.

So, as you get ready
to get set
and to go now
into that trance
where you can
start to listen
carefully
to what I say
and stay relaxed
along the way
and stay on track,
there is no reason,
is there,

to not go there
but to be there now
instead
as effortlessly
and comfortably
as you wish
wondering about the things
I am saying
or going to say next.
[*Go to a direct approach, metaphorical
anecdote script, or trance termination
procedure.*]

C.

Now,
as you sit there,
with your eyes closed,
and begin to drift

into trance,
in your own way,
in your own time,
you can take your time

to allow
that letting go to occur.
(*Pause while relaxation and trance develop.*)
Because your conscious mind
can do anything it wishes,
while your unconscious mind

continues to hear,
and to understand,
those things I might say.
[*Go to a direct approach, metaphorical anecdote script, or trance termination procedure.*]

D.

Here now,
as you relax
and begin to remember
the experience of trance
from there before,
you can reexperience
those same changes,
in thought, feeling, and sensation
and drift down

into that trance again,
perhaps even more comfortably
and effortlessly
than before.
(*Pause for trance to develop.*)
That's right.
[*Go to a direct approach, metaphorical anecdote script, or trance termination procedure.*]

E.

Relaxing
drifting down,
letting go,
allowing thoughts
to drift,
images to appear,
not too fast
and not too slow,
just right for you,
and then not needing
to do anything at all
for a while.

(*Pause*)
Not even needing
to wonder
what you will learn
as my voice
drifts down
with you
and you drift
along with it.
[*Go to a direct approach, metaphorical anecdote script, or trance termination procedure.*]

F.

And now
how do you allow
your mind to focus
on that feeling
of trance

now . . .
(*Pause*)
[*Go to a direct approach, metaphorical anecdote script, or trance termination procedure.*]

CATEGORY IXA. TRADITIONAL SELF-HYPNOSIS TRAINING SCRIPT

Applications: For training clients how to surreptitiously enter and use a self-hypnotic trance to relax in stressful situations or to prepare for performance situations. Self-hypnosis also can be used to manage urges and for therapeutic self-exploration. These procedures should be used only with individuals who have entered trance several times before.

Today,
as you drift into your trance,
I would like to help you learn
even more than before
about how to allow
this alteration to occur
anytime at all
that you need to
or want to.
That's right,
because today
you can drift into that trance
in a different way,
all by yourself.
And you can learn
how to drift into that trance
for a brief time,
or a long time,
anytime, anywhere
that is useful to you
to be able to utilize
your own unconscious mind
to do so many things
for you.
And so,
before you drift down completely,
what I would like you to do
is to make a fist
with your right
or your left hand.
That's right,
a tight fist
with that hand.
And pay very close attention
to the tightness in that hand,
in the fingers,

in the back of the hand,
in the muscles of the forearm,
and feel that tightness.
And now
as you relax that hand
and pay close attention
to that relaxation
as it occurs
more and more completely,
and that relaxed heaviness
begins to spread
up through the arm
into the shoulder,
and the back,
and the other arm.
That's right.
And that relaxation
can continue to increase
as your legs relax,
and your neck relaxes
and your face relaxes,
as you relax everyplace,
and continue to drift down,
more and more completely,
more and more deeply
into that trance state of mind,
where the mind relaxes as well,
and it becomes
easier and easier
just to allow
the unconscious mind
to assume more and more responsibility
for guiding and directing awareness
and providing those experiences
that are useful to you.
That's right,

you can continue
to drift down quite effortlessly
and you can drift upward as well,
up toward the surface of awareness
where you can have the opportunity
to practice that ability
to create your own trance
experience.
And as you drift back now
to the surface of wakeful awareness,
you can make that tight fist again . . .
[*Wait for the subject to make a fist again.*]
And you can pay attention again
to that tightness
and to the spreading relaxation
as you relax that hand
and feel that drifting back down,
drifting back down into that trance
in your own time,
in your own way.
And I would like you
to continue to experience
that ability to drift down
on your own
as I sit here
quietly for awhile
and you continue to learn
how to let go in that way
and I just sit here with you
for a while.
That's right.
[*Pause for at least a minute,*
unless the subject begins to
reawaken, then continue.]
And so you have learned,
how to make that fist,
and how to relax that hand
and drift down with that relaxation,
into your own trance state,
an effortless state
of not needing to do
anything at all
as you let go
more and more completely

and drift down and back up
in your own time
and in your own way,
in whatever way
your unconscious mind knows
is the right way for you.
Because as you learned
how to drift down
in that way,
your unconscious mind
becomes more and more available
to you now,
and anytime, anywhere you wish
you can utilize that ability . . .
you can make a tight fist,
you can drift down into trance
with the understanding
that your unconscious mind
can do those things needed.
All you need to do
is to let go completely
with the thought or idea
of providing an opportunity
for your unconscious mind
to take care of those things
for *you.*
All you need to do
is to ask it to do so
as you drift down
and then drift back upward
now,
in your own way
in your own time, . . .
back toward the surface
of wakeful awareness
and alertness
bringing those learnings
with you.
That's right,
back to wakeful alertness now
with a relaxed, refreshed feeling
of comfortable self-awareness.
And as you reach the surface
of wakeful awareness,

you can allow
the eyes
to open
now.
[*After the subject becomes reoriented, it is
helpful to immediately have him or her
practice the self-induction process again once
or twice. This solidifies the learning and
makes it a skill available to the conscious
mind.*]

CATEGORY IXB. RAPID SELF-HYPNOSIS TRAINING SCRIPT

[This is a highly modified version of the Rapid Self-Hypnosis approach described by Martinez-Tendro, Capafons, & Cardena (2001). We find it to be especially useful with subjects who manifest a high degree of imaginative involvement.]

Sitting up straight in your chair,
eyes open,
relaxed and ready,
breathing in deeply now . . .
That's right.
And letting it out.
And as the air leaves,
each time you breathe out,
you can notice, you may feel
your arms become heavy,
heavier with each breathing out,
and one becomes so heavy,
one arm heavier than the other,
that it begins to feel like
it would be difficult,
even impossible to lift,
a lead-like heaviness,
a heaviness that indicates
you are entering a trance,
the kind of trance
you have felt before,
so as you feel that heavy arm
become more and more
heavy,
then you will know
you are now ready
to use that trance
in whatever way is best for you
at the time,
wherever you are at the time,
whatever you need at the time.
So feel that heaviness now,
and feel that trance developing now
as you use that heaviness
to remind you of a trance
and take you into a trance
whenever you wish,
because beginning that trance

anywhere at all,
will be as easy for you
as thinking about a heavy arm,
remembering that feeling
of a heavy arm,
like you can do right now
to discover how easy it is
to feel that heaviness again,
and to drift right down again,
and then to drift back upward
when your unconscious is through
doing things for you,
because ending that trance,
is as easy
as counting from one to three,
now,
one,
two,
three,
taking a deep breath,
now,
and becoming awake,
now . . .

[After the subject becomes reoriented, it is helpful to immediately have him or her practice the self-induction process again once or twice. This solidifies the learning and makes it a skill available to the conscious mind.]

5

DIRECT APPROACHES
TO CHANGE

In the previous chapter we discussed how to induce hypnotic trance. In this chapter, we explain how to follow an induction with direct statements, suggestions, and/or similes designed to replace distress with more pleasurable thoughts, perceptions, and actions.

Direct approaches are used to correct misconceptions, convey important ideas, provide new understandings, give paradoxical assignments, assign ordeals, create pleasing or comforting alterations in perception, alter response patterns, or make comments designed to elicit rebound effects (i.e., offer messages that will create the intense emotional reactions needed to motivate the client to take charge of the situation and resolve the problem).

Direct hypnotic approaches are especially useful under certain circumstances. When the solution to a problem is relatively straightforward and involves the clear communication of one simple idea; one behavioral assignment; or the modification of one response, sensation, or perception; then a direct approach is the most parsimonious. This is especially true when the client is a highly compliant hypnotic subject.

Furthermore, as a result of television and movie portrayals of hypnotherapy, many clients seem to expect that direct approaches will be a part of the process. When this is the case, it makes sense to use them, if for no other reason than to satisfy that expectation.

There are at least three different types of direct approach: direct statements, direct suggestions, and similes. Each has a different structure and application.

THE NATURE OF DIRECT STATEMENTS

Direct statements are used to convey a specific understanding, attitude, or behavioral assignment. They are straightforward messages regarding the nature of a problem or its solution. Because they are blatant attempts to tell the client what to think or do, they often are messages the client might resist, argue with, or ignore in the waking state. However, such messages are much more likely to penetrate conscious resistances or "sink in" and have a long-term effect when the client listens to them from within a relaxed, passive, and relatively receptive trance state of mind. We frequently present these direct statements as comments a third party (another therapist, perhaps) might tell a client if given the opportunity. It seems to be harder to reject a message when the message bearer is not present.

In addition, we usually include reassuring reasons why it is possible and appropriate to eliminate or replace the undesirable responses. The idea is to motivate the client to comply with the suggested alteration or response for some reason other than merely because you say so. Thus, the client should be informed that the symptoms or false beliefs can or may now fade because: (a) they no longer are needed; (b) they are based upon an erroneous idea; (c) the client now knows how to avoid creating them in the first place; or (d) there are better ways to accomplish the same purpose. When followed by an indication of what the client can think or do instead, this approach often promotes rapid resolution of the problem.

EXAMPLE OF TREATMENT USING DIRECT STATEMENTS

The use of direct statements is demonstrated in the following case. An 18-year-old college student was referred for treatment of panic attacks that had not been reduced by relaxation training, desensitization, or psychotherapy by previous therapists. A Diagnostic Trance exploration revealed that his attacks were triggered by any event that seemed to provide evidence consistent with his secret fear that his overuse of marijuana for several months had done irreparable and major damage to his brain. He knew consciously that this belief probably was unwarranted, but he remained terrified that it might be true.

A light trance was induced and he was told in no uncertain terms that he no longer needed to experience panic attacks because he was not brain damaged, all of the things he thought might indicate brain damage were more easily explained by other things, and he was not adequately trained to make such diagnoses in any event. He was then told that whenever he began to think he was brain damaged he would hear the therapist's voice telling him this was not true. These admonitions were repeated several times with professional conviction, made possible because the therapist genuinely believed them to be true, and he was aroused from the trance. He immediately expressed feelings of relief, and since that time he has not experienced a single recurrence of his symptoms.

It should be noted that this client responded to direct requests for change because the changes requested were appropriate and acceptable to him. Had the suggested changes been inappropriate, contrary to his ethical or moral principles, or potentially dangerous, it is unlikely that he would have complied. In fact, inappropriate or untenable suggestions may result in animosity on the client's part. Just because a client is in a trance and thus is more amenable to suggestions and new ideas does not mean that he or she has become a mindless automaton. People in a trance may become more willing to accept and act upon ideas that are desirable or helpful, but also they seem to become less willing to respond to ideas that are inappropriate or intrusive.

THE NATURE OF DIRECT SUGGESTIONS

Direct suggestions are efforts to straightforwardly elicit hypnotically induced alterations in perception, thought, emotion, or behavior. They are typified by commands such as, "Your right hand will now feel numb, completely numb . . ." or, "You arm is too heavy to lift." These alterations are supposed to happen automatically without conscious intention or control. Thus, direct suggestions are what most people think of when they think of hypnosis. The hypnotist orders the subject to lose all feeling in a hand or arm, forget something, see something that is not there, or become unable to stand up.

Some people assume that this approach to hypnotic suggestion can be used to simply direct subjects to stop being afraid or depressed, or stop smoking. Unfortunately, such direct frontal assaults on the presenting symptoms do not work and are to be avoided. When they are used, direct suggestions are not used to eliminate or block symptoms but to insert experiences that reduce, disrupt, or replace those symptoms.

For example, hypnotically induced amnesias can reduce some sources of emotional discomfort. An altered sense of taste may eliminate smoking or overeating problems.

A sudden immersion in a highly pleasurable sensation or an unexpected feeling of intense amusement may enable a client to break out of a pattern of anxiety or become unaware of pain. And, understandably, hallucinating the members of an audience sitting in their underwear can greatly reduce speaking anxiety.

Although the list of potential applications of direct suggestions is quite long, there are many potential problems with their use. First of all, and perhaps most importantly, relatively few novice subjects are able to comply with suggestions for such dramatic hypnotic alterations. They simply do not know how to experience the phenomena being requested. Significant alterations in sensation, perception, and response seem to require a higher level of hypnotic responsiveness or imaginative involvement than most people are able to experience. In addition, because they are so blatant, the likelihood of conscious resistance is very great. Unless the suggestion is acceptable to the person on a conscious level or the person is so responsive to hypnotic suggestions that the conscious mind is unable to prevent unconscious compliance, they will not work. For these and other reasons, we rarely use them.

If you do decide to use direct suggestions, however, it is recommended that you surround them with distracting metaphors or embed them within an anecdote. This minimizes the possibility of conscious recognition and resistance and maximizes the probability of an unconscious response.

On the other hand, significant alterations in perception, memory, and even symptoms often can be obtained very directly through the use of similes. Direct suggestions given within a simile are less likely to create resistance and are more likely to produce the results desired.

THE NATURE OF SIMILES

Similes are statements that compare or equate two different things using terms such as "like" or "as." When we say, "That is as soft as a baby's behind," or "He is like a rock," we are using a simile to ascribe a quality of one thing to another.

Similes are used in a hypnotherapeutic context instead of, or in addition to, direct suggestions because they help clients figure out how to use trance to create the requested alterations in perception and experience. For example, Kay Thompson, one of Erickson's early followers, taught her hypnotized dental patients how to experience self-induced anesthesia by explaining that nerves are like tiny wires that lead to a switchboard in the brain and that all they needed to do was find the switch on that switchboard that would turn off all sensation of pain in the tooth on which she was going to work. Not surprisingly, this approach is much more effective than simply telling someone to stop feeling pain. Similes offer an imaginary way of accomplishing things that otherwise might seem difficult or even impossible.

Clients themselves can often generate useful similes. When a client was asked what his depression felt like, he said that it felt like a dark, damp, heavy cloud that surrounded everything around him. During trance he subsequently was able to imagine how it would feel to have that cloud begin to evaporate in the warmth of a summer sun. Although the relief he felt was only temporary and did not permanently replace his depression, the experience did give him hope and the realization that he had the capacity to feel better. Similarly, a twenty-five-year-old woman experiencing severe anxiety described herself as feeling like she was full of electricity. When asked to imagine turning down the generator inside her body that was sending this current through her, she immediately felt calmer and more relaxed.

Similes provide a way for clients to use their imagination to accomplish useful or pleasant alterations in sensation, perception, thought, behavior, even memory. Such alterations do not always lead to a resolution of the problems being experienced at the time, but they typically do offer at least a brief respite from them. For this reason, we often use such an approach in the early stages of treatment. At times these similes also provide the basic foundation for a more elaborate metaphorical anecdote that can be used later on.

Hypnotherapists are not the first or only people to use similes in this healing manner. An example recently described in a local newspaper involves a Native American grandfather explaining his feelings to his grandson. The grandfather commented that, "I feel like I have two wolves fighting in my heart. One is vengeful and angry, the other is compassionate and loving." The grandson asked which would win and the grandfather answered, "The one I feed." Similes offer a degree of self-control that is difficult to manage otherwise, a fact that has not gone unnoticed by other cultures.

In the remainder of this chapter we present examples of direct approaches (primarily direct statements) for use with clients in general and for intervention with specific types of problems. It should be noted that the scripts for direct suggestions and statements maintain roughly the same rhythm and phrasings used for trance inductions and for the metaphorical anecdotes presented in later chapters. They also often incorporate plays on words and double meanings to convey the message in a somewhat indirect, but basically obvious manner. The goal is to help the client remain in a trance state while listening to these straightforward messages. Although more emphasis may be added to certain words to enhance the impact of the message, you should be careful not to shift into a conversational pattern that might disrupt the trance and reduce the receptivity of the client.

A DIRECT APPROACH FOR CREATING A PLEASANT EXPERIENCE

Application: May be used at any time with any client. The purpose simply is to give the client a chance to experience something positive in his or her life.

Sometime later today,
perhaps this evening,
and tomorrow too if you like,
I would like your unconscious mind
to have an opportunity
to give a surprise to you,
a present, a pleasant gift,
something special, something nice,
an unexpected pleasure,
a wonderful feeling,
a particular taste perhaps,
or a brilliant color,
something that suddenly stands out,
and gives you a warm pleasure,
that special feeling
of a special treat,
so nice to be alive to experience that,
a brief moment perhaps
or a long one,
a giggle of amusement
or a luxurious sigh.
So keep an eye out for it,
for that time
when your unconscious mind,
sneaks up on you
and opens up your mind
to that special feeling then.
[*Go to the trance termination sequence.*]

A DIRECT APPROACH FOR ESTABLISHING GOALS:
POSTHYPNOTIC PREDETERMINATION

Application: This approach may be used with clients to determine their preferred life or therapy goals and to insert the hypnotic suggestion that their unconscious can take the steps necessary to accomplish these goals. This approach is not recommended for depressed or suicidal clients.

You do not know
exactly what to do
that would allow you
to feel the best you can,
so here is what I want you to do.
I want you to pay close attention
to how you would like to feel,
that feeling of freedom
and calm satisfaction,
the actual physical sensations
that you will feel
when you finally accomplish your goal,
and know you have done so,
as you leave here
for the last time,
having finally gotten things arranged
in the right way for you.
That's right, that all right feeling
as you walk out the door
knowing you've made it,
finally found your place,
and as your unconscious
forms that feeling, that image, that idea,
and lets you see you there then,
like watching you on TV
doing and being who you are
when you are what makes you feel best,
as your unconscious watches
that TV with you
and helps you remember
the things you did along the way,
the things you started doing today,
and did a few days from now,
that led you from here to there,
the steps that took you there,
quite automatically and effortlessly.
And as you watch yourself remember

what things happened to you,
what things you decided to do,
that let you have that feeling,
that let you accomplish that goal,
and shows them to you
on that TV too,
I would like your unconscious
 to have the opportunity
to begin to plan for you
to do those things *for* you,
to review the steps needed,
and later on
to take full advantage
of any situation, any opportunity,
to lead you effortlessly,
toward that goal,
a gift, a surprise present
of accomplishing what you need
in the present
without even needing to know
exactly where you're going to go,
to do what you see
on that TV
and knowing how good you will feel
when you get to be there . . . (*Pause for
    thirty seconds.*)
[*Go to the trance termination sequence after
pausing.*]

A GENERIC DIRECT APPROACH: #1

Application: May be used with virtually any client to elicit unconscious assistance in the therapy process.

Now,
as you continue
to go deeper into trance,
I want you to tell me
in very specific detail,
a very comprehensive description,
of exactly what you wish
and expect to happen
with regard to your problem,
then as you continue
to go deeper into trance
I want you to tell me again
in even more exact detail
what you want and expect,
what you wish to happen,
with regard to your problem,
then I want you to tell me
a third and final time,
exactly what you wish
to happen,
then you can awaken
and open your eyes,
and wonder how
your unconscious mind
will see to it
that those things happen
sooner than you might expect.

A GENERIC DIRECT APPROACH: #2

Application: May be used with virtually any client to elicit unconscious assistance in the therapy process.

Tonight, perhaps tomorrow too,
your unconscious can give you a dream,
a very special dream
that clarifies the problem
indicates the source perhaps,
but tells you quite clearly
how to solve that problem now,
and each night afterward,
until you understand it,
until you decide to do it or not,
that dream can return to you
in one form or another,
and every day
as you go about your business,
your unconscious may find something,
some thought, perception, awareness,
a taste perhaps or a sensation,
or even a color,
that seems familiar
and reminds you of that dream,
reminds you of what your unconscious
       mind
is trying to tell you,
until you finally understand
and use that understanding for you.
[*Go to the trance termination sequence.*]

A DIRECT APPROACH FOR DEPRESSION

Application: Especially useful with clients who persist in depressive patterns of thought and behavior.

Now, whether you like it or not,
it is entirely up to you,
but if you really want to feel better
what you probably need to do,
at least what Milton Erickson,
a world famous therapist,
would tell you to do,
is to pay closer attention
to what you think
and what you do,
like tuning the TV of your mind
to channels that feel better,
because you can choose to watch things
that make you sad and feel bad
or you can begin to think and do things
that make you feel good.
Erickson would tell you
it is entirely up to you.
You can tune in to sad thoughts,
you can remember bad feelings,
or you can watch things
you enjoy instead.
You create the space you live in.
You have the ability
to direct your thinking,
to decorate your mind
in whatever way *you* choose.
You can change what you do,
you can do things for you.
And so tonight, tomorrow, this week,
what I want you to do is this . . .
Every evening,
when you eat your dinner,
your unconscious mind
can automatically remind you,
perhaps with a particular sound,
a particular thought,
a particular image,
a stop sign of sorts,

an alarm,
that that is the time for you to decide,
what you will do that evening.
You can decide to do or think about
something interesting
or something fun for a change,
it is completely up to you,
whether to enjoy yourself doing some-
    thing different,
something amusing, interesting, or fun,
or to continue to practice making
    yourself feel bad.
So what makes sense to you to choose?
Those things that make you feel bad,
or those other things
you can think about and do
that make you feel good?
[*Go to the trance termination sequence.*]

A DIRECT APPROACH FOR LOW SELF-ESTEEM

Application: For individuals who appear to be convinced that it would be "wrong" for them to ever praise themselves for a job well done or to appreciate any of their positive attributes.

It is easy to pay close attention
to things that are wrong.
It's easy to be a critic,
to find fault with everything.
It's easy to find reasons
to not feel good,
to not feel comfortable,
to hide from oneself and others.
It's easy to not like yourself,
or to not trust yourself to be OK.
It's harder to have the courage
to see things in a different light.
It's harder to take a risk
and to enjoy yourself,
your life, and other people,
It's harder just to say what the heck,
to not care what anyone thinks,
it's hard to give yourself permission
to feel good no matter what,
or is it?
Maybe it's easy,
maybe it's easy to do
but you have been afraid to do it,
because you do know how
and you can do it now
but sometimes it feels wrong
to really believe you're OK,
when you might be wrong
but who's to say,
and so from now on,
I want you to know it's OK
to do that crazy thing,
to let yourself feel that way.
You can do it now, today,
and you can do it tomorrow.
You can see what is OK about you
and what you do.
You can see those things quite clearly,
and feel quite comfortable too.

You can alter your mind
and alter your mood,
even if you have to pretend, for a while,
that this new way of thinking and
      feeling
is because of something you took,
a pill perhaps,
or something that was done to you,
hypnosis perhaps,
and you really can't help it,
that's just the way you feel,
confident, happy, and pleased,
knowing that feeling is real.
So you can do it now,
or you can let your unconscious do it
      for you,
so you don't have to know
what's gotten into you
when your whole way of thinking about
      you
—*changes now and then!*
[*Go to the trance termination sequence.*]

A DIRECT APPROACH FOR ANXIETY

Application: Potentially useful with clients who are physiologically highly sensitive or reactive and have been unable to focus on potential pleasures instead of potential dangers.

We both know now
that you can scare yourself,
because you have an active mind,
and a reactive body,
and if you think that scary thing,
even for a brief moment,
it has been scaring you.
But we also both know
that there are other things you can think
that are comfortable and calming,
relaxing and reassuring thoughts or
    images
that you can use instead
to replace those other thoughts,
to help yourself relax
to maintain that relaxed, calm feeling.
You can let your unconscious mind
    learn
all it needs to know
to be able to distract you from those
    scary thoughts,
to be able to provide you with those
    relaxing thoughts.
And I think you will enjoy
being happily unconcerned,
unable to remember to worry
in exactly the same way or at the same
    time.
So from now on,
when you enter that situation,
you can enter it knowing you're pro-
    tected
and can tell that part of you
that tries to do its job by telling you
that there are things to be afraid of
    here,
that you really don't need it anymore,
and don't want to hear it anymore,
and so it can either go away

or find a different game to play,
and remind you now instead
of the good things that might happen
    here,
or the fun things that might occur later,
because those old thoughts and fears
aren't useful anymore.
So you can relax and forget it
and go on about your business,
surprised to discover, perhaps,
that you have been thinking
about something else entirely
and you will know at that point,
deep down in every cell of your body,
that you won't ever have to feel that
    again,
that it is over and done with,
more rapidly that you expected,
though not as soon as you would have
    liked.
You can do it now,
and you can do it later.
You can frighten yourself with that
    thought,
or you can calmly relax yourself
with a different thought.
That's right,
so practice and choose,
because it all belongs to *you*.
[*Go to the trance termination sequence.*]

A DIRECT APPROACH FOR VICTIMS OF ABUSIVE CHILDHOODS

Application: For clients who do not blame themselves for what happened but who do continue to think about it frequently and, thus, continue to be constrained by it.

Nothing can undo
what happened to you.
What was done to you
was done *to* you back then.
But that was then and this is now
and you can stop it here and now,
you can stop the pain and fear,
you can put an end to it, *now*,
and you already know how,
you know how to forget to pay attention
to particular things,
you know how to shut doors and
    windows
and you can shut those on the past,
you know how to see things now
for what they are now,
and your unconscious knows how to
    walk
forward in time across that line,
a boundary line
that marks a new beginning,
that lets you join the present,
as you let go of the past,
like a butterfly
coming out of that cocoon,
that lets you see a future,
when you will remember
how good it felt today
to let go of that past,
to say goodbye to it,
and to let yourself feel OK.
So go ahead now
and keep going ahead later on,
because that past is through
and you are just you here and now.
And when you get home,
there is something you can do
to put this away and get on with the
    future,

some way for you, a ritual perhaps,
a ceremonial letting go,
throwing something away
to let yourself know
that the past is done
and the future has begun,
and you will do that,
whatever feels right
to get rid of it all
once and for all,
will you not?
[*Go to the trance termination.*]

A DIRECT APPROACH FOR IMPOTENCE AND ANORGASMIA

There is a wisdom to the body,
it knows exactly what to do
to do those things sexually
that you want to have happen,
so I am going to say some things now,
and I want you to pay close attention
to what happens to you,
because you have come here
wanting to be able to respond
and once you learn that you know how
you can never forget how to do it,
you will always know that you know
how to pay attention to that place,
how to realize that you really can feel
everything that goes on there,
every tiny sensation—
every small change in sensation—
that you can watch and see
in the mind's eye now,
as I begin to tell you
that there are certain images you can
          see,
certain fantasies you can have,
that change those sensations,
make you more aware of things there,
that allow you to put your finger on the
          idea
that causes you to stir.
Some thoughts enter your mind,
and penetrate deeply into your aware-
          ness,
thoughts you ordinarily wouldn't allow
can begin to stimulate imagination,
to arouse your interest in that feeling,
that before you would never notice
in that comfortable, quiet way,
but will later on today, or tonight,
when your unconscious mind
can demonstrate to your surprise
that it knows what to do,
if you allow it to
create those images for you

and let you begin to feel
those thoughts spread down across that
          line
and grow larger and larger
as it becomes harder and harder
to tell where one begins
and the other ends
as the two begin to touch
in that private, special way,
and at that point you will know
that you can leave here today
having learned that you do know
how to feel that special way
very deep within
and again and again,
whenever you want
to allow yourself to do so.
So go ahead now
and discover more on your own,
in your own way,
in whatever way
works for you.
But don't do it too well
or you may have to walk around
excited all the time.
And just imagine what that would be
          like,
what you might do,
if you were that full of desire.
It could be embarrassing.
[*Pause until client shifts position or shows
some reaction, then proceed to the trance
termination procedure.*]

A DIRECT APPROACH FOR PREMATURE EJACULATION

We tell a small child
to not get so carried away,
to not get so excited
that it ends up yelling and screaming
with happiness and glee.
And I think that every man
should have as much self-control
as a small child.
But it's not like there is something
       wrong
with being highly sensitive,
or very responsive,
because I am going to suggest
something to your unconscious mind,
that will make it difficult
for you to feel those sensations,
or to respond in that way,
something that will make it hard for
       you
to have an orgasm at all.
Something you won't hear or
       understand . . .
consciously,
although your unconscious mind can
       hear
and can understand and do it now,
and there's nothing you can do,
but I do want you to pay close attention
next time you have sex,
to make sure that the cure
isn't worse than the problem.
Because as your unconscious mind,
makes you feel more and more numb
       there,
and less and less able
to feel that coming feeling,
you may end up being stuck
with an erection for a long, long time,
too long, perhaps, for comfort.
So I want you to try not to be too
       worried,
but to worry enough to pay attention

to make sure your unconscious
doesn't do its job too well,
and you end up never coming again,
in which case,
we'll have to try to undo this,
so next time pay attention
and let me know
if you think it is starting
to take too long,
or not happening at all,
even after a lot of effort,
because we wouldn't want you
to forget how to do it . . .
entirely.
[*Go to the trance termination sequence.*]

A DIRECT APPROACH FOR UNEXPLAINED INFERTILITY

The next time you make love,
I want you to imagine,
that you are a sexy, turned-on teenager,
in the back seat of a car somewhere,
doing things you've never done before,
almost out of control with desire,
letting him do things,
going all the way,
wanting desperately to go all the way,
but hoping and praying first
before you say yes, do it now,
and giving in to it later,
that whatever happens
you don't get knocked up now
please not that, not now.
And you know how that would feel,
do you not?
So I want you
to think about that each time,
just before it's too late to stop it,
that you can't help it,
but do not get pregnant yet
or you will ruin this whole thing,
it would be a naughty thing
to do right now.
Remember that!
[*Go to the trance termination sequence.*]

A DIRECT APPROACH FOR INSOMNIA

So here is what you need to do.
Tonight, and every night this week,
as you lie down to go to sleep,
and pray the Lord your soul to keep,
I want you to try to stay awake
for at least *one long* hour.
And during that time
I want you to think about nothing but blue,
just let your thoughts fill with blue,
and make sure you try to do that for an hour
before you finally let go.
I know it will be difficult,
to experience nothing but the color blue,
but I know you can do it for a while.
So when my words come back to you,
at night as you drift off to sleep,
you will remember to try to stay awake,
at least for a while,
and to be aware only of blue,
like the blue in the sky,
or robin's egg blue
or the deep blue sea
and you can promise to do that now,
and then you can open your eyes
and be comfortably wide awake again
can't you?

A DIRECT APPROACH FOR SELF-CONSCIOUSNESS

As you know only too well,
no body is perfect,
but you have yet to be
imperfectly imperfect,
so what you need to do is this
in order to become more comfortable,
this weekend, when nobody will see you,
I want you to buy some bright red lipstick,
the brightest red you can find,
and you rub just a little of that lipstick
on that part of you you think is ugliest,
rub it on your most embarrassing part,
and walk around with it red,
red for an entire day,
and every time you see something red,
remember that red place on you.
You will do that,
even though you do not understand
why I might be telling you to,
will you not?
Good for you!
[*Go to the trance termination.*]

A DIRECT APPROACH FOR PSYCHOPHYSIOLOGIC DISORDERS

As you relax
in a deep trance now,
deep enough anyway,
I would like you
to give your unconscious mind time
to examine this problem of yours carefully,
until it can find a beneficial solution,
a solution you can use,
a solution it is willing and able to use,
to use for you to solve this problem,
and to solve it comfortably and well,
and when it knows
that it can and will do so,
has decided what to do
and has decided to do it for you,
it can indicate that knowing,
that decision,
by creating a movement
in a hand or a finger,
or an arm may be moved,
or even a leg or a foot,
just some small movement
so that you and I can know,
so that it can indicate
that it knows what to do
and is going to do it.
So let's go ahead
and just wait patiently,
waiting for that unconscious signal,
keep waiting until you know,
until it lets you know somehow,
that it knows how now
and will do it for you . . . (*Pause*)
[*After you detect a small unconscious
movement or restlessness of some sort on
the part of the client, go to the trance
termination sequence.*]

A DIRECT APPROACH FOR PROCRASTINATION

I could tell you
that you will have an irresistible urge
a driving desire to do those things
you complain you keep putting off.
And I could tell you,
while you drift in and out of trance,
that you will get great satisfaction
out of doing those things you haven't,
that nothing else will seem to be as much fun,
and that may work,
but the only way we'll know for sure,
is if you do your very best
to fight that idea, that impulse,
and to not do those things better for a while,
if you can,
or to not do them very well,
if you must,
because I know it will be difficult
to not do these things for a while,
so I am going to give you permission
to go ahead and do some things,
but just those things you have to do.
So remember to just do what you need to do,
and to try to force yourself
to put off everything else,
so that those hypnotic suggestions
have time to build up in force,
while you resist them as much as possible
and just do some things,
whatever things you feel you have to do,
but keep fighting that hypnotic urge
to do everything at once
as much as you can.
[*Go to the trance termination.*)

A DIRECT APPROACH FOR REHEARSING FUTURE PERFORMANCE

Application: This approach may be used with virtually any therapy client to promote therapeutic progress when the activities needed for that progress already have been identified.

So now you know what to do,
you know what needs to be done,
and all you need to do
is to do it right for you,
to let yourself do it
in the way that you can,
so I would like to give you an opportunity
to carefully review and rehearse,
to imagine every movement,
to experience every sound,
to see it all clearly in your mind
like watching something
on your mind's VCR,
to let your unconscious
go over it with you,
to review and practice it carefully,
step by step,
and to rewind and play it back
all the way through,
or even to stop the action
here and there
so that you know
exactly what to do,
and know that you can do it,
and know how you will do it.
So go ahead now,
review every part,
go over it as often as you need to,
to know it is a part of you.
Take your time . . .
do it thoroughly . . .
and when you are through
let me know
by allowing your eyes to open
and wakeful awareness to return.
So go ahead now
while I wait for you
to review it all . . .

6

GENERAL-PURPOSE METAPHORS

The metaphors and anecdotes (actually metaphorical anecdotes) presented in this chapter can be used with virtually any client. They are designed to convey universally applicable messages about the nature and source of therapeutic change and to stimulate the use of inner resources for self-healing.

We recommend that you use one or two of these general-purpose metaphors first. If therapeutic benefits are not apparent by the following session, you may wish to begin using the symptom- or problem-specific metaphors presented in later chapters. Initially, however, it is best to introduce clients to the hypnotherapeutic process via general-purpose metaphors such as these. They are relatively nonthreatening and thus establish a comfortable familiarity with the hypnotherapeutic procedure.

You may select whatever script you believe will capture the interest and attention of your client or use the script that is most comfortable for you. Because these are general-purpose metaphors, there are no specific reasons for choosing one over another aside from individual preferences and tastes.

As with the induction scripts, we have attempted to present these scripts in a format that conveys a rhythm and phrasing consistent with a trance state. Nonetheless, as with the induction scripts, it is not absolutely necessary, and perhaps not appropriate, for you to read them verbatim to your clients. Feel free to embellish them or to change the wording in whatever way you like.

JUST TRUST THE UNCONSCIOUS

As you sit there
continuing to relax
and think about the problem
that brought you here,
I wonder if you know
that tip-of-the-tongue feeling
when trying to remember
a name or an idea
or the answer to a question,
the solution to a problem
that you know you know
but it is just out of reach,
though you can taste it,
and know you know it,
but the harder you look for it
the further away it goes,
it is like it hides until you stop
then it pops into your mind.
Suddenly you know what it is
that you could not find before.
It is like your unconscious mind
waits until you look away,
waits until you give up
or stop trying so hard,
then it gives you the answer,
the way in Ireland they say
you can only see elves
out of the corner of your eye,
off to the side where they hide.
You can only see them
when you are not looking
right at them,
or the way a perfect present
for someone you know
jumps out at you
when you are looking for something
    else,
but when you go shopping
for their birthdays or holidays,
there is nothing more difficult
than finding the right thing.
A part of us knows,

and will give us what is needed,
will give the answer to you,
when you just relax,
which may be why Zen koans
work the way they do,
questions like "What is the sound
of one hand clapping?"
or "What is a mouse that roars?"
that the students ponder and wonder
    about
and try to figure out
and cannot make sense of
until they give up
and then the answer comes to mind,
a mind-blowing answer
that answers everything
and gives them peace of mind,
so knowing that you already know
exactly what you need to know,
even if you do not know
exactly what the question is
or where the answer is,
you can feel it deep down below,
and ask your own unconscious mind
to show you what is needed
then forget about it
for a moment or two,
or even a day or two,
and then suddenly there it is,
a wish come true,
a gift for you
from your own unconscious,
that just comes through
into awareness
now . . .
[*Go to the trance termination.*]

LAKE LIFE

I can remember
and remind you as well,
that many years ago
a family I know
took a vacation
at Kentucky Lake,
with their young children,
to get away from it all
at a small resort,
with rustic cabins
and a fishing dock,
small motorboats to rent,
a beach and swings,
and everyone found something
to enjoy,
until one day
a terrible smell appeared
from underneath the dock
and when they complained
the owner just laughed and said,
"That's lake life!"
and walked off chuckling,
and even though
whatever was making that smell
eventually went away on its own
by then all those people
had learned to just ignore it
and had stopped worrying
or even thinking about it
and had begun playing happily
enjoying the beauty around them,
laughing at the pleasure of it all.
And many years later,
now living on a lake,
their children grown and gone,
laughing together
as they sipped their lemonade,
their boat rocked gently by waves,
looking out at a red-streaked sunset,
watching the geese and herons fly by,
this couple laughingly announcing
to the gulls and the warm breeze,

"That's lake life,"
knowing now how
to enjoy the joys of life,
no matter what the waves wash up,
accepting unpleasant things
at times,
then after those times go away,
celebrating the wonders
that make life
a vacation every day.
[*Go to the trance termination.*]

BUILDING A HOUSE

It can be very relaxing
to watch someone working.
Educational as well.
And I wonder
if you know
what is involved
in building a house, a home,
a place to live, to be.
I don't know
everything involved,
but I remember watching,
as a child,
the way they marked it off
with stakes at each corner
on the vacant lot
and then dug the foundation,
deep in the soil,
and poured truckloads of concrete
for the basement floor,
and the thick walls,
reinforced with steel bars
to prevent cracking
or crumbling.
That house
was built to last.
A solid foundation
to rest upon,
to build the rest of a life upon.
And as you rest there,
continuing to relax,
your unconscious mind
can use that time
to examine closely
your foundation
of thought,
ideas, and beliefs,
values and experiences
defined by the blueprint,
the design,
of what is wanted
and where it is built,
already or planned.

Because someone
had to foresee,
to see before
in the mind's eye,
what was to be,
what could be
how it would look,
where it would sit,
how it would function,
that house,
sitting there,
a place to live,
a place to be,
for someone to enter,
and relax comfortably,
welcomed
and protected within,
arranged and organized,
for living within.
So if the walls
could talk
they would soothe,
and observe
a smooth, effortless flow
from one room to another,
one space to another,
a living space,
living room,
the private places,
private rooms,
where private events,
and private thoughts,
can occur safely,
and be kept
safe and sound.
Where a child
could go,
to explore and play
room after room,
floor after floor,
hidden spaces,
crawl spaces,

storage places,
full of memories,
and things put away until later.
Some remembered,
some forgotten,
old toys, school papers, pictures, and
     books
some used, some ignored,
each with a feeling,
that also was stored,
a memory of happy times,
playful events,
laughter and joy.
A house full of places,
empty spaces,
to be filled
and transformed
to meet the needs,
the desires,
of those who choose
to live within,
within oneself,
to weather the storms,
to work on ideas,
to let the mind wander,
gazing out at the sky,
or the people walking by
or coming in, and sharing and talking.
And as I talk
that solid foundation
begins to take form,
the ground floor takes shape
the plans that tell
where things go,
how things will be,
what and where
is the key.
A key question,
what will be done,
what are the plans
that guide and provide
a solid foundation
to build upon
for the future.

All from a few stakes
that mark out the place
where the stakes are high
but the payoff enormous,
where they dig a hole
deep down
in the ground,
where all the dirt was once,
but is now replaced
by a new place to be,
a new space to see,
A relaxed place to be
even now as you relax
even more
and drift in thoughts
about what will be
and what was found
that can be used later on.
Because I don't know,
what your unconscious mind knows,
or what it shows you,
when you wander and wonder
what you want,
what you will be
what it will take for you
to live comfortably in there,
but you can know,
or begin to know,
all you need to know
now . . .
[*Go to the trance termination.*]

THE TRAIN TRIP

And there are
different ways of relaxing
and taking a trip someplace else.
You can watch the passengers
pass the time waiting
for a train to board.
It is plain to see
that some are excited,
some are bored,
and some use the time
to see what they can see.
Some sleep in their chairs,
some watch their watches closely,
anxiously wondering
when they'll get where they're going,
while others relax
and enjoy the opportunity
to have nothing to do
except relax and learn.
And it's easy to see
even before the train arrives
who will enjoy the trip
and who will worry or fret
all the way there.
Some pace around,
can't sit down,
can't sit still,
not trusting the engineer
to do things right,
or the train
to stay on track,
or their own planning ahead,
to get them there
at the right time
or in the right way.
Always worrying,
worrying in all ways,
whether this leaning left. . .
or right . . .
speeding up . . .
or slowing down . . .
and what about that sound?

While someplace else,
another mind sits,
passing the time relaxing,
thinking things through,
or looking out the window
at the scene going by outside
as the fields and farms
drift by the view
where the farmers plow and sow
and plan ahead and know
that some things
can't be helped,
that there are some things
they *can* do
and other things they cannot,
and that worrying
about the weather
won't make it rain,
but that pulling on the reins,
can stop a horse in time.
And so at night they sit back
in a comfortable chair
and relax, wondering
at the wonder of it all,
and learn to trust
themselves,
what they know,
what they do,
automatically.
And that person can see
all that and more
from that view through
the image of themselves
reflected in the window,
relaxed, barely aware
of where they are
in space and time.
While someplace else,
another mind can decide
what to do and when,
the right way at the right time,
for *you.*

To relax and enjoy the view,
to do what you can,
to look down within
and discover
how much more there is
than there was before
to you, within you,
to use in whatever way
is the right way
for you
to do those things needed.
That's right . . .
Go ahead and take some time,
your own time,
to watch and learn and decide.
[*Go to the trance termination.*]

ERICKSON'S WISDOM

And so, while you relax
I can wonder,
as I often do,
what that master hypnotherapist,
Milton Erickson,
would say to you, now.
Because he often had his clients relax,
and he spoke to them of many things
while they drifted into a trance
and became aware of things
that otherwise would go overlooked,
or ignored,
or hidden from view.
Because he almost seemed
to see into their minds,
to see through them, into them,
where they kept hidden
their secret hopes, dreams, and fears.
And he knew what to say,
what to do,
to help them learn to use
their hidden talents,
their hidden knowledge,
to get them to face
what they tried to ignore,
to get them to do
what they needed to do
but would rather pretend
they could not.
He always found some way around
their usual ways of hiding
by telling them stories
about things he knew
or about childhood experiences
full of symbols and signs.
And they always knew
that he was talking to them,
showing them things,
teaching them things
that they needed to know
but didn't know they knew,
or knew but were saying no to

even though it was not new to them.
And so,
I imagine he would talk to you
about the unconscious mind,
those thoughts and ideas
that come into view
as you relax
and begin to become aware,
that somewhere in there
are memories and learnings
and things you know
and things you can do.
If only he were here
to talk to you,
because I don't know,
but you do know,
the things he might say,
the things he might do
to point out just to you,
those memories and abilities,
to help you decide
what to do and how.
A wise old man
who was not afraid
to help others see themselves
to help others accept
responsibility
for doing what was right.
A wise old man
who could talk to you
about what you knew as a child,
running and playing
or watching clouds,
how hard it was
to learn those things,
to resist some things,
to do the right things,
and how good it felt
when you felt or knew
that you were in charge of you.
But I'll save my stories,
and you can save yours,

for those times at night,
drifting in dreams,
when the mind relaxes
and images flow
and a knowing occurs that changes things,
that reveals things unseen and unheard before.
And in some unknown way
you'll know that he knew
and said to you
what you needed to hear,
what you needed to know,
because something changes,
rearranges,
in the mind's eye view
and you begin to do things—differently,
to experience things—differently,
to face things—differently,
to be able to do
what you could not do before.
You know and I know
that you know
that it all belongs
to you.
To hold on
or to let go,
to move on
or to stay put,
to put on
or to take off on your own,
or to change those things that you do
to avoid doing what you need to do
to change what is happening to you,
within you,
around you,
because it all belongs
to *you* . . .
[*Go to the trance termination.*]

THE MOVEMENT OF IDEAS

And even as you relax more and more,
the mind automatically moves toward
those thoughts, ideas, images
that clarify most clearly for you,
the very things you know and do
that seem to get in the way.
Awareness migrates toward
things that need attention,
in the same way animals migrate.
Automatically,
without thinking or trying,
they seem to know
when to go and where,
and what to do to take care of them-
    selves.
An inner voice, an inner awareness
that moves the birds,
the butterflies,
the whales,
the herds of animals
from one place to another,
that makes them restless,
something not right
that draws their attention
toward that uncomfortable feeling
and sets them in motion,
moving toward a place,
perhaps the ocean,
an expansive inner space
of quiet comfort
and effortless relaxation.
And they move
hundreds of miles, thousands of miles,
taking care of their young,
taking care of themselves.
And everyone thinks
that no one really knows,
exactly how it feels
to be an otter, or a whale, or a butterfly,
that suddenly knows
the time is right
for a change,

that suddenly knows
the exact change needed,
but they do know
and so do you,
just like you know
when you are uncomfortable
or need something to eat.
So we can relax and imagine
how it might feel
to gradually or suddenly feel that
    feeling,
that inner awareness,
that restless recognition,
that something needs to change
and needs to change now.
And we can imagine
how it might be
to know without knowing
what needs to be done,
to be told without hearing,
by an inner voice, an inner feeling,
to do this *now*.
And we can imagine,
how it feels
to have actions flow
from those feelings,
responding effortlessly, automatically,
to that inner awareness,
that inner knowing,
that tells us what to do
and when
and how to do it.
We are born
with that knowledge,
we can trust that feeling,
comfortably aware of oneself,
one's inner guide,
that subtle voice
that we too often ignore
that knows what is good for us
and what is a mistake
and everything becomes easier,

though no one ever imagined
that traveling a thousand miles is easy,
but the decision to go
takes no effort at all.
A decision, a knowing
that is a part of each being
that guides and directs automatically
toward those things needed.
A migration of thought,
of awareness,
which presents memories, ideas,
understandings for you to use
for you.
That's right.
Even as you relax
and the unconscious mind
automatically provides that awareness
that you can use later on
or right now.
[*Go to the trance termination.*]

VACATIONS

And anytime
you drift off someplace . . .
deep inside the mind,
it is like a vacation,
going off to a different place,
experiencing different things . . .
and forgetting for a time
the cares and concerns . . .
discovering something new
or remembering something old, forgotten.
Because it is comforting to let go,
to enjoy a new way of seeing,
a new way of being
that you can experience . . . now,
like the woman I know
who traveled alone
down to Florida.
She'd never left the Midwest before,
but as soon as she got off the plane
she began to experience and explore
new things . . .
and she began to change
her way of thinking,
her way of being.
The warm salt sea air
full of sunlight
brushed her skin
with its new smell,
and gentle heat,
the palm trees caught her eye,
the sand glistened in the sun
and she felt strange,
alive and alert to every new thing,
new sights, sounds, smells,
new ways of doing things.
She walked on the beach,
she waded into the ocean,
she stopped and talked
to people . . .
from many different places
who then stopped being strangers
and became her friends,

and she felt her world,
her inner world,
expand . . .
as she became aware
of how much more there is
than she knew before.
She examined every detail
of every shell, plant, and face,
she looked through the shops
and the windows
of every brightly painted home,
and as she made friends . . .
people from all over the world
with new ideas,
new ways of speaking,
new places to show her,
new experiences to share,
this shy Midwest farm girl,
had her eyes opened,
her mind opened,
to a whole new world,
because everything was so different
she could ignore it no more,
she could deny it no longer.
And even while swimming in the ocean
she continued to learn,
that things are not always
what they seem,
or may seem to be one thing
but turn out to be another,
like the strange things she felt
as she walked through the water,
and her mind could imagine
what lurked beneath the surface
tickling her feet, wrapping around her
    legs
with strange and frightening sensations.
But when she really looked
to see what was there,
it was beautiful sea grasses
rolling with the waves,
and soft fern mosses,

not the stuff of her imagination
not what she had feared,
just something wonderfully new . . .
like the new thoughts she had,
the new feelings she felt,
as she relaxed on the beach
and let her mind go,
let her mind wander deep down below,
where things go overlooked,
ignored or unused.
And those deep down thoughts
and those deeper down feelings
began to bubble up,
to drift up into her awareness,
things she had never thought before,
things she's never allowed herself
to see or think or to feel,
remembering things . . .
new things about old times,
old things in new ways
good times and bad times,
in good ways and bad ways,
wanting things, new things,
experiences and pleasures.
She discovered treasures
buried deep inside,
she experienced pleasures
she had always denied.
She let herself begin to know,
although it was difficult at times,
and took a long time
to look at it all in all ways
so that she would always know
what it was she knew,
and what she needed to do
now that she knew
so many new things.
She returned home
but what she learned
stayed with her . . .
how to relax,
how to allow her mind to teach,
her mind to guide,
herself to know,

herself to trust,
and she changed
her way of doing things.
She returned home,
but she stayed on that vacation as well.
And you can stay relaxed,
comfortably relaxed,
as your mind drifts
in the sands of time,
and brings those learnings
back with you
now too . . .
[*Go to the trance termination.*]

7

MANAGING CHRONIC
AND ACUTE PAIN

The scripts presented in this chapter are examples of an entire hypnotherapy session for pain management, including the induction, metaphorical implications, direct approaches, and trance termination procedures. As such, they demonstrate how these various components of a hypnotherapeutic intervention are integrated into a treatment session. Furthermore, because our Neo-Ericksonian approach to therapy is based on the observation that pain is the primary symptom of all therapy patients and the creation of pleasure is the primary goal, we suggest that learning how to use hypnotic approaches to help people manage, escape from, or replace pain is an appropriate place to begin.

The following scripts reflect the fact that hypnotic interventions for physical pain usually are much more straightforward than hypnotherapy for emotional or psychological suffering. Nonetheless, pain and pain management are complex topics that extend far beyond the scope of the material presented here. Before you attempt to use hypnosis for pain management training, you should become familiar with the available literature. In the meantime, however, there are several points worth stressing.

First of all, pain is only a signal, a neurophysiologic event that must be noticed and interpreted cognitively before it turns into suffering. Thus, pain control involves either learning to not notice the signal at all or learning to interpret it in a benign manner.

Learning to not notice a pain signal really amounts to learning to notice something else instead. When a patient's attention is fully focused on something other than the pain signal, such as something dangerous or highly significant, the pain will not be noticed and, consequently, it will not generate any suffering. Erickson once asked a woman how much pain she would feel if she saw a tiger coming through her door licking its chops. She admitted that she would not notice her pain at all. Similarly, a chronic pain patient whose back and pelvis had been severely damaged in a fall from a roof was surprised but pleased to discover that he felt no discomfort at all when he began piloting a plane.

The experience of pain also vanishes when attention is absorbed by something pleasant or comforting. One man reported that his pain was reduced to almost nothing whenever he became immersed in playing his electronic keyboard and, of course, as mentioned previously, there are numerous references in the literature to the use of humor and pleasant memories as a form of pain relief. Erickson (1983, p. 104) recommended that during a hypnosis session, "you can give progressively more and more attention to the ease and comfort and less and less attention to the pain." The scripts presented here follow this recommendation.

When a pain signal is noticed, the suffering it produces stems largely from the anger, fear, and other reactions people experience when they cognitively interpret that sensation. Morphine, for example, does not "kill" pain. Rather, it puts people in a state of mind where they no longer care about it or think about it. The pain signal is still there but it no longer concerns them. Thus, when you eliminate the negative cognitive connotations of the pain, much of the emotionally based suffering is eliminated as well.

Hypnotic trance can be used to reduce suffering by revising negative connotations as well as by directing attention elsewhere. If they know it is safe to do so, people in a relaxed trance can learn to remain calm and unaffected by a sensation that otherwise might terrify or enrage them. In that calm state of mind they can learn to redefine their pain as an itch, a cramp, a hot sensation, or even a meaningless irrelevancy. Sometimes they even can learn how to not experience it at all. They can disconnect from it completely, "forget" how to locate it, or generate a feeling of numbness in the affected area. When given an opportunity to rely on their own experiential backgrounds and abilities, people can creatively use what they have learned from their previous experiences to generate a remarkable range of solutions. When patients know it is safe to ignore the pain signal and are given access via hypnosis to other possibilities, they will readily accept and use those other options.

This brings us to our second point, that pain can be a meaningful signal or have no value at all. If the sensation is an alarm, then it means that something is wrong physically that can and should receive attention; if it means that tissue is being destroyed, then it is meaningful.

It is difficult and potentially dangerous to ignore or eliminate a meaningful pain signal. By definition, meaningful pain is an alarm calling attention to a situation that requires corrective action. On the other hand, pain in an amputated foot or pain originating from a strangulated nerve that cannot be corrected is meaningless. The short-term pain from a surgical procedure, a dental procedure, or childbirth also usually lacks real significance. Although there is damage being done, there is no reason to attend to it. Awareness of the pain will not improve an operation and lack of awareness will not ruin it. As Fisher (1991) teaches his hypnosis patients, the surgeon is not attacking them. The surgery is a source of help and healing, not a life-threatening assault. In that sense, the sensations from the surgeon's incision are meaningless and it is safe to ignore them.

As long as a patient believes that a pain is important or meaningful, it will be difficult for that person to learn how to use hypnosis to manage the experience of it. For example, one patient was able to learn how to reduce his discomfort only after he was thoroughly convinced that the sharp twinges he felt did not mean that bone fragments slowly were severing a nerve in his injured back. Patients need to be consciously reassured prior to the use of hypnosis that an inability to feel a sensation will not result in any undue damage. So do hypnotherapists.

When a pain does have meaning, care must be taken to preserve the cautions or restrictions created by that signal even as you reduce the suffering. Various types of back pain, for example, serve as a warning not to move in certain ways or not to lift too much weight. Ignoring these signals could result in serious muscle, nerve, or disc damage. Instead of attempting to block these signals out entirely, an effort can be made to transform them into alternative protective signals such as tightness or warmth.

Finally, pain may be a short-term, situation-specific phenomenon or a long-term, chronic experience. Most people can manage short-term discomfort rather easily, especially if they know it is not a danger signal requiring curative action. A stubbed toe may lead to curses, but it is soon forgotten if nothing is broken, even though that toe will continue to be painful for several hours or days. Chronic pain, however, carries with it the memory of past pain and the anticipation of all future pain. It permeates the entire body and takes over the person's entire existence. The hypnotic approaches used to deal with these two different types of pain must take into account these differences as well as the meaningfulness of the pain signal itself. Thus, we provide different scripts for chronic versus acute pain.

Because chronic pain patients automatically are drawn into an awareness of their pain as soon as they are told to close their eyes or relax, the pain itself is used as their initial internal focus. By directing attention toward the pain while encouraging relaxation and calmness, patients are allowed to learn that the pain signal will not destroy them. This removes the tendency to struggle angrily or fearfully against the pain, which can itself cause muscle cramping or spasms and further pain. As patients learn that they can be highly aware of the pain and yet remain calm, their suffering diminishes. Treatment then becomes a matter of guiding them through a series of internal events (images, thoughts, perspectives, and so forth) until one or more is found that creates the comfortable relief and pleasure sought. An opportunity to practice using these newly discovered abilities is then provided before they are brought out of trance.

The procedures used to help patients prepare to control an anticipated short-term pain, such as childbirth or surgery, typically involve a brief trance induction followed by a series of comments or suggestions designed to enable the person to accept the pain sensation as irrelevant and recognize different ways that sensations can be altered or numbness created. The effectiveness of these approaches cannot be monitored directly by subjects because pain is not yet present. Hence, the therapist may provide a painful stimulus or, as in the script presented here, direct the client to do so in order to "test" the degree of pain control created. The discovery of an effective approach is followed by a practice session wherein the pain control is successively removed and reinstated until the subject has mastered the internal "shift" that produces the desired lack of sensitivity. This procedure is comparable to the rehearsal procedure used during the trance termination phase of hypnotherapy.

It should be apparent that there is a tremendous similarity between these hypnotic pain management processes and hypnotherapy for emotional or psychological discomforts. The underlying logic, goals, and procedures of each are virtually identical. Whether the incident responsible for the pain is brief or long-standing, a powerful internal physiologic reaction, unpleasant thought, imagined event, terrifying memory, or horrific external event, the individual's suffering is a result of ongoing attention to, interpretations of, and emotional responses to that event. When those painful interpretations are replaced by more comforting ideas and the attendant debilitating emotional reactions have abated, attention then can be diverted toward enhanced pleasure and even joy. Physiologic and emotional pain may have different names, but the nature and treatment of each are basically the same.

The scripts presented in this chapter are designed to help people learn the skills required to master chronic or acute pain. As indicated previously, however, cognitive or emotional issues with regard to the source of the pain may make it difficult for a patient to apply such techniques effectively. For example, fears, misconceptions, confusions, frustrations, or anger regarding the surgical or dental procedures to be used, the nature of an injury or illness, or the process of childbirth may interfere with a patient's ability to learn or use the pain management skills presented in the following. Such problems must be recognized and dealt with before pain management can be successful. Scripts for this purpose are presented in Chapter 14.

CHRONIC PAIN MANAGEMENT SCRIPT

Applications: For use with long-term pain such as back injuries, nerve damage, phantom limb pain, cancer, and so on.

With your eyes closed,
as you begin to relax,
you probably notice
that the first thing you notice
is how difficult it is
to not become aware
of that pain and discomfort,
and that's fine.
You don't need
to fight your mind,
which is always aware
of those sensations there
for you
because as you relax,
you can begin to discover
that each time you relax
a muscle in an arm . . .
or a leg . . .
or your face . . .
or even a foot . . . or a finger,
that you can drift down
more and more deeply than before,
into that sensation there
in a more relaxed and comfortable way.
Because there really is no need
to make the effort it takes
to try to stay away
from that feeling
or try to fight that feeling,
which almost seems to guide and direct
awareness down toward it,
more and more into it,
and as you drift toward it,
toward the center of that feeling,
the very tiniest center
of that feeling
the very small middle of it,
the source of it,
a place that does not mean
to be mean to you,
is not an evil monster
trying to kill you,
or something for you
to fight with, to destroy,
to hate or fear,
because it will not destroy you
it just wants to tell you
what you already know,
that something is wrong there,
so just relax into it,
let yourself go to it,
embrace it and let it know
that you appreciate its help,
and thank it for its concern,
but there is nothing left to do,
that you know
all you need to know
and it can now relax,
can let go, can quiet down,
and you can too,
you can relax,
relax more and more,
as you begin to discover
that it really is OK
to let go in that way,
to let that pain go its own way
while you go another
and leave it alone,
let it do its thing
while you do yours,
and allow yourself to relax
every part of your body
and drift down through that center,
down through that place
into a place beneath it,
a wonderful place beyond it
of quietness and calm awareness,
down through that feeling,

and out the other side,
drifting into a space
of relaxed letting go,
of comfortable relaxation,
where the mind can drift,
the way waves drift
from one place to another
as that body relaxes
and the mind becomes smoother
and softer,
able to absorb events,
even those events,
easily and comfortably,
becoming absorbed
in thoughts and images,
as the mind reflects
the clear wonder of a child,
a young child,
watching a flock of geese
as they soar
across the sky
and fly away into the mists,
the rhythm of their sound
becoming softer and softer,
as soft as the down
in a pillow in a place
where you can rest and relax,
a most comfortable place
for a child to relax
and drift in dreams
through the mind, protected and safe,
where letting go
allows the flow
and the soft floating upward,
where the mind drifts free
of the things far below,
and seems to soar
in a sky as clear as glass,
so smooth and calm
that it disappears
when you look at it,
and what appears instead
is the deep blue shine
of the warm soft sun

in a quiet sky,
a star far beyond
that reaches out and provides
that warm soft light
as you drift down
and feel the comfort
of a deep sound sleep
that your unconscious mind
can provide to you
whenever you relax
and drift into a trance like this.
Because your unconscious mind
can lead you down,
down through that feeling,
into that healing
into that space,
that relaxed comfortable place,
as you relax
and allow it to do so
just for you.
That relief and relaxation,
that drifting down through
that comes to you
whenever you allow it to,
just as that drifting upward
occurs as well,
a drifting back
toward the surface of wakeful
    awareness,
as your unconscious mind
reminds you to drift up
in a relaxed, comfortable way now.
Back toward the surface now,
bringing with you
that comfortable relaxation,
that effortless change in sensation,
even as the mind drifts upward,
and the relaxation continues,
as the mind awakens
and the eyes open
but the body remains behind, relaxed.
That's right, eyes open now. (*Pause*)
But before you come back completely,
you can close those eyes again,

and feel that relaxation again,
and recognize that ability,
that ability to relax,
to let your unconscious mind
find the way to provide you
with more and more comfort,
more and more relaxed,
following that path back,
letting go and going down.
That's right.
Aware that you can do so,
anytime, anyplace you need to or want to,
you can return to that place.
So here is what you do,
later on today, tomorrow, next week
and for the rest of your life,
whenever you need to or want to,
you can close your eyes
for just a moment, perhaps,
and feel that comfortable feeling,
that change in sensation,
that change in awareness,
return to you
as you drift into that light trance
or a deep trance
where your unconscious mind
can take care of you,
make things comfortable for you,
where you can stop fighting
and stop reacting,
and feel comfort return
and then you can return
to the surface of wakeful awareness,
not needing to make the effort it takes
to try to tell if that feeling is there or not,
just as you return now
back to the surface,
comfortably rested and refreshed,
remaining relaxed perhaps,
even as the eyes open again,
and wakeful awareness returns,
now!!
That's right,
Wide awake now.

ANTICIPATED SHORT-TERM PAIN MANAGEMENT SCRIPT

Applications: For use with childbirth, dental work, surgery, sports injuries, and so on.

Now, your eyes are closed,
and you are sitting there comfortably
        aware
that you have come here today
because you want to learn
to use your own hypnotic abilities,
to eliminate some future sensation
that otherwise might feel uncomfortable
but can go away from you
as you go away from it and just let it be.
And so, as you begin to relax
and to drift down into a light trance,
or a medium trance,
or even a deep trance,
I want you to take your time doing so.
Not too quickly yet,
because there are some things
you need to listen to carefully first.
For example, you need to understand
that you already have an ability
to lose an arm or a hand,
to become completely unaware
of exactly where that arm is positioned,
or the fingers,
and you have an ability to be
        unconcerned
about exactly where that finger went
or that hand or leg,
or your entire body,
which may seem to take
too much effort to pay attention to at
        times.
Because you also have an ability,
an unconscious ability
you can learn how to use,
and that ability is the ability
to turn off the feeling
in an arm, a leg, or anywhere,
just like turning off a light
by following the wires that lead

from that hand,
that right hand perhaps,
and carry those signals,
those pain signals,
up past the wrist,
past the elbow,
up to the upper arm,
a larger wire now
as it follows the path
up the spinal column
and into the brain,
up to that special circuit board
where all the switches are
for all the parts of the body,
and all you need to do,
as we follow that wire to that switch,
is turn off that switch
and wonder how it feels then
for the pain to be blocked there,
for all pain from that hand
to be stopped right there
and to not get through into awareness,
not at all,
that switch turned off,
a kind of numb, comfortable feeling
anywhere, anytime it is useful to you,
a comfortable tingling feeling perhaps,
or a heavy, thick numbness,
that might seem to grow and spread
        over time,
until it covers that hand, the back of the
        hand,
or anything else you pay close attention
        to,
but you don't really know how it feels
        yet,
to not feel something that isn't there,
so here is what I want you to do.
I want you to reach over to that pain-
        free area,

to that hand with the pain switch turned
　　off,
that's right, go ahead and touch it,
and feel that touching,
because the touching switch is not turned
　　off,
just the pain switch,
so now begin to pinch yourself there
and begin to discover,
that you feel no pain there at all,
no matter how hard you pinch it,
that's right, the pain is turned off,
go ahead, pinch a bit harder,
explore that more and more,
get used to how it feels
for the pain to be turned off,
so you begin to know, *really* know,
that you already do know
how to allow pain to disappear
from that hand there, or anywhere,
you know how to trace those wires
that carry pain
and find that switch,
and turn it off,
anywhere on your body at all . . .
And once you are convinced
that you have that ability,
you can begin drifting up,
up to that point
where wakeful awareness will return.
So go ahead now, as you relax,
and continue to drift up,
in your own time,
in your own way.
That's right, take your time to learn,
and then drifting back upward, eyes
　　opening.
[*Pause until the client opens his or her eyes.
Then immediately continue.*]
Now, before you wake up completely,
I would like you to close your eyes again,
and allow that drifting down again,
re-entering that place of calm relaxation,
because there was a young boy on TV

not long ago,
who learned how to control *all* his pain.
He described the steps he went down in
　　his mind,
one at a time down those steps,
until he found this hall at the bottom,
like a long tunnel,
and all along the tunnel on both sides
were many different switches,
　　switchboxes,
each clearly labeled.
One for the right hand, one the left, one
　　the leg,
and one for every other place on the
　　body,
and he could see the wires to those
　　switches,
the nerves that carried sensations
from one place to another
all going through those switches.
And all he needed to do
was to reach up in his mind
and turn off the switches he wanted to
and then he could feel nothing there at
　　all
no pain could get through from there,
none at all,
because he had turned off those
　　switches there,
just like you,
he used his mind's abilities
just like you,
he said he didn't know how he did it
　　exactly,
all he knew was he relaxed and
　　disconnected,
turned off that switch and that was that.
And it really doesn't matter
exactly how you tell your unconscious
　　what to do,
or how your unconscious does it for
　　you.
The only thing of importance
is that you know you can

lose painful sensations
as easily as closing your eyes,
and drifting down within
where something happens
when you disconnect that wire
that allows that numbness to occur,
and then a drifting upward now,
upward toward the surface
and slowly allowing the eyes to open
as wakeful awareness returns
with a comfortable continuation
of that protected feeling
of safe, secure relaxation
and an ability to quiet a hand,
or anything at all,
with no need to pay attention
to things that are just fine,
that somebody else can take care of
while you drift in your mind
and then return when it is time
to enjoy that comfortable drifting upward
where the eyes open
and wakeful awareness returns
quite completely *now*.

8

RECOVERING FROM TRAUMA AND GRIEF

Just as hypnosis can be used to alleviate the physical suffering caused by physical injuries, it also can be used to alleviate the emotional suffering caused by tragic life events. As the examples of metaphorical anecdotes presented in this and the following chapters demonstrate, the logic and the approaches used are similar no matter whether the pain is physical or emotional. In each case, the goal is to promote a comfortable awareness of the underlying pain, offer clients a clearer view of themselves in general, and encourage a more straightforward understanding of or experience with potential sources of relief and resolution. Although these messages are directed primarily toward the unconscious mind, the metaphors often are specific enough to gently challenge the conscious mind a bit as well. They plant the seeds of a specific idea or understanding that can grow from unconscious to conscious awareness.

Some people are haunted by vague or clear memories of excruciatingly painful events. The memories of terror, horror, victimization, or loss may be ambiguous or quite specific, the events recent or long past, but the impact on a person's life can be dramatic and ever-present. Nothing will ever undo what happened in the past, nothing can bring back lost loved ones or prevent a previous attack from happening, but there are ways to undo what the past is doing to a client in the present. There are ways a person can reduce the pain.

Healing the effects of a past trauma is neither simple nor easy. Sometimes it involves the development of a new perspective on what happened in order to remove all blame from the victim, direct the anger outward, and empower the person now and in the future. At other times, it involves an acknowledgment that the past cannot be understood or changed and must be mournfully released. On top of all this, disturbing memories and images of the event itself typically must be banished and overridden.

Almost invariably, however, recovery from trauma also involves the reestablishment of some precious inner resource that the traumatic event tore away from the client. Child sexual abuse often shatters the feeling of one's innocent goodness and leaves a pervasive sense of guilty vulnerability. Physical and sexual abuse or assault may destroy all awareness of personal safety, self-worth, and joy. Loss of a loved one can disconnect the person from the ability to love or feel connected to anyone or anything. The damage done varies from client to client but the therapeutic goal remains the same: to prevent further suffering by helping that client rediscover the ability to enjoy life events and look forward to a promising future.

It is difficult enough to cope with the random destruction and death caused by natural events, but nothing seems to compare to the disturbing images, terror, and rage people experience following physical assaults or acts of war and terrorism. The pain people experience under such circumstances can be more devastating than any other form of pain imaginable. Their entire physiology may be altered, patterns of thought disrupted, and emotions amplified beyond tolerability. To escape from such suffering, the natural tendency often seems to be to try to ignore what happened, put it behind them, not let themselves or the rest of the world know about those events, much less the ongoing effects of those events. But because their initial trauma was so intense and thorough, their subsequent suffering can continue at an unspoken or even unconscious level long after an apparent conscious resolution of the issues involved. This suffering may be reflected in nightmares, unwarranted anxieties, and even self-hatred. The initial trauma is ignored, perhaps denied at times, but the painful consequences live on.

For this reason, metaphorical hypnotherapeutic interventions, such as those presented in the following, can be of considerable value. They gently bypass any efforts to ignore the devastating impact of what happened and offer unconscious suggestions for healing. We do not want to imply that these techniques can be relied upon exclusively to resolve such problems. They are, however, an effective adjunct to the many forms of support and intervention specifically tailored to the needs of survivors of assault and those in the mourning process.

LITTLE DREAMS

A metaphor script for adult survivors of child sexual abuse.

Now, you've told me many things about
    your life
and listening to the truth about
    someone's life
is a privilege and an honor . . .
and though you don't need my thanks
I really do thank your conscious mind
for sorting and categorizing so much
    information
and I thank your unconscious mind
for what your conscious mind
can discover later on.
And there are so many things
a person can discover.
I remember the time,
five or six years ago
when I first discovered
what it would be like
to live an entire life
feeling different every day
because that's when I met Annie
and she was the only dwarf I'd ever
    met.
And I learned that in childhood
it really hadn't been a problem
cause everyone was small and little
    then,
but friends grew up
and Annie stayed small,
and had to go on living her life
in a world of big people.
She had a special stool in the kitchen,
she pushed it around as she moved
from counter, to cabinet,
so she could jump on top of it
and reach out for the things she needed,
so she could look into the freezer,
and reach the burners on the stove.
She had a special sewing machine
and she made all her own clothes
from her own designs

since nothing else would fit.
At a party she couldn't reach the punch
    bowl,
and she sometimes had to crawl onto a
    chair
where her feet never touched ground.
And I really wanted to learn from her
about living such a life,
and she told me,
"There's just one thing you can say
about people like me,
there's always going to be
something that comes up."
And I thought a long time about that
and what it might mean in a life.
Now a client I worked with a while
    back
told me about a dream he'd had
where he'd awakened in his bedroom,
but the entire room was covered with a
    dense fog.
And when he first felt the fog he was
    quite angry,
finding himself damp and uncomfortable
and unable to see a foot ahead of him,
and the anger just grew and grew
until he felt nothing but rage,
and that heavy fog enveloping him.
He wanted to run screaming from the
    room,
but when he opened his mouth to
    speak
nothing came out,
and who would he tell?
He was so alone.
And how could there be so much fog?
Would anyone believe him?
And these thoughts occupied his mind,
he couldn't move, he couldn't cry,
he could only feel his anger,
rusting like a nail in the dense fog.

And just when things seemed darkest
he became aware of a breath of warm air
hovering around his face.
And you can imagine his surprise
to discover that that warm, moist air
was his own breath mingling with the
    fog.
And he continued to breathe
deep, strong breaths, blowing that fog
    away
with every inhalation and exhalation
as the fog lifted
and light began filtering into that room,
anger lifting, breathing calmly, peacefully,
and he awakened from that dream
with a new understanding.
And it was about the same time
that his sister received the letter
about the inheritance.
Now he and his sister were orphaned
at a very early age,
and they had impressed upon me
that their expectations from childhood
didn't include having anyone
look out for them,
or take care of them.
They were all alone in the world,
on their own in the world,
or so it seemed to them,
until the day they got the letter telling
    them
they were to receive a large inheritance.
And their puzzlement grew and grew,
since they were orphans, alone in the
    world.
But adults so often forget the things
they knew so well as children,
just as they'd forgotten the times
they'd saved a penny here, a nickel there,
and left them for safekeeping
with a kind, old woman up the street,
who'd taken their money and invested it
with her own
until she could return

their own savings to them
multiplied into the thousands and
    thousands.
And with so many resources to rely on,
a child, robbed of a parent,
became rich as an adult,
safe, and comforted now.
And though you sometimes dream in
    darkness,
that is one of your lives by now—
it is not the time that you know best,
so much of the journey
has been in shadow . . .
now you are safe
you know life in light,
where there is no pressure, no rush to
    change,
only the time without shadows.
[*Go to a direct approach or trance
termination.*]

AN APPLE TREE

A metaphor script for adult survivors of a recent assault.

I suppose you already know
that sometimes children can be
    thoughtless,
and at times even cruel,
but I can remember a time,
very long ago,
when I was very young,
and I watched a boy much older than me,
much bigger than me,
a kid I never did like,
Donny was his name,
attack a tree with a hatchet
because he was mad about something,
who knows what,
but he hit it over and over,
knocking off bark from the trunk,
chips flew everywhere,
sap started running down,
and then he chopped of a few branches
and threw them on the ground,
and I think he even stomped on them,
and climbed up in the tree
and hit it some more.
He was yelling and screaming,
cursing and everything,
and he scared me because he seemed
so totally out of control,
so I just stood back and watched him,
even though that tree was an apple tree
in my own back yard,
one I had climbed many times,
one that gave us apples
when we played football out there,
but I did not care,
I stayed away,
confused and afraid of him,
which was nothing new
because he was a bully anyway,
but I just waited
until he quit and left,
then I got scared that my father

would think I had done it,
so I carried the limbs out back,
and picked up all the pieces I could,
and just stayed away from that kid
from then on
and tried to forget all about it.
But years later
when I went back to my home town
to visit some old friends
I drove over to my old house,
got out and walked around
and that apple tree was still there
in the back yard
taller and bigger
and covered with apples
that looked delicious,
so I went over to that tree
and picked an apple
that was juicier and sweeter
than I remembered
and only then did I notice
the faint lines in the bark
that were healed wounds,
the small bumps
where limbs had once been,
now replaced by many more,
and then I remembered
what I had tried to forget about,
Donny's angry fit
which had vanished from my mind,
just about,
until that tree reminded me,
and that reminds me
that later I found out
that Donny is now in prison,
and will be for quite a while,
which makes me wonder
if you know
how a tree smiles.
[*Go to a direct approach or trance
termination.*]

PREDICTION AND CONTROL

A metaphor script for adult survivors of disasters and acts of terrorism.

And so, as you relax,
it becomes easier to think about
many different things,
even scientific things,
or science itself,
because science is a way of thinking,
one way of knowing,
one that involves an effort
to predict and control,
to predict what is going to happen
and to control what does happen,
because people do not like things
they do not understand
and they cannot control,
people really hate things
that go out of control,
like cars that spin and flip over,
or machines that do not start,
or fires that explode across the land,
or animals that misbehave,
or weather that tears lives apart,
so we have many different sciences
and many different scientists,
all trying to understand
why things do what they do
and how to predict
what they are going to do next,
and we even have psychology,
the science of human behavior,
where they try to figure out
why people do what they do
and how to get them to stop
or go in different directions,
but the sad fact is
that chemicals in a test tube
are one thing,
but the events of everyday life
and the actions of people
are another,
much harder to understand
more difficult to control

than even black bears
in national parks,
the ones that learn
that cars contain food,
like hot dogs and candy,
that is easy to get
if you break a few windows
or tear off a few doors
and so they teach their young
how to do it too
and there really is no way
to stop them from doing it
and so they just catch them,
and ship them very far away,
because we understand why
they do what they do,
they do not mean to hurt anyone,
they are just trying to get food,
but what about the bears
that decide to attack people?
They really scare us
because it makes no sense
for them to do that,
and we don't really know
what they might do next,
so we eliminate them
if we can bear to do so
and we become more careful,
but we refuse to be afraid all the time
of all the things that might happen,
we decide to not hide inside,
like bears trapped in a cave,
or stop living life to the fullest
when the odds are on our side,
so we talk about it with each other,
find out how others feel
and what others want to do,
and we keep going back,
returning to the beauty
of the forests and mountains,
enjoying the lakes and rivers,

doing what we want to do,
hoping all the other animals and bears
will behave themselves,
or misbehave someplace else,
the way we go back after a fire
has destroyed thousands of acres,
sad that it happened,
but glad it is over,
watching nature heal it,
until one day
from under the ashes
a flower pushes up
and opens to the sun,
which reminds us all,
even the scientists there,
to be more open to life,
because life is tough
and will survive
even the worst of times
to bring back all the beauty,
and replenish the earth
with the things that bring us joy
and the things that bring us pleasure,
and the feeling
of being free
to be
once again.
[*Go to a direct approach or trance termination.*]

SAYING GOODBYE

A metaphor script for adult victims of child abuse and childhood trauma.[1]

Now,
as you sit there with your eyes closed,
and begin to continue to allow your
    body to relax,
your mind to relax,
and experience the awareness
of many different things,
you may begin to wonder,
how many different ways there are
to heal a wound,
a wound from long ago that never healed
but remained behind
to change the way you think and feel,
like a woman I know
who always wondered why
she was the way she was,
until one day when she discovered a
    child within—
a sad child, an unhappy child,
an angry hurt child from long ago.
A child she always heard in the
    background,
a child she protected and did everything
    for today,
a child who made her feel so sad
and she would do anything to keep that
    child quiet,
to keep that child happy,
to give that child what it wanted and
    needed.
And I asked her what needed to be done,
and she said she needed to say *goodbye*
    to that child,
she needed to *hug* that child,
to *hold* that child
and to *tell* that child how very, very
    sorry she was
that those things had happened to it.
She felt so badly for the pain,
so badly for the fear,
so badly for the anger.
But she knew she had to say goodbye,
    finally,
she had to leave it behind
and go on with her life.
She knew there was nothing she could do
to save that child,
to change the past,
to undo what was.
What was, was, and there was nothing
    she could do.
So she hugged that child, and said
    goodbye,
and walked away, and cried and cried.
The hardest thing she had ever done
was say goodbye, leave it behind,
abandon it to the past.
She felt awful, but she knew
that was what she had to do.
There was nothing she could do to
    change the past,
nothing she could do to undo
what that child went through.
But afterward she was free,
felt free, to do what *she* wanted.
The child was gone
and she was free,
free of the past,
free to be.
And so as you relax,
and continue to drift down,
your unconscious knows what you can do,
your conscious knows it too,
and you can feel the freedom
of that relaxed letting go
in your own way,
even as you drift more deeply at times
    than others.
[*Go to a direct approach or trance
termination.*]

[1]A modified version of this procedure was included in the *Handbook of Hypnotic Suggestions and Metaphors*, edited by D. Corydon Hammond, Ph.D., published in 1990 by W. W. Norton & Co. as an official publication of the American Society of Clinical Hypnosis.

BURIED TREASURES

A metaphor script for adult victims of child sexual abuse.

I wonder if you have ever seen
the small fragile glass figurines
that artisans sell at fairs and in shopping
     malls,
made of tiny strands of clear bright glass
all carefully laced together
to form the shape of a ship or an animal,
or even a house or a tree,
that seem to fascinate children
with their delicate sparkles and shapes
like priceless jewels, valuable
     possessions,
to be carried in velvet cases and
     protected,
kept safe from loss or damage,
tiny treasures, a gift to someone,
like the treasure carried in ships across
     the sea.
There was a program on TV several years
     ago,
about a man who spent twenty years
searching for such a ship, a lost treasure
     ship,
one of hundreds that had been lost along
     the coast
because of accidents and disasters and
     wars.
He researched it very carefully,
and thought he knew exactly what had
     been lost.
He also thought he knew what had
     happened
and where the treasure had sunk.
But it was hard to find that ship,
it had been lost for so long.
It had gotten buried with mud and coral,
and there were many other wrecks in the
     area,
any one of which could have been the
     one,
but wasn't.

So he spent many years searching,
and he raised thousands of dollars from
     investors,
because he was convinced
there was something of great value
     down there,
lost treasure of immeasurable worth,
and he convinced others it was there
     too,
family, friends, and the divers who
     worked with him,
searched for it year after year,
until finally one day
the divers returned to the surface
shouting and screaming and holding up
     gold bars.
They had found that ship,
and it contained more than you can
     imagine,
tons of gold bars, silver bars, gold coins,
precious jewels and elaborate jewelry,
priceless objects, treasure untold,
things from the past that had gone
     untouched,
that had not been seen for hundreds of
     years
suddenly were there for people to hold
     and feel.
And they held them with reverence,
touching them gently and silently,
as if these things that had been lost for
     so long
contained some memory of the past,
something special that people need,
something special to protect,
like those tiny glass figures
that you see at fairs and malls.
They seem to be so fragile,
so easily broken by someone rough,
but they actually are quite sturdy
and can survive for years and years,

even when lost or hidden away,
like the treasures at the bottom of the ocean,
hidden deep down below,
something precious and valuable inside,
a part of you, before,
that belonged to you, before,
because there is a kind of glass
called Pyrex
that is as strong as steel,
that can withstand the hottest fires
without cracking,
without breaking,
that can be bumped and dropped,
mishandled and misused,
that looks and feels fragile,
like those inner treasures may seem
to you
yet it still stays strong and clear and bright,
beautiful to look at
wonderful to touch.
And the joy of its discovery,
the recovery of that buried treasure,
the pleasure of knowing it belongs to you,
that it is you,
is something you can bring back with you
that warm good part of the heart of the matter
that children sometimes lose for a time,
or have taken from them at another time,
but it always lies there waiting,
waiting to be brought back to the surface
where it can be touched and felt and enjoyed
and kept close within you forever, now,
because it all belongs to you.
[*Go to a direct approach or trance termination.*]

LETTING GO

A metaphor script for unresolved grief or bereavement.

As you already know
if you have ever watched a baby grow,
it is much easier for that child
to hold onto something
than it is to put it down
or to let go,
they are born with the ability
to hold on tight,
to get a firm grip on anything
placed into their tiny hands,
they cling to a parent's finger
or a piece of cloth
or a rattle,
in a kind of reflex response
that keeps them attached and safe,
and it is quite a feat
to learn how to let go,
so it is interesting,
as the child gets older,
to watch that child
hold on to one toy
and want to pick up something else
but not know how to let go
so that they can hold on to something
     else,
but eventually that child does learn
because holding on and letting go
create a balanced flow
from one place to another,
like breathing in
and breathing out,
so when they cross
those monkey bars,
they have to learn to let go
of that bar with one hand
so they can swing across to the next
and continue to make progress
from one end to the other,
in a balanced flow
of holding on and letting go.

And then a few become acrobats,
high-flying trapeze artists
who also have to let go,
and have to do so
at exactly the right time,
not too soon, not too late,
let go of that bar
as they swing across the sky
so someone can catch them,
hold on tight to them
and not let them go,
because if they hold on too long
they might miss that connection,
and missing means falling,
and falling means hurting
when you are up so high.
So the smart ones use nets,
large soft places to land,
that catch them if they miss
so they won't get too hurt
when they miss that connection
and fall toward the earth,
because they know
you never know
when something might go wrong
and it is a good idea
to be prepared for that,
to know where your net is
and what it looks like
and how to land in it
to get the support needed
to break the fall,
because breaking up
is hard to do
and can be hard on you too,
but having a safe place to land
after you let go
makes it easier to do
and softens the blow,
and lets you move forward

across those jungle gym bars,
and on to other things,
just like all those playground toys
get left behind eventually
when we move on to other things
and get on with living life
whatever it brings
in its ongoing flow,
the flow of a stream
where things drift down,
swirl around for a while,
then move on out of view,
gone and yet quickly replaced
by something new
that drifts into view
in that irresistible flow
of holding on
and letting go,
of letting go,
and holding on
to what that flow
brings to you
now.
[*Go to a direct approach or trance termination.*]

9

—

DEALING
WITH DEPRESSION

The metaphor scripts presented in the present chapter were constructed for use with depressed, self-effacing, self-blaming clients whose underlying pain stems from critical self-evaluations and pessimistic attitudes coupled with recurring memories of past failures, rejections, or disappointments. These scripts emphasize the well-established correlation between such patterns of thought and subsequent painful feelings of depression, helplessness, or worthlessness. They also stress the realization that it is up to the client to replace these painful, self-destructive thoughts with internal and external sources of pleasure and satisfaction.

Many depressed clients are reluctant to change their way of thinking. They seem to cling to their misery either because they believe it is their right to feel awful given what life has done to them or because they feel that somehow it would be wrong to feel better. In some cases, the resulting behavior often seems like a justifiable temper tantrum given the client's past or present circumstances. In other cases, the client apparently has learned to feel miserable and blame or belittle himself or herself in order to protect or please someone else (often a parent). The scripts that follow speak to these and other issues.

THE WICKED STEPMOTHER

A metaphor script for depression with underlying self-criticism.

So, as you relax there,
you may become aware
that we all have a voice in our head,
like a radio commentator,
the people on while we drive
from one place to another,
one that always seems mad
or sad and angry,
always criticizing everything,
especially you,
saying everything you do,
everything that is,
is wrong,
not what it should be,
and nothing else is right either,
not even what I am saying,
or what you are thinking.
That broadcast voice
is not nice
to you or anyone,
and you may think it is you,
but it reminds me
of that evil stepmother
in the tale of Cinderella,
who told her she was bad,
that she would never
amount to anything,
and deserved nothing
except to clean up after others
and do what she was told,
although of course,
as we all know now,
she did amount to something,
got rescued into happiness,
found by something good,
loved by many ever after,
turned out to be more beautiful
than those stepsisters too,
like it is easy for me to imagine,
easy for me to think,
that something good can happen
to a beautiful you as well
before we are through,
a wish come true
from a wishing well,
although it may be hard for you
right now,
to not know
what it would be like
to replace that voice
with another
from another channel,
with another tale
from another time,
from another place
in time and space,
a voice that fits like a glove,
or a glass slipper,
slipping into place,
fitting right in,
saying different things,
and in this story,
what words would you bring in
if you could tune in
or broadcast on your own?
What things would you say instead?
What thoughts
would fill your head
to soothe and comfort
that Cinderella . . .
that might also comfort you?
Because it now belongs to you,
an opportunity to rewrite history,
and write your own fairy tale too,
a chance to replace that wicked voice,
to replace that state of mind
with another tune, another line,
a peaceful place to be,
just by changing the channel,
tuning in to something else,
changing
what you are willing to hear,

what you listen to,
what you say to you
about you
and everything else too,
just by tuning in,
now,
and changing
what you allow
your own thoughts to be.
Try it and see,
just to see how it feels,
while your unconscious mind
repeats after me,
an echo in that static space
of relaxed awareness,
hearing that new voice,
saying to you,
that you are doing fine . . . ,
you are doing well . . . ,
you are fine too,
so you can relax
and feel how it feels,
to hear that said
to you by you,
sent to you from you,
that you are doing fine,
you are doing well,
you are fine,
and you are well,
and then feeling well,
because as you can tell,
Cinderella is a very different story
when you replace
that wicked voice,
that critical menacing voice,
with that other one instead,
that godmother good mother one,
a comforting one,
a loving one,
that admires you,
and speaks to you with respect,
and knows that you can do
what you need to do
to take care of you,

Now!
[*Go to a direct approach or trance termination.*]

THE WRECK

A metaphor script for depression associated with a sense of failure and helplessness.

And so, as you know, how we feel
about something imagined or real
is really up to us.
Like the man I've heard about
who bought a new car,
a fancy sports car,
that he waxed and polished and cleaned,
at least once a week, sometimes more.
He was so proud of that car,
until one day
somebody backed into it,
put a big dent in it,
a big scrape along the side,
and he was so hurt and upset,
that he flew into a rage at first,
refused to drive it for a week,
and when he finally did drive it,
he drove it hard and fast,
and refused to wash it or wax it,
and every time he saw that dent,
a big depression along the side,
he became very sad and angry,
and sometimes he even cried.
It changed his whole life,
nothing made him happy anymore,
nothing seemed like fun.
He kept looking at that dent,
which reminded him how bad he felt,
how mad and upset he was.
Every time he saw it,
he felt a twinge inside,
and he thought to himself,
"Why bother?" "Why me?"
"Nothing ever goes right anyway."
That scraped up dent began to rust
and became an ugly hole
that he glanced at every day
and felt that sad, mad feeling again.
and after a while,
he didn't want to go anywhere,
he didn't want to do anything,
because each time he went out

he saw that hole again
and he felt bad again,
and just wanted to go inside and hide.
It was like he wanted to feel bad,
felt like he had a right to,
and he was right
but he could have done something,
because he did have insurance
unlike the people who live
next to rivers in the flood plains,
where everything washes away
whenever the river rises above its banks
and they lose everything they have,
but move back when the water recedes
telling reporters they are just glad to be
    alive,
borrowing money freely from banks
to rebuild their lives.
I guess it is hard to be mad at a river
or take a flood personally.
They call it an act of God
and continue to go to church
where they pray it won't happen again,
but know that it probably will,
because rivers flood,
like people make mistakes or do things
    wrong.
It's just their nature, the way they are
and nobody thinks a river should be
    different
or gets angry or hurt when it does what
    it does,
and nobody worries that they caused
    the rain,
the rain that caused the flood.
They just move back in
and get on with their lives
and go swimming or boating,
glad that the sun is back,
the damage undone.
[*Go to a direct approach or trance
termination.*]

ROYAL SERVICE

A metaphor script for depression associated with self-defeating efforts to please or protect others.

Now, some people get a lot of pleasure
taking care of others in different ways.
Even tiny children,
who need to be taken care of themselves,
seem to genuinely enjoy doing little
    things
for those they love, those they care about,
those they want to protect,
I know about a young boy, Michael
who found a baby rabbit in his yard,
its mother had been hit by a car.
So he brought it inside to his room
and he made a soft warm bed for it,
and he went to the library
and read about taking care of it,
and he bought a tiny bottle to feed it
with the money he had saved
from his allowance.
He fed it every four hours,
even set his alarm clock
and got up to feed it at night.
He was so happy as it grew,
and he spoke to it in those gentle tones.
It would have all been perfect
if it hadn't run away,
after it grew
the way most baby rabbits do.
So he cried when it left
but his parents made sure he knew
that it wasn't his fault,
that he'd done everything there was to
    do,
and they were very proud of him,
which may be why
he still rescues baby animals
and raises them to be set free,
and seems to feel better about himself
as a result.
But that's a very different experience
from the little girl

raised by a self-styled queen.
That little girl was raised in luxury,
pampered and spoiled in a lot of ways,
but she was never allowed to know
that she was prettier or nicer, or
    smarter,
or more talented than her mother ever
    had been.
And somehow that little girl knew
that she had to do whatever she could
to protect her mother from the truth
from being better than her
and made sure she said she wasn't.
It wasn't just that it was dangerous
to offend the "queen" and make her
    mad,
the little girl really wanted to take care
    of her
and make sure she never got sad.
So she acted stupid and silly,
and she put on lots of weight,
and whenever she did something well,
she explained to everyone
why it didn't count.
Little Linda became very good at one
    thing;
at criticizing herself and what she did,
she mastered that skill
at putting herself down
and not giving herself any credit for
    anything,
but try as she might she still excelled
and accomplished great things
in spite of herself,
which made it harder not to feel
like she'd done something wrong,
even years after her mother died
because there was something deep
    inside
which said it was bad and mean

to be better than mother in any way.
And she continued to feel that way
until one day she finally got mad,
after sitting in a trance for a while,
and realized what her mother had done,
and she decided that she had a right
to take care of herself
as well as she had taken care of others.
So she learned how to praise herself,
to speak to herself in those gentle tones
and be happy
about what she was able to do,
and when she crawled into
her soft warm bed,
she was able to allow herself
to feel glad to be herself
and to tell her mother she was sorry
that she had grown up to be
so content with her life and herself,
but that now it was time to be free.
[*Go to a direct approach or trance termination.*]

THE HEARING TEST

A metaphor script for low self-esteem.

And what about Beethoven
who became increasingly deaf
as he got older,
but kept on working, writing music
that he could not hear.
Until one day, one evening,
he conducted the symphony
as they played his newest work,
a concerto.
And when it was finished
the crowd erupted in applause.
They stood and cheered,
but he could not hear.
He stood there facing the orchestra,
unaware of the audience approval
until someone walked out
and turned him around.
Only then did he know
what everyone needs to know
but sometimes cannot hear,
like the woman I have heard of,
black hair, black eyes, stocky build,
a bright professional woman
who hated herself
and hated her life.
She thought she was ugly and awful,
and she thought it was why
so many awful things had happened to
    her.
But one day
she was having lunch with a friend,
an artist she had known for a time,
and she said to her friend
that there were so many beautiful
    women
and they seemed to be on that street
    that day,
and her friend simply said,
"I think you're the most beautiful
    woman
I've ever seen,"

and went on eating, as if it were
    nothing.
And that simple observation,
that simple statement of opinion,
matter-of-fact not flattery,
wouldn't go away,
couldn't be undone.
Her friend was an artist
who knew what beauty was,
so she could not ignore it,
and she could not forget it.
Instead she began to look at herself,
each day in the mirror
and she began to look at others,
how they looked, who they were with,
and it was very hard and scary at first
to realize how wrong her mother had
    been,
how wrong she had been about herself
in so many different ways.
But over time she began to accept it,
she was not ugly,
she was not stupid,
she was not a bad person,
she was attractive and likable and nice,
and she did not have to settle
for less than she deserved.
How she thought changed,
how she felt changed,
what she did changed,
her life changed,
all because of one brief comment,
one brief glimpse of herself,
a clear admission of something
she had been unable
to let herself know before,
that truth is beauty
and beauty truth,
and the truth about oneself, one's
    beauty,
is in the eye of the beholder.

But what we hear
is not measured on a hearing test.
Beethoven heard things in his mind
that his ears could no longer hear,
and many animals can hear sounds,
that the human ear cannot,
and all we ever need to hear
is that there is nothing else we need to do,
except hear the beauty of what is.
[*Go to a direct approach or trance termination.*]

10

ALLEVIATING UNWARRANTED FEARS

The metaphor scripts presented in this chapter explore the creation and removal of fear. They were designed to help people learn how to prevent the thoughts, images, and behaviors associated with their anxiety and replace them with more comfortable and useful patterns of response.

Sometimes the chronic anticipation of unpleasant future events is the result of previous unpleasant events. Essentially, the person is constantly worried that that highly unpleasant event will occur again. When such worries and anxieties are the result of an assault, disaster, or accident, the scripts presented in Chapter 8 are more appropriate than those presented here, at least at first. Even when such worries are the result of what might seem to be a relatively minor unpleasant event, such as a dog bite or dental session with too little anesthetic, they also may be an appropriate way to begin treatment.

Many people, however, simply have mastered the art of worrying in a well-intentioned but misguided effort to prevent anything unpleasant or bad from ever happening to them or anyone they know. They are able to clearly imagine numerous worst-case scenarios for any situation. As a result, they unwittingly create discomfort by constantly trying to avoid it. This is especially a problem for individuals who have the capacity to become highly absorbed in their own imaginings; that is, people who are highly hypnotizable. The constant anticipation of unpleasant outcomes can create adrenalin surges and high levels of anxiety in anyone, but individuals who experience high levels of imaginative absorption are often especially prone to the development of problems in this arena. These people can imagine such outcomes so clearly that their autonomic systems go into high gear. For other individuals, it is the other way around. A high and unpleasant level of autonomic activity, perhaps the result of inadequate inhibition of neural circuits in the limbic system or high levels of carbon dioxide in the blood caused by breathing and cardiovascular problems (e.g., sleep apnea, asthma, mitral valve prolapse, or paroxysmal supraventricular tachycardia), stimulates an imaginative search for explanation and superstitious attempts at control. In either case, avoidance or ritualistic responses are developed in a doomed attempt to counteract, control, or prevent those unpleasant experiences.

The Diagnostic Trance process (Chapter 2) may help establish whether fantasy or physiology lies at the core of the problem. If there is a physiological condition that can be corrected, the associated thoughts and behaviors may disappear by themselves. On the other hand, because the thoughts and actions associated with these conditions usually become overlearned (hence unconscious) activities, hypnotherapeutic interventions are especially appropriate and useful no matter what led to the fears in the first place.

THE WORST THING

A metaphor script for anxiety disorders.

And as you sit there,
relaxed, listening very carefully
with your eyes closed
and your mind open,
I can think about
what you have told me
about yourself,
and remember a young woman
who went for therapy several years ago,
and told her therapist
she was afraid to drive,
afraid to leave home,
afraid to do anything,
afraid of everything,
but really the thing
that frightened her the most,
and really was the only thing
that scared her at all,
was the idea that she might,
get an upset stomach,
and someone would see,
someone would know,
and wouldn't that be the worst,
the absolute most terrible,
the most awful horrible thing,
at least she thought it would,
and so she did anything she could,
everything she could,
to avoid that awful possibility,
even though it ruined her life,
made her miserable all the time,
kept her from doing anything fun,
and kept her upset,
always worried
no matter how hard she tried
to just forget about it.
So that therapist told her
to close her eyes and relax,
to just listen very carefully,
and he told her a story

about a woman he treated years before,
for something very similar,
by having her relax and close her eyes
and listen very carefully,
then saying to her
how impressed he was
by her ability to make something
huge and overwhelming
out of something small,
like a mad scientist,
or a funny magician,
turning thin air
into brilliant colors,
when all there was really
was nothing there at all,
and that perhaps she could use
her own imagination
to invent and create things
that were a bit more fun,
and less like blowing up
balloons full of hot air.
And then he explained
in great detail that she was
not going to die,
not going to go crazy,
if that thing happened to her
that she was trying hard to avoid,
because her brain and her body
were unfortunately quite healthy,
not worth worrying about,
very well designed,
perfect in many ways,
her body able to heal itself,
to get rid of poisons by itself,
to cure itself,
to enjoy itself,
to amuse itself,
and to take care of her
in the right way
at the right time,

and that maybe now
it was time for her
to do so as well
with the magic of her own
imagination.
And do you know,
after listening carefully,
but not really remembering
what had been said,
for some unknown reason
that young woman
began to get better,
day after day,
until one day she said,
she had worried last week
about losing control
and getting sick in public,
and then surprised herself
and pleased herself
when the thought came through,
loud and clear and sure,
"Who cares?
It doesn't matter really,
it does not really matter,
I just made it up,
and I can just take it away,
stop believing is the same way
I once stopped believing in the Tooth
    Fairy,
or the Easter Bunny,
and even Santa Claus."
She never knew what changed exactly,
why what once seemed so awful
and had to be avoided
suddenly did not matter any more,
was not important any more,
did not have to be avoided any more,
did not throw her off any more,
but it did go away,
it just floated away like a balloon of hot
    air,
something that once seemed all
    important
no longer mattered,

and that was all that mattered,
and that was all she needed,
she was through believing
something bad would happen,
or that it would be disastrous if it did,
no matter how she felt about it
she knew, really knew,
it was through,
not worth thinking about any more,
it was through,
and I wonder if you
can see the smile
on the face of that balloon
as her cares and concerns,
like yours,
floated right away too . . .
[*Go to a direct approach or trance
termination.*]

INFLATED RESUMES

A metaphor script for social phobias.

Now,
about this business
of being afraid
of what others will see
or what they will think,
I wonder if you know
that Notre Dame once hired a coach
for their football team
and fired him five days later
because they found out
he lied on his resume,
said he had done things
he hadn't
tried to be something
he wasn't,
like all those men
who tell everyone
that they fought in the war
when they were not even
in the military,
just made up stories
and got caught
and made fools of
by their own efforts
to be something they were not,
all because they thought
that what they really were
was not good enough,
but the fact is
that what we all like,
what we enjoy most,
are people who are not afraid
to just be what they are,
not always lying
or pretending to be
perfect in all ways
or any way at all,
like the professor I know
who forgets to go to class,
so his students just smile

and go to his office to get him,
and even then
he sometimes starts a lecture
that belongs in another course,
so of course
his students just smile
and remind him where he is
and then he gets back on course
and gives a brilliant discourse
on the topic at hand,
and always gets the highest ratings
of any professor in the university,
because students enjoy the fact
that he just doesn't care
to try to be something
he is not,
he is just right there,
perfectly imperfect,
like a small child
learning something new,
bowling, for example,
enjoying rolling that ball
no matter where it goes,
because a gutter ball
is just as fun to see
as pins falling down
when life is too mysterious
to take things very serious,
because the only people
who worry about
not making mistakes
not being just what they are,
and try to be something else,
or worry about others seeing
that they are not perfect
in some little way
are the ones who think
they should be perfect,
which they are not,
and don't want other people

to see their flaws,
when it is those very flaws
that keep them
from being artificial,
the way artificial diamonds
can be perfect,
but not very valuable
or artificial flowers
are too perfect to be right,
so as you relax,
your standards can relax as well,
and becoming perfectly imperfect,
or is it imperfectly perfect,
is so comfortable
it feels just right.
[*Go to a direct approach or trance termination.*]

A QUIET BIRTH

A metaphor script for generalized anxiety and panic attacks.

It has been suggested,
by a French physician,
that when babies are born,
they should *not* be held upside down,
in a cold, bright, noisy operating room,
and spanked to make them cry.
Instead, they should be born
into a warm, quiet room
with soft, gentle lights
and put into a warm bath,
because when they are babied that way,
they open their eyes and look around.
they seem amazed and happy,
they even seem to smile.
they lie there quietly relaxed,
and they grow up to be happier
and more secure
all because they were treated gently,
protected and taken care of,
not hurt or scared,
but just allowed to be safe
and quiet for a while,
a natural way of doing things
that seems to work out well,
because almost all animals
have their babies on warm spring nights
when it is safe to be born
and the mother can take care of them
and help them get used to things,
get their arms and legs
under control.
And then they learn to hide quietly
in the tall grass,
how to remain very still,
even when there is danger near,
and they learn to play happily,
secure in the awareness
that someone is nearby, protecting
    them,
calmly watching out for them.

and become more quiet inside and out,
as they use everything they've learned,
because even a brief moment
can provide a lesson to be used
to keep oneself calm and quiet inside,
The way warm water
can seep throughout a soft towel,
even though only a small corner
rests gently in that warm bath
where a newborn child rests and smiles,
with a warm glow of safe comfort.
And as they get older and wiser,
they seem to calm down themselves.
[*Go to a direct approach or trance
termination.*]

FORTUNE TELLING

A metaphor script for phobias.

Because the unconscious mind
is interesting to observe
as you drift down into that trance,
where those unconscious thoughts,
images and ideas
flash through the mind so rapidly,
like schools of fish
darting through the mind so rapidly,
startling as they suddenly appear,
their strange forms and shapes,
and then disappear, replaced by others.
Some schools of thought are about the
    past,
others about the present or even the
    future,
wondering what might happen then,
what might come of what is going on,
like the frightened fortune tellers,
always seeing the end of the world
written in tea leaves and palm prints,
all the signs everywhere of doom
and disaster.
And what to make of the fact
that if you look at the horoscopes
in the paper,
they always suggest wealth and success,
prosperity and potentials at every turn,
while the doomsayers walk the streets
with hand printed signs
announcing the end of the world,
those who get paid and paid attention to
have a different point of view,
but at least their messages are easy
    to see,
not like subliminal images or words
that could be hidden in movies or TV,
telling us to be afraid of this or that,
reminding us to be concerned
that something awful is about to happen,
something awful or terrible,
like the shape of a hawk circling above,

a shape that scares all birds
from the time they are born.
They do not have to learn to be afraid,
nature does that for them,
to protect them from real danger.
Some buildings have a cutout of that
    shape
pasted on large windows,
to keep birds from flying into them
and hurting themselves.
That shape scares them away,
and it cannot be unlearned,
but some things can be unlearned.
We know you won't fall
off the edge of the world
when you sail out to sea,
and we know that tomatoes are not
    poisonous,
and toads cannot create warts,
or that just believing we can fly,
doesn't make it so,
even though Peter Pan and Tinkerbell
can still be fun to watch,
like anything can be fun to watch,
and any knot can be undone, untied,
as the unconscious mind
finds its own way
to unlearn for you
and see things in a different light,
a warm comfortable light
that allows a feeling to change,
to rearrange those thoughts and images,
to change that feeling,
or make it fly away,
like the fortune tellers said,
allowing the mind to foresee
that change in the future,
and to enjoy noticing
that future changes do occur.
[*Go to a direct approach or trance
termination.*]

ALIEN THOUGHTS

A metaphor script for obsessive-compulsive disorders.

Now you have come here today
for help with your problem,
because you say
you just cannot help doing
or thinking the things you do
and I know a bit about
how it feels
to be unable to stop,
everyone knows a bit about it
because everyone has tried
to not sneeze,
to not yawn,
to not scratch an itch,
but that just scratches the surface
of what it is like for you
to feel so uncomfortable
that you have to do what you do
to make it feel better,
or so it seems,
because you know on the one hand,
and you have told yourself to stop,
but none of that has worked
because what you are doing
is not really you,
even though it feels like it,
and that makes me wonder
if you have ever seen the movie
"The Body Snatchers,"
where aliens invade human bodies,
take them over,
somehow get inside
and take over their brains,
control them from the inside,
in scene after scene
people do things
they would not do otherwise,
unable to control themselves,
because they are not themselves,
although they can still think clearly
on the one hand,
whereas on the other

their thoughts and actions
are controlled by the other,
the aliens are in charge,
the way they say zombies
lose their will,
lose their way,
under a voodoo spell
that they do so well,
but are still conscious and aware
of everything going on,
just unable to control themselves,
and how to rebel,
to take charge again
is not something they can tell,
at least not at first,
although there is always a way,
isn't that the way it is
in any good story,
because there is always something,
something that can be done,
if only they can focus their energy
on doing that one thing
that will drive out that alien
or undo that spell,
that one thing that the alien
is keeping them from doing,
or anything that spell
is forcing them to avoid,
so they go toward water
if that alien force says stay away,
or they start to move
if the force says stay,
they just do whatever it is
they are not supposed to do
or refuse to do
what the alien is trying to do,
because they know
if they can just do it just once
and loosen its grip,
and then do it again,
and feel that spell letting go,

and do it again and again,
and feel that being begin to squirm
and finally breaking free
it just starts getting weaker,
just a tiny bit at first,
then eventually evaporates
into nothing,
and I always wonder
just how it must feel,
to feel that happen
as that other source of thought,
that other thing inside
begins to let go,
begins to run and hide
and you begin to feel free
to think for yourself
and at the same time
feeling that alien
fighting for control,
trying to trick you
into allowing it
to be in charge again,
trick you
with all those different sensations,
all those terrible thoughts,
while the rational you,
that knowing part of your mind,
keeps forcing that body
to do those things
that feel awful and hurt,
like holding a hand
over a candle
or jumping off a cliff
but going ahead anyway
in spite of the pain,
in spite of the terror,
because breaking away
or getting unstuck
when you are stuck on something
or it is stuck to you
can be a difficult thing to do
so you can just close your eyes
and do it all at once,
and get it over with

rip it right off,
rip it right out
fight against it
and replace it
once and for all . . .
[*Go to a direct approach or trance termination.*]

11

CONCENTRATION AND SUCCESS IN WORK, SCHOOL, AND SPORTS

Those who achieve and excel are those who become completely absorbed in the pursuit of a goal and who supplement their inherent abilities with an investment of time, energy, and faith in themselves. They have a clear vision of their own possible future and they are willing to do whatever it takes to make that vision into a reality. The appeal of that successful future gives them the dedication and energy it takes to practice an activity long enough for the unconscious to master it. Once they have attained some degree of mastery, their faith in themselves allows them to trust their own well-trained unconscious to accomplish their goals. Finally, they are able to focus intently on the task at hand and stay relaxed enough to not get in their own way. They are rewarded for all of this by amazement at their accomplishments and a sense of well-being along the way (cf. Csikszentmihalyi, 1990, 1993, 1997).

Procrastination, lack of motivation, anxiety, and self-consciousness often block performance and prevent people from living up to their own expectations. Several of the metaphor scripts presented in the following are designed to replace these obvious blocks to success. The first one is designed for use with clients who procrastinate because they are faced with something that they must do but do not really want to do. Other scripts are offered for those who are blocked by a fear of failure, performance anxiety, or other self-imposed barriers to their own success.

It should be noted that clients' expectations of themselves sometimes are inappropriate. When that is the case, a lack of progress toward their goals may be a beneficial self-protective measure. Before an effort is made to remove barriers to performance, therefore, it should be established that the activities or goals involved are both feasible and appropriate.

Replacing roadblocks is only the first step. If one hopes to succeed in any activity, that activity must be studied, rehearsed, or practiced to the point of mastery. When knowledge or skills are mastered, they become automatically available or "unconscious." Walking and talking are examples, as are reading and writing. No conscious effort is involved in walking. In fact, conscious effort tends to disrupt the smooth utilization of mastered abilities and information. Furthermore, even the acquisition of new skills and information is best accomplished without a lot of conscious criticism or interference. The person must pay attention to the task at hand and to the feedback received regarding progress toward the goal, but distracting and disruptive thoughts must be kept to a minimum or eliminated altogether. Thus, both learning and performance are best accomplished in a completely relaxed yet highly observant state of stable awareness, a state of mind comparable to the hypnotic trance state.

One advantage of a trance state is that it allows a person to experience a realistic immersion in imaginary practice or rehearsal sessions. Although imagined practice does not produce as much new learning as actual practice, imagined rehearsal of a successful performance enhances self-confidence and reduces performance anxiety. Furthermore, this technique can be used with beneficial results for virtually any activity, from practicing the piano to rehearsing a speech or anticipating successful performance in a football game or on a test.

In some respects, the use of metaphorical anecdotes is a way to immerse clients in imagined therapeutic responses when it would be difficult to get them to do so directly. However, when a client is quite willing and able to relax and vividly imagine engaging in an activity or performance, there is no real need for metaphors. The solution or the desired activity can be rehearsed imaginatively, improved upon imaginatively, and incorporated into response sets. Indirect messages or metaphorical scripts are not necessary. Simply help the person enter into a trance and provide direct instructions about what needs to be imagined to improve performance. [For additional information and guidance regarding the use of imaginary practice, the reader is referred to Walters & Havens (1993), *Hypnotherapy for Health, Harmony, and Peak Performance*. NY: Brunner/Mazel.]

Although imagined rehearsal can reduce performance anxiety and increase self-confidence, the critical ingredient for peak performance in virtually any endeavor appears to be the ability to enter into a highly focused but observant state of mind. Gilligan (1987) referred to this state of mind as "controlled spontaneity," Gallwey (1974) called it "unfreakability" and "relaxed concentration," and Csikszentmihalyi (1990) labeled it "flow." Athletes sometimes call it "being in the zone" or "streaming."

No matter what we call it, this passively observant yet highly attentive condition allows for a noncritical or nonjudgmental liberation and utilization of unconscious abilities and capacities for learning and mastery. During this process the conscious mind becomes a quiet member of an appreciative audience, an observer of the self as "unconscious" capacities for learning and performance are unleashed, unfettered by conscious concerns or considerations. The basketball player sees the ball go through the hoop before it is even released, the archer feels the flight of the arrow, the writer hears the insights and phrases offered by an inner muse, the student knows the answer before the question is completed, and the dancer becomes the dance.

Although repeated experience with hypnotic trance may facilitate the tendency to become absorbed in this manner, the final script in this chapter is specifically designed to do so. That script is derived from an approach first used by Havens (1991) in a brief pilot study. In this study, post-session and follow-up ratings of absorption and "flow experiences" increased significantly for each of his nine participants. The rest of the scripts in this chapter are derived from interventions used with clients for the problems mentioned.

RAISING DOGS

A metaphor script for procrastination.

So we won't put it off any longer,
this movement into a deeper trance,
where you can relax completely
and I can explain
to your unconscious mind
a story I heard from a friend
who had a friend whose son was in
    school
at a distant university.
He was failing his courses
because he would not go to class
and he would not do his homework,
although he said he wanted to,
so he went to see a counselor
who told him to drop out of school
and to raise dogs or lions
because they would growl and attack
if he didn't take care of his business.
This put him off at first,
made him angry,
so angry he went to class instead,
did all his homework,
got all As
to prove what an idiot that guy was.
And each time he found it hard,
to do what he needed to do,
he thought about raising puppies,
and all he would have to go through
with their little piles here
and their little messes there
as they just did what they wanted to do
whenever and wherever they wanted,
although he did know from experience,
that even a tiny puppy
can eventually be trained
to behave itself, to control itself,
even if it is hard to do
what it really doesn't want to do,
to wait and do it
in the right place at the right time,
because who would want to live with it,

if it never did learn
to behave itself
and to stop acting
like a spoiled soiling pup.
And so even the most rebellious pup
has a willingness to take care of itself
and to just do what needs to be done
if for no other reason than its own
    comfort,
its own security,
its own sense of self-worth.
And I've often wondered what
    happened to him,
because I know he did not quit school,
and he did not raise dogs,
so I guess he learned his lessons well
and took good care of himself from then
    on.
[*Go to a direct approach or trance
termination.*]

THE INVISIBLE BARRIER

A metaphor script for removing self-imposed boundaries to achievement and fear of success.
[*This type of metaphor may be used with all clients in an effort to help them become more committed to their therapeutic goals, or with individuals such as athletes or students who have specific goals they wish to pursue more diligently.*]

I wonder if you are familiar with fences,
especially the electric fences used with
    horses.
These fences have a few tiny strands of
    wire,
and through that wire goes a current of
    electricity.
Not the kind of electricity that is dangerous,
just the kind that gives you a jolt,
like static electricity you get from walking
    on rugs,
a sudden, sharp spark.
These wires stretch all around the field,
and as the horses walk from place to place,
they quickly learn where they can go,
and where they don't want to venture.
All it takes is a few brushes against the
    wire,
a few sudden, startling zaps,
and being very smart animals,
they learn to look but not touch.
They learn so well, in fact,
that after a while,
the farmer can turn off the electricity,
or even replace the wires with string,
and those horses will stay put,
fenced in by nothing at all,
stopped in their tracks by a thought,
by the feeling that some places are off
    limits,
that where they are is safe,
as long as they just stay put,
satisfied to be where they are.
An invisible barrier or boundary
created by the mind,
but once one horse goes through it,
then they all will follow behind,
that barrier shattered and broken,

with no restraints on where they go next.
But where to go next is a problem,
a problem everyone faces,
and not everyone knows how to solve,
which is probably why . . .
you can earn a fortune these days,
telling people their fortunes
and giving advice on what they should do,
We don't know how a horse knows
    where to go,
but we do know
that once they know where they're
    going,
it is difficult to stop them or rein them in,
because once a tired, hungry horse
sees that stable or barn at the bottom of
    a hill,
all you have to do
is give it free rein
and it will take you there,
as quickly and surely as it can,
because it wants to be comfortable,
and it wants to be fed,
and once it knows where to go
to get what it wants,
even an imaginary boundary
can be leaped over
on the way to that goal.
What fun to hold on tight
and just let it run
trusting that it will take you there,
swiftly and surely.
That is a pleasure
every child can treasure
and so could most adults,
if they allowed themselves to do so.
[*Go to a direct approach or trance
termination.*]

CONTENTS UNDER PRESSURE

A metaphor script for test or performance anxiety.

What to say to someone
who is afraid to take a test
is not a difficult thing to decide,
but deciding how to say it
in a way that will be heard
and accepted deep inside
is the real issue,
because there are things we all know
with the conscious mind
that do not always change
how we feel when we get there
or what we do when the time comes,
like the way children never believe
what is written on all spray cans,
where it says "Do not incinerate,
contents under pressure,"
which means that it will explode
if thrown into a fire
or heated beyond its capacity
to hold that increased pressure,
but even adults are tempted
to throw it in the fire
just to see what will happen
because they have never seen
a can explode that way
and wonder if it will,
or what it will be like,
even though they know
or have heard stories about it
because experience is the only teacher,
and how to teach you
that you need not toss
a mind full of facts and information,
more than you can ever imagine,
smarter than you will ever know,
into the fires of imagined worries
that create an unnecessary
and uncomfortable amount of pressure
when you could instead
be relaxing with a mind full

of many wonderful things,
like the delightful pleasure
of spring flowers and summer breezes,
of playful kittens and carefree feelings,
looking forward to an opportunity
to play a game for fun,
to use your head in new ways,
enjoying the ways it feels to be
a child with a new toy,
eager to discover how to do it,
happy to figure it out
to solve a puzzle,
to do something new,
to use those abilities
to learn what to do,
to play and pretend
to be someone else,
like when children play house
and begin acting and talking
like the adults they have seen,
like you used to do
and still can too
when you start to enter that room
and begin to pretend
to be somebody new,
forgetting the old you,
becoming new,
a person you knew
who always seemed able
to do what was needed,
enjoying the chance
to enter the dance,
somebody who trusts and enjoys
 your abilities and learnings
and knows how it feels
to be free to do well,
to do just as well
as you possibly can do,
without having to do
anything else at all

except see it all through
whoever it is
you will pretend to be
the next time you want to
let all the pressure right out,
and feel free to just use
what you know all about.
[*Go to a direct approach or trance termination.*]

CLIMBING MOUNTAINS

A metaphor script for fear of failure in any endeavor.

It is my understanding
that when someone begins
the dangerous sport of rock climbing,
or mountain climbing,
that the first thing you learn
is how to do things
that protect you
from the inevitable fall,
the slip, the misstep,
the overestimation of abilities,
the brief loss of concentration,
the unpredictable loose rock,
the gust of wind,
the patch of ice,
the slippery slope,
the jagged sharpness,
the hardness and difficulties every-
     where,
the everything that could happen
to bring you down,
or cause you harm,
because what goes up
must come down at times,
as everyone knows,
because there is no such thing
as never making a mistake
in anything you do.
So climbers have a calm acceptance
and willing realization
that eventually a fall will happen,
and the only thing to do
is to do everything there is to do
to make sure that when it does
there are plenty of things there
to keep you safe,
to break your fall,
to catch and hold you securely,
so you can survive unharmed
and learn from your mistakes,
and that is why they have ropes,

special climbing ropes,
that stretch to absorb a fall,
that are strong enough to hold your
     weight,
ten times over,
and why they have created harnesses
to connect the ropes to you,
and things called belay devices,
and different types of strong clips,
and carabineers and crampons,
wedges and protectors and more,
all because everyone knows
that if something can go wrong
it will,
and so the wisest thing to do
is to take every precaution to protect
     you
so you can climb to the top
and know that if you slip
you will be safe and will survive,
so you can relax and focus
on the things that you need to do,
to get where you want to go
without worrying about what might
     happen
if you make a mistake or two,
because then you can continue
the rest of the climb
and you can rely on all those skills,
all that strength and ability,
to see you through to the top,
because as long as it is safe to fail,
anyone and everyone can succeed,
so the only thing you need to do
to enjoy being you,
is to realize how safe you really are,
how well protected you can feel,
when you stop and pay attention,
to all the things you already have in
     place,

all the protections needed,
to make it safe to climb,
all those abilities and capacities,
all those strong and reliable devices,
that already exist within you,
within the unconscious mind,
designed to take care of you,
to keep you safe and secure,
so you can relax,
and rest assured,
that no matter what,
you are safe and protected,
which makes it OK
to not worry and just do
whatever you need to do
to enjoy the opportunity
to climb higher every day
and to reach for the stars,
the peak of experiences,
the pleasures of being alive.
[*Go to a direct approach or trance termination.*]

KNOT PERFECT

A metaphor script for worries about being imperfect.

Let's just talk for a while,
because everyone needs to relax at times,
even Olympic athletes,
who are under a great deal of pressure
    to perform,
and sometimes must be perfect to win,
need some way to relax
and put things into perspective,
to recognize that it is just a sport,
a game,
and not a matter of life and death.
Because death is one thing
and a game is something else entirely,
where even the biggest mistakes
are just an opportunity to learn
and not the end of everything at all.
Those athletes really can afford to relax,
because they know
that they already know
all they need to know,
to do what they need to do,
and all they need to do
is let their mind and body do
what they already know how to do.
There are very few places in the world
where mistakes cannot be allowed,
and it is comforting to note
that almost everywhere,
an error is just an opportunity
to do it differently later on,
because perfection is rarely required
and perfection is seldom needed,
and even Olympic athletes,
are never perfect all the time,
and do things wrong even when they
    win,
like the Navahos when they weave a
    rug,
who always leave a knot, an
    imperfection,
so the gods won't be angered

and think they are trying to be gods
    themselves.
But that is another story
about what is really important
and what is not
and how it feels to give permission
to enjoy the feeling of the freedom
to feel safe doing those things
knowing that the world won't end,
if you leave a knot someplace,
so the gods can also relax
knowing you are not challenging them,
just relaxing,
allowing your unconscious mind
to do the best you can,
and letting it go at that.
[*Go to a direct approach or trance
termination.*]

MICROSCOPES

A metaphor script for nervousness about public speaking and sales presentations.

Relaxed, with eyes closed
it is much easier
to pay close attention
to all those tiny sensations,
all those sounds and thoughts
that are clearer and larger
than before,
the way even the tiniest object
can look huge
when seen through a microscope.
I remember when I took biology
we looked at cells and paramecium,
tiny living things you could barely see
with the naked eye,
that suddenly were enormous
under that lens,
and you could examine
every detail, every movement,
zero in on one,
intensify the magnification,
and see things
you never could have seen,
legs, feelers, tiny hairs for swimming,
and wondering how it feels
to be under there,
watched that way,
examined that way,
to have every movement,
every tiny hair and every breath
noticed and analyzed,
but as far as I could tell
those tiny things
really did not notice
that anyone was watching,
and probably did not care
even if they knew,
sitting there on that slide,
doing their own thing,
it is easy to do that well,
not trying to impress anyone,
not worrying about anything,
just going about their business,
whatever that was,
not putting on an act
or putting on a show,
just being themselves,
completely unaware
that anyone is even there
or anyone is watching,
or perhaps they are aware
and really do not care
because just being what they are
is all they need to do,
trusting that what they are
is good enough,
is exactly what is needed,
because all we need
as we watch them closely
is for them to stay
where they are
doing what they do,
so we can get to know them,
can begin to feel closer to them,
because we will, of course,
like them,
we can't help it
as we look as them
and get to know them,
it just happens automatically,
just like things happen
automatically to you
as you continue to relax
and become aware
that you have been
quite comfortable
sitting there with them,
under that microscope
that magnifies everything,
illuminates it all
like a spotlight,
without a care
in the whole wide world . . .
[*Go to a direct approach or trance
termination.*]

MAGNIFYING GLASS

A metaphor script for enhanced concentration.

Now, as you relax,
and your mind slowly slows
and it becomes easier
to pay close attention
to your thoughts,
to where your mind goes,
and I wonder if you can
begin to notice
that each thought,
each sensation,
seems to stand out
to become bigger than before,
the way tiny images
become enlarged
when viewed through the lens
of a magnifying glass,
the kind used by private eyes
to look for fingerprints and clues,
to carefully study every object
one at a time,
to examine things in detail,
to not miss a thing,
the way you can be aware
of everything I say,
listening to each word,
hearing every sound said,
focusing in as I begin
to explain to you
that you can too
pay close attention to
whatever you need to,
whenever you want to,
by quieting down
and zeroing in
and becoming still inside
like this,
as the mind finds it easier
to be aware of one thing at a time,
like it is easier to listen to me
and examine every detail,
that the mind can find

through that magnifying lens
that even a child can use
to explore tiny worlds
and enjoy discovering
how it all fits together,
how things stick together,
and sticking to a job,
seeing it through,
dealing with every detail
right to the end,
becomes easier over time
as the mind begins to play
with its own ability
to just stay put,
to be intently still,
as you realize how easy it is
to continue doing so,
even as you begin to be aware
that the mind can comfortably stare
at anything at all,
absorbing it all,
enjoying it all,
the way you continue to hear,
the sound of my voice,
and the meaning of my words,
each one letting you know,
even more than before,
that you *can* do that now,
are paying attention fully,
a magnifying lens you can use,
anywhere at all.
[*Go to a direct approach or trance
termination.*]

ABSOLUTE AMAZEMENT

A metaphor script for experiencing "flow" or getting into the "zone."

And I wonder if you can remember
    now,
as you continue to relax
and listen carefully
to the things I am saying to you,
how it feels to watch someone
do something utterly amazing,
like in a circus
or a magic act,
where you sit there in the audience,
eyes fixed, mouth open,
mind absolutely still,
stunned into total silence
by the incredible thing
happening right there,
someone doing something
you thought could not be done,
balancing or lifting,
twisting or turning,
in ways never seen before,
and you just sit there watching,
amazed by it all,
entranced by the performance,
like you are in a trance now,
and can return to that memory
of how it feels now
whenever you begin to do
something old or something new,
learning or doing,
because many years ago
people began to learn
that when they want to learn something
or do something,
they do not need someone yelling,
someone telling them what is wrong,
not even that tiny voice
they carry in their head,
that just prevents you
from paying attention
to what you are doing,

so the secret they discovered
was how to relax,
and go along for the ride
with your eyes and ears open
and your mind quiet inside,
just watching quietly,
and allowing events to occur,
a silent passenger,
a fascinated tourist,
the way it felt to ride a horse,
which I did as a child,
out across the fields,
then winding through the woods,
and no matter how far away I went
or how lost I was,
I just turned that horse around,
relaxed the reins
and let it go where it wanted,
because it knew the way home,
even when I did not,
and it knows what to do
when you do not,
and you can trust it
like you rarely have before,
your own unconscious mind,
when you let yourself
relax this way
and let it do
what it can do
for you,
more than you can imagine,
things to watch in amazement,
mind absolutely still,
silently enjoying
totally fascinated
by those abilities to learn and do,
whatever you want it to do.
So as you relax and remember
the mind absorbed this way,
a sponge on water,

soaking it all up,
clear and still,
learning to do this at other times,
in other places,
and discovering how it feels,
to be amazed and thoroughly enjoy,
what that unconscious mind performer
can do for you
as you allow it to.
[*Go to a direct approach or trance termination.*]

12
———

OVERCOMING SEXUAL PROBLEMS

Sexual problems may be the result of many things, including a physiologic condition, unpleasant associations to past experiences, a value-laden set of beliefs and emotional reactions to sex itself, ignorance or a lack of experience, a problem in the relationship, and/or a self-conscious concern about being able to perform adequately. No matter what the source, it is possible that an appropriate medical intervention, such as a prescription for Viagra or testosterone, will resolve the condition effectively and swiftly. When such interventions are insufficient, however, hypnosis is an appropriate option.

Many clients presenting with sexual problems need to learn how to stop trying to do something that would occur naturally if they simply allowed it to do so. These clients must learn to relax and trust the unconscious to make it happen automatically. Paradoxically, the more we try to control something that is supposed to be automatic, the more we disrupt it. This is the case for simple things like walking, breathing, and falling asleep, but it is especially true of various forms of sexual function. For example, trying to not have an orgasm may speed up the onset of one, whereas trying to have one may actually delay or prevent it from happening. Under such circumstances, focusing attention on the opposite of the goal response or on just relaxing and letting nature take its well-designed course can significantly increase the probability of the desired response. (There is a possibility that the counterproductive effect of conscious intention may apply even to the basic biological processes involved in pregnancy. Erickson once told a highly proper young couple who had "engaged in marital union" regularly for three years in a very conscious, intentional, stilted, and unsuccessful effort to "procreate" to go home and "fuck for fun and pray to the devil that she isn't knocked up for at least three months" [Haley, 1973, p. 166]. The wife became pregnant less than three months later.)

Other clients need to learn how to turn off the anxiety or worry that blocks or prevents the spontaneous occurrence of sexual responses. This may sound easy, but it is not. Sexuality and self-esteem are highly interrelated in our culture. A sexual failure can be extremely damaging to self-esteem, especially if that self-esteem is already fragile. Furthermore, low self-esteem itself can produce anxiety and self-consciousness that then leads to poor sexual performance and a further reduction in self-esteem. Thus, failure sexually is something to be worried about and avoided at all costs, even though that worry is virtually guaranteed to produce failure. For such clients, a script dealing with self-esteem issues and/or anxiety may be necessary before sexual responses can be dealt with at all.

When a sexual problem occurs only within a specific relationship, it is obvious that the problem lies within that relationship, not within that person's sexual responsiveness. Feelings of rejection, betrayal, or resentment can block a sexual response even if the person genuinely wants to have sex with the other person and is consciously unaware of or denying the underlying feelings. A hypnotherapy session designed to reveal the disruptive emotion and heal the relationship may be more effective than one focused on the presenting problem itself.

Previous negative experiences or a strict moral upbringing may conflict directly with sexual responsiveness. Undoing the inhibitory influences of these factors obviously is the first order of business. Before a person can begin to relax, focus on pleasure, and enjoy exploring what happens naturally, that person must be reassured that it is appropriate and safe to do so.

Finally, although sexual responsiveness is a natural and normal part of human functioning, simply relaxing and allowing it to happen is not enough. As with all human endeavors, information, practice, and skill produce a more mature, intense, and satisfying approach to sexual activity. Learning the attitudes and behaviors involved in giving and receiving pleasure is necessary to the resolution of sexual disorders in general.

It also is worth mentioning that the conditions responsible for sexual arousal and response are somewhat different for men and women. In general, males tend to be more visually oriented and responsive to localized genital stimulation, whereas females tend to be aroused by a wider array of physical sensations and perceptions and tend to be more emotionally and intellectually involved in the interpersonal aspects of the process.

Given all of these variables, it is obvious that the scripts presented in this chapter cannot cover every possible situation. Each is based on an approach used successfully with a specific sexual problem. Thus, these scripts contain material designed to embed trust in one's natural capacities or inclinations, convey a more mature attitude or approach to sex, and redirect attention in ways that are more likely to produce the desired outcome.

DINNER FOR TWO

A metaphor script for improving male attitudes about sex.

Now we could talk about sex
while you continue to relax
and I am quite sure
you would listen carefully
to everything I have to say,
because you and I both know
that you do not know
how to do things for her
that you really want to do
but I think that first
you need to slow down a lot,
you need to take your time here,
you need to consider
the difference between a gourmet meal
and a quick hamburger
at a greasy fast food joint,
because everyone knows
that when you want to impress some-
    one
and have a wonderful time yourself
you take them out to a four-star place,
a restaurant where they serve you in
    style,
with fancy tablecloths and silverware
and lots of expensive items on the
    menu,
but not everyone knows
how much more impressive it can be,
satisfying and rewarding as well,
to fix a wonderful meal at home,
taking the challenge,
wondering if you can do it,
to take the time and thought
to select a menu,
to set the table,
to light the candles,
to arrange the flowers,
so the light is right
and the perfume just right,
to prepare the food,

to serve it,
to make it look beautiful,
to share it with someone,
to think about it ahead of time,
to enjoy the anticipation,
to select the appetizers she might like,
to offer several different ones,
to watch her look at each one
see her taste each one,
close her eyes,
and see her lick her lips
with absolute delight,
as the tastes melt on her tongue
and she feels it with her mind,
and pouring the drinks
and then serving the meal,
savoring the taste of each,
the ones that melt in your mouth,
the ones that are salty or sweet,
the ones she thinks are just right,
you can tell by how she reacts,
so you give her more of that
until she has had
as much of everything as she wants,
then you take your time,
give her time to recover,
time for things to settle,
there is no rush at all,
perhaps sipping some coffee,
dancing a bit to soft music,
moving legs and hips together
and bodies together
in a slow rhythm of movement
in the soft light of candles
and bringing out desert at last,
the best for last,
something she can't resist
even though she feels satisfied
she will always have room for that,
so there is no hurry,

just taking your time,
all the time in the world to enjoy,
seeing her delight,
enjoying her pleasure,
and discovering you can do it,
can really impress her
can make her feel special,
can feel the pleasure
of doing it so well
that it becomes a special time,
a special memory for her
and you as well,
and even if you never do it,
never serve her a meal
just thinking about it
you can appreciate
how much better that is
than a greasy burger
at a fast food place.
And so you already know
all you need to know
without even knowing it
and all you need to do
is to decide to do it
in a way that you know
will do that too . . .
[*Go to a direct approach or trance termination.*]

LEARNING TO RIDE

A metaphor script for sexual inhibitions in general.

There are many different ways
to do what you want to do,
but there is only one way
to let it be done for you,
because there are many things
we don't know how to do
and so we can learn to trust
and allow them to be done.
They will be done
when you allow them to,
like learning to ride a horse.
At first it can be difficult
to just relax and ride,
but the horse
has its own rhythm
and its own power
and once you find that rhythm
and relax into it,
that horse will carry you
wherever you want to go.
Like your own unconscious mind,
it has the power and ability
to do those things automatically,
although at first
it can be rather scary,
and you may want to hold on tight,
wondering about every move,
every thing that happens . . .
wondering if it is supposed to be that way
or if that horse can be trusted.
But after a while you do learn . . .
how to relax
and enjoy those things that occur
quite automatically,
that effortless movement,
that automatic flow . . .
and the mind relaxes,
drifting off someplace else entirely,
enjoying thoughts or images,
like riding a bus,
looking out the window,

enjoying the scenes and sights,
knowing the driver knows
where to go and when,
knowing it is safe to just watch,
or to drift off in dreams,
a dream of joining the circus perhaps,
to walk a tight rope,
which looks harder than it is,
and only is hard because it is so high,
so high you begin to try
but trying to do it
makes it hard to do,
and doing it without thinking,
allowing the unconscious to take over,
makes it easier and easier.
Just like typing or playing the piano,
where the fingers skip over the keys
in an effortless flow of rhythm
until someone asks which finger
you use for F or P.
The body knows,
but you don't know,
and so doing what you want to do
is just going along for the ride,
letting it be done to you,
as your unconscious mind
allows you to forget to remember
to try to do what you cannot do,
because you can forget,
or your unconscious mind can forget
to remember it to you,
so that in a short time,
you can just relax
absorbed by the sights and sounds
of your own mind's eye
while that horse continues on
and you ride with that rhythm,
go with that flow
anywhere at all.
[*Go to a direct approach or trance
termination.*]

BEAUTIFUL GIFTS

A metaphor script for premature ejaculation.

The unconscious mind
guards a variety of treasures,
like a guard in an art museum,
standing in a room full of sculptures
and paintings of beautiful women.
They get to observe the reactions
of people as they walk into that room,
and hear the sudden exclamations,
the "oohs" and "aahs" of appreciation
that just burst forth from their lips
as soon as they see those things
that are so beautiful it takes the breath
    away.
It is easy to demonstrate our appreciation
with that unexpected, uncontrolled response,
the same kind of reaction you see in
    children
when they receive a special gift, a toy
    perhaps,
a birthday present or a Christmas present.
I love watching their uncontrolled
    excitement
as they tear off the wrapping paper
and throw it everywhere
and jerk out that toy
and start playing with it at once
and probably break it
before they even have a chance to say,
    "Thank you!"
But sometimes it can be more satisfying
watching a friend or lover receive a gift,
carefully examining the package,
appreciating the beauty of the wrapping,
and slowly undoing it,
savoring each moment of anticipation,
enjoying the pleasure of each step,
stretching it out over time,
not giving in to the temptations,
but taking their time to enjoy each step,
pausing every now and then to say
    something,

to express their appreciation,
wondering out loud what it could be,
and then finally opening the box,
taking out the gift slowly, gently,
softly expressing their pleasure
in a deep and genuine way,
letting the giver receive attention for a
    time,
telling them how wonderful and
    thoughtful.
And then, and only then,
when everything else has been done,
finally exploring the present completely,
enjoying themselves thoroughly,
like real art lovers
who also take their time,
they allow the beauty to sink in,
they sit and ponder and enjoy each one
for hours and hours on end.
With a quiet reverence and respect
they pay tribute in a quiet way,
that takes them far away
from the crowds of noisy children
skipping through yelling "Look at this
    and that."
And through it all
the guard stands back
watching and protecting,
knowing that sometimes a teacher
    comes in,
calms the children, gets their attention,
and slowly and carefully explains to
    them
how to look at the beauty quietly,
how to see what's really there,
so that they too can sit and stare
and feel the pleasure grow
as they slowly begin to know
how to control their own awareness.
[*Go to a direct approach or trance
termination.*]

EXPLOSIONS

A metaphor script for female anorgasmia.

You have told me that sometimes
you almost get there
but pull back at the last minute,
become afraid of the intensity,
afraid to lose control,
and I can understand that
because everyone has been afraid
to cross a line at some point,
even little children get afraid
of something entirely new,
especially if it is too loud
or too noisy
or just too different
from what happened before,
especially if it changes everything,
from the top of their head
to the tips of their toes,
the way a small child feels
about getting into a swimming pool,
especially diving in the first time.
I remember a program on TV
about children learning to swim
and they showed a young boy,
about seven or eight years old,
standing at the top of the ladder
of a diving board
with all the parents along the pool,
and all the other kids too,
all yelling for him to do it,
cheering him on,
and he was scared,
scared as scared could be,
he was shaking with fear
as he stood up on that board
only three feet above the water,
and he stood there frozen for a while
then took a tiny step forward,
all hunched up and stiff,
afraid he would fall off,
you could tell,

and then another tiny step,
standing there shivering for a while,
another small step forward,
closer to the end,
and another and another,
and standing on the very end,
his whole body shaking,
every muscle stiff and rigid,
then finally taking the leap,
jumping off feet first,
and everyone applauding
yelling hurray at him
as he came up to the surface
and made his way to the side,
and later they asked him on camera
what he was thinking out there
and he said quite seriously
that all he kept thinking was,
"I think I am going to die,
I think I am going to die,
I think I am going to die . . ."
And he really did think
he was going to die
but he jumped in anyway
because he also knew
that others had done it before
and had come out alive,
even seemed to enjoy it
like he enjoyed it now,
smiling and happy and thrilled,
and going back up and doing it again,
again and again,
laughing now as he walked to the end,
yelling with joy as he plunged in,
even going head first a few times,
because every child eventually learns
that the best pleasures in life
are the things that seem dangerous
at first
but are just new and different,

from learning to ride a bike
to learning to swim and dive
to learning how to drive,
and once you learned
that you could survive
that is all the learning
you need now . . .
[*Go to a direct approach or trance termination.*]

LOOKING

A metaphor script for impotence.

They say a watched pot never boils
but the truth is
it is heat that makes the water boil
and all the watching in the world
can't stop that bubbling
once the pot reaches 212 degrees.
Waiting and watching only makes it
    seem
like forever,
like it will never happen,
but a good cook knows
that once you start the fire
and put the pot on
all you need to do
is peel the carrots and onions or thaw
    the peas
or eat a few to enjoy yourself
while you wait happily for what is
    bound to happen,
as that heat continues to rise and rise
to the boiling point.
But some people still are afraid to
    watch,
to pay close attention as the steam rises,
and the first bubbles begin to form,
liquid condenses on the sides.
They seem to believe
they should not pay attention to such
    things,
even though sometimes you have to
    watch,
you have to participate fully
if you really want it to be a success,
even if it is only in your mind,
imagining what is happening there,
or what you want to happen,
and what would it be
that would make it happen,
so you can add things to the pot
when the temperature is just right

or pull them out when they are done.
And you have to pay close attention
to get a feel for cooking that way,
the way you do
when you want to examine the texture
    of something
to see if it is smooth enough or rough.
So you close your eyes and taste it,
or touch it softly with a finger
and focus fully on that feeling,
so even the tiniest sensation gets
    noticed,
aware of it all.
And everything is magnified
as it becomes the full focus
of all your attention,
and you can just allow those tastes,
those pleasant sensations to grow,
to become the only thing you feel
as you observe them with pleasure
and look forward to that meal
and desert afterward.
A good cook can almost taste it
in the mind's eye,
and when that happens
the salivary glands
begin to fill the mouth
with the anticipation of something
    wonderful,
which makes it harder and harder
to wait any longer
until you can finally
let yourself take that first bite,
and feel the relief and satisfaction
or perhaps the surprise
of a new sensation,
a new reaction to a situation,
and once it occurs,
gives rise to that awareness,
nothing can stop it,

nothing can interfere,
hard to imagine
the power of a good stiff one
at the end of a meal
like the great gourmets of the world
who learn to appreciate
fine wines with fine food,
and all the other pleasures
available to you now.
[*Go to a direct approach or trance termination.*]

13

ENHANCING
RELATIONSHIPS

When the presenting problem involves a relationship, we prefer to work with both people at the same time. This is true even if the primary source of the problem appears to be the unwarranted insecurity, jealousy, or blocked emotions of only one of the two people involved. Thus, most of the metaphor scripts presented in this chapter are appropriate for use with couples who have participated in a trance induction together and are now ready for the therapist to clarify the situation and offer suggestions for alternative resolutions. These metaphors also can be used with individuals seeking help because of a history of insecurity, jealousy, or fear of commitment; however, we recommend that interpersonal difficulties be dealt with in an interpersonal manner, that is, with a partner, whenever this is feasible. By involving a partner in the process, it becomes possible to alter the outcome of the undesirable behavior and break the dynamic that has supported it in the past.

For example, insecure individuals seem unable to trust themselves or the relationship. Their constant and insatiable demands for reassurance can exasperate even the most loving and comforting partner and eventually drive that person away. This outcome then further reinforces their insecurity. Similarly, jealousy tends to produce the very outcome the person is trying hardest to prevent. Suspicious efforts to control the thoughts and behavior of the partner almost invariably result in a rebellious assertion of the partner's rights to do whatever he or she wants. Finally, blocked emotional involvement or the withholding of interpersonal commitment frequently seems to be a protection against getting hurt. But by holding back emotionally the person virtually guarantees that his or her partner eventually will withdraw as well. Once again, the original concerns are confirmed in a self-fulfilling prophecy and the outcome the person is trying to prevent is exactly what occurs. The interpersonal conflict continues even though neither party is sure exactly why they are fighting.

The metaphor scripts presented in this chapter convey this self-defeating, self-fulfilling prophecy quality of the behavior involved and offer each member of the relationship suggestions for an alternative approach. The goal is to break the destructive cycle and pave the way for a meaningful, safe, and rewarding relationship.

It should be noted that the phenomena of jealousy, insecurity, and blocked emotional involvement often occur together in a relationship in an interactive manner. For example, blocked emotional involvement by one person may result in insecurity or jealousy from the other. Likewise, insecurity or jealousy may prompt the partner to withdraw or block further emotional involvement. Any or all of the following metaphors may apply in these situations.

It also should be noted that emotional unavailability can be the result of an addictive involvement, rather than being a self-protective emotional withdrawal. When addiction to alcohol, drugs, another person, or some outside activity is the reason for emotional withholding in a relationship, that addiction must be the focus of the intervention. The following scripts are not relevant to that difficulty.

Finally, not all problematic interpersonal relationships involve only adults. Many parent–child relationships are equally difficult to deal with at times, as reflected by our inclusion of a script designed to foster parental tolerance toward children.

WORLD WAR I

A metaphor script for interpersonal conflicts perpetuated by old hurt feelings.

Now, I do not know
if either of you
know much about history,
about World War I, for example,
or what can be learned from it,
but I do know about something
that happened during that war
that is worth thinking about,
is worth learning about,
because no one on either side,
not the soldiers doing the fighting,
nor the generals or politicians
who sent them off to battle,
really knew what the war was about,
or exactly how or why it got started,
they were just there, fighting,
for some reason,
the Germans and the English,
shooting at each other in France,
living in filthy mud trenches,
cold, wet, and hungry,
thousands dying each day
to gain an inch or two of land,
losing it the next day
as the mortars and shells
fell everywhere,
and friends fell in the muck,
broken by the blasts
that no one could see coming,
until one night before Christmas,
the fighting slowed just a bit
as both sides opened presents,
food and candles and candy
sent from home,
from loved ones and strangers,
more than they could use
before it would spoil,
and both sides began singing,
Christmas carols,
"Silent Night,"

in German on one side,
English on the other,
throwing songs back and forth
instead of bullets and bombs,
then the Germans put candles
on small Christmas trees,
they lit up the night,
gave away their positions,
but the English did not fire,
instead they were curious,
crawled through the barbed wire,
across no-man's land,
to sneak a peek,
to see what was going on,
and the Germans saw them
and did not fire either,
crawled out to meet them instead.
They talked,
and then they agreed
to meet back there
the next morning,
to bury all the dead
that lay everywhere around them,
their relatives and friends,
to clean up that place
so they could get together,
and at dawn on Christmas day
that is what they did,
silently, reverently,
with no bitterness,
just sorrow,
burying their own
and those of the other side too,
saying prayers and singing hymns,
and when it was done,
they exchanged presents
and talked some more,
then they began to play football,
soccer we call it,
right out there where the war

was supposed to be,
all along the front line
games of football began,
and when the day ended
they were friends
who refused to fight,
refused to take shots
at those they had played with,
refused to try to hurt
those they had shared with,
and the generals were furious,
took them off the front lines,
replaced them with new recruits
who had no idea
what had happened,
who did not know
about the other side,
and began killing each other again
until ten million more had died
and both sides finally decided
to just give it all up.
So neither side really won,
everyone lost,
dead and wounded everywhere,
entire cities gone,
cathedrals destroyed,
friends and lovers gone,
for no particular reason
except spite,
and a refusal to accept
that both sides could be friends,
could say they were sorry
and shake hands and embrace,
like those soldiers did
on that one cold Christmas day,
when they felt sad and sorry
for what was going on,
and just refused to go on,
and revealed to us all
what happens
when we stop being angry
and put down our weapons,
when we declare peace for a time
and spend some time

enjoying someone
without fighting.
[*Go to a direct approach or trance
termination.*]

TERRITORIALITY

A metaphor script for jealousy.

Now, as each of both of you
continue to listen to me,
I can begin to wonder
if either or both of you,
separately or together,
have ever had the experience
of watching a dog mark out its territory.
Because dogs, and many other animals,
spend a lot of time establishing
    boundaries,
using scents to say this belongs to me,
it is not yours,
it is not you.
Some animals have special glands
that give off a peculiar scent,
and others just urinate here and there,
and then act like that land belongs to
    them,
the same way countries put up fences,
and draw imaginary lines on maps,
and then say that everything here,
belongs to us
for us to use any way we want,
and everyone here has to do what we
    want, too,
whether they want to or not,
they have to do what the dictator says,
what that petty dictator wants,
until there is a revolution
or the people simply move someplace
    else
or the dictator changes the rules
and lets the people do as they want,
lets the people make the decisions
and declares freedom throughout the
    land,
which requires a lot of faith and trust
that the people will do what's best,
and won't just up and leave
as soon as they have the chance.

But if that leader believes in them
and they believe in their leader,
if they respect each other and
    themselves,
then democracy seems to work
and people vote for who they like best,
like a popularity contest
or the way we select our favorite movie
    stars,
who may seem to be one thing,
but turn out to be another,
like the big, tough man's man
who actually is soft and gentle,
just afraid of being left,
or the handsome leading man
who doesn't even like women,
and what about the high school star
who shows up at the class reunion,
and turns out to be a bum,
never even had a decent job,
but he still wants to tell everybody else
what to do and how to do it,
because one of the things you learn
as a therapist
is that things sometimes are not what
    they seem.
We imagine how happy the rich folk
    are,
and we think we know what goes on
    there,
but when you really talk to people,
in private where they tell the truth,
you discover that what we imagine
is rarely accurate or even close,
and that just because we can imagine
    anything,
that doesn't make it so,
even though we can find evidence for it,
in trashy papers and magazines.
What we really see behind the scenes

is that everyone needs something special,
and that all the boundaries dissolve,
when the dog finally lets you pet him,
and you scratch his back or behind his ears,
and play with him for a while,
he doesn't growl anymore
when you cross his urinary line,
or enter into his territory
with a bone or something sweet,
and you let him lick your hand,
and play a few games
so that later on
that friendship allows each of you
to come and go as you wish,
comfortable in the knowledge
that there is a trust in each other
you can bank on,
and that it makes good sense
and is in your best interest
to do so.
[*Go to a direct approach or trance termination.*]

PLAYGROUNDS

A metaphor script for insecurity and mistrust.

Each of you has a brain,
that you use in everyday life,
that thinks, and understands, and
    remembers,
and you depend upon it,
to provide you with the abilities needed,
to take care of things for you.
But I wonder if you know
that the neurons in that brain
can inhibit each other
or excite each other
so that when some neurons fire
they excite others,
but when other neurons fire
they inhibit the others
and keep them from responding at all.
And so there are times
when the harder those cells try
to do one thing,
the more difficult it becomes,
while at other times
not doing anything at all
gives the desired results.
And if one neuron is stimulated too much,
it may become exhausted
and stop responding completely,
just like the cells in a muscle
that get tired of doing the same thing
over and over again.
This is true even for little children,
who may be afraid at first
when their parents take them to the
    playground
and turn them loose to run around.
You can watch that tiny toddler,
unsure of itself at first,
unsure of the parent too,
afraid that parent may disappear
if it gets too far away.
So at first you go with them,
you reassure them that it is OK
to go off to play in the sandbox
or explore the swings.
And that toddler keeps coming back,
but staying away longer and longer,
beginning to play with others,
even getting on the teeter totter
and learning how to balance,
each trusting the other
not to get off suddenly,
the kind of trust it takes
to invest your life's savings
in a business with a friend,
Not the kind of thing you'd do
with a total stranger,
but there are some people
who we know that we can trust
because they have earned that trust
like interest in a bank
that you count on to be there,
even though you know
that banks do fail sometimes
but it is pretty rare,
so we trust them,
unless we have a good reason not to,
just like that child trusts others.
They are all friends
unless they prove they're not,
and when that friend gets tired
of doing the same thing over and over,
they go off together
and do something else,
on the swings, or in the sandbox,
knowing their parents are there,
waiting at the picnic bench
to take them home when they're tired,
to bring them back when they're not,
and because that all goes without saying,
they can enjoy themselves
quite completely.
[*Go to a direct approach or trance
termination.*]

DROUGHTS

A metaphor script for difficulties with emotional commitments.

There are some plants
that find it easier to survive a drought
because they have deep roots
burrowed down into the soil,
down where it stays damp and moist
even when the ground is hard and dry.
But most grasses have shallow roots,
fine roots that go down just below the
    surface,
so they dry out when the rains stop
and are unable to get nutrients,
the things they need to stay alive.
Because once the nutrients stop flowing in,
the growing stops as well
and the dying starts,
just like any living tissue
which is why you loosen a tourniquet
once every three or four minutes at least,
and let the blood flow through again
to nourish the cells
and to take away the wastes,
even though it may mean
that the bleeding starts again,
because we all have lots of blood
and we can stand to lose a bit,
but we can't stand to block the flow
of those things needed very long.
And the marvel of it all
is that we can donate to each other,
we can give each other what we need
and never miss it at all,
the way a plant with deep roots
can give us moisture even in a drought,
while shallow-rooted grass
becomes dry and rough
and tends to catch on fire,
like the grasslands of California
where fire is always a hazard
but it is a different state of mind
to be in a place where you can play
and enjoy the sea breezes
in the fertile valleys
that are so close to the ocean
but still need to be irrigated
so that the ground can support the
    gardens
that feed an entire nation
and provide the fruits
we enjoy in the winter months.
So much food
they could never eat it all,
so they don't need to hoard it,
they can share it, sell it,
and reap great profits in return,
because no one would say
they should just give it all away
because they need to save some
just for themselves,
and they need to get something out of it
just for themselves.
But they seem to be very proud
of all they provide for others,
things from deep inside
the center of that state
and the more taxes they pay
the more they know they earned that day
but nobody likes withholding money
just to throw it away
with no return on their investment
so sometimes they put it away,
deep in vaults in the biggest banks,
to keep it safe for later,
the way a snail hides in a shell
protected and yet available
ready to come out again
when the rains return
and the soil softens
and the nutrients flow rich and deep.
[*Go to a direct intervention or trance
termination.*]

BECOME AS LITTLE CHILDREN

A metaphor script for parental attitudes toward their children.

Many years ago
a professor told me
that people never really become
mature, responsible adults
until they have children of their own.
And I wondered
exactly what he meant,
if he really thought
that people have to endure hardships
or take on great responsibilities,
or put up with crying and messes,
or say no a million times
before they can mature,
but even Christ once said,
"Lest you become as little children,
you shall not enter
the kingdom of Heaven."
So I decided maybe
he knew something
worth paying attention to,
or thinking about a lot,
because it is not apparent
how to raise a child,
although wild animals,
like coyotes and elephants and deer,
have families that they raise
year after year after year,
showing them how and where
to find food,
how and where to hide,
what to do and where to go,
playing with them
and protecting them,
while their children watch
and learn by example
exactly how to behave,
to do exactly what the parent does,
because that is what children do,
and how do those parents know
what to do and when,

with no instruction manuals,
no specific directions to follow
like you even get with plants you buy
that tell you how much sun
and how much water,
although it can be fun
to get one of those bags
of wildflower seeds
and just scatter them about
in fertile soil
and just wait and watch
to see what grows,
and those little sprouts come up
and there is no way to know
what each one will be,
so you just water them
and protect them,
wondering what they will become,
looking forward to that day,
as they grow bigger and stronger,
when they finally burst into bloom,
no two exactly alike,
but each one
a colorful miracle,
no instructions needed
to take good care of things,
to protect them and care for them,
to keep them healthy and unharmed,
that is something anyone can do,
even a small child,
or an animal in a zoo
like that gorilla did
when a small boy
fell fifteen feet into its enclosure,
a place where many gorillas lived
        together,
with artificial cliffs and caves,
tree limbs to climb on,
and that boy lay there,
right where he fell,

on that hard concrete,
and that enormous male gorilla
walked over to him
and looked him over,
touched him with a huge finger
and grunted softly several times
as if to wake him up,
and the crowd of people above
were horrified and afraid,
expected the worst,
especially when that gorilla
reached down and picked up that boy,
took him in his arms,
and people screamed
as he cradled that child
and roared at the other gorillas
to make them go away,
people terrified above,
while below that gorilla
gently carried that injured child
right over to the door
and laid him on the floor there,
and backed away,
and kept the others away,
until the keepers could open the door
and retrieve the child
who turned out to be fine,
and all the people there that day
said they learned something new
about what we call a dumb animal,
who turned out to be
not dumb or cruel at all,
but someone any professor
would be proud of
and respect
as a mature adult
who knew how to protect
the little ones,
although the little ones
can teach the parents too,
or at least give them a good excuse,
to run about and laugh and play,
which they do a lot every day
because parents soon discover

they can have fun too,
can play and laugh as well,
the way children can and do
when watching cartoons,
like Wile E. Coyote
and the Road Runner,
which makes children laugh so hard
that even parents learn to smile
and rediscover joy
all over again.
[*Go to a direct approach or trance termination.*]

14

MEDICAL ISSUES

The relationship between the mind and body is circular and the boundary between them is permeable. Actually, they probably are best thought of as inseparable, unitary, or identical. The mind influences what the body does and what the body does influences the mind. In other words, the mind can modify or influence virtually any physiologic function from blood flow to the production of antibodies and, conversely, even small changes in our physiology can affect how we think and feel. Although few people know how to influence these relationships consciously, the unconscious mind often can figure out how to do so when given the opportunity.

Anyone genuinely interested in using hypnosis to treat psychophysiologic disorders should consult *Mind-Body Therapy* by Ernest L. Rossi and David B. Cheek (1988) and/ or Rossi's *The Psychobiology of Mind-Body Healing* (1986). Rossi's coverage of this topic in particular includes a thorough discussion of mind/body linkages and a detailed description of his unique and elegantly simple hypnotic formula for accessing unconscious solutions. In essence, his approach involves a relatively straightforward request to the unconscious to do whatever it can to resolve the current problem. This request is followed by an expectant pause to allow the unconscious time to determine what needs to be done and to signal its discovery of a solution.

As emphasized in Chapter 3, we recommend that a minimalist approach such as Rossi's be used initially with *all* types of problems. If this minimalist or permissive strategy does not succeed, however, then it may be necessary to employ appropriate metaphorical communications with the unconscious in a further effort to elicit its aid.

It also is clear that replacing stress, anger, and fear with relaxation, pleasure, and optimism can improve our physical health and even our response to surgery, medications, or other medical interventions (cf. Hafen, Karren, Frandsen, & Smith, 1996). Several of the scripts presented in this chapter emphasize this route to improved health and more useful reactions to various types of medical treatment.

PROTECTIVE ANTS

A metaphor script for increasing immune system responses to infections.

There is a tree in Africa
that has a special relationship
with a particular kind of ant.
The ants spend their entire lives
living on that tree.
They build their nests
out of its leaves,
they only drink
the particular kind of sap
that tree produces and secretes
or eat the special tiny berries it grows.
They never leave that tree,
because that tree provides
everything they need.
And this type of ant is the only insect
that does live on that tree.
Whenever any other insect
begins to crawl upon it
or lands on one of its leaves
the ant sentries send out an alarm,
and all the other ants come running.
They attack those foreign bodies
and either destroy them
or drive them away
and in this way
they protect that tree
from any invaders
that might attack it
or even destroy it.
They save the tree
and the tree saves them.
There are many other examples
of the same thing throughout the world,
where one tiny creature
protects a large one
from dangerous invaders.
And in each and every case
they always seem to have a way
of paying very close attention
to anything that could be harmful

so that they know immediately
if something is wrong,
and they know immediately
where something is wrong,
and they know what is wrong
and they pay close attention to it
so they can do something about it,
to eliminate it or fix it,
just the way people do
when they notice a pain in a foot
and they pay close attention
to that discomfort
so they can tell what it is
and get rid of that stone in the shoe,
as long as nothing gets in the way,
and they continue to pay close attention
to the way the body reacts
and amplify that reaction
the way they amplify the sound of an
    engine
to hear what's wrong
and let that body take care of itself
with the same amazing grace
that those ants take care of that tree,
automatically and continuously,
rushing to do those things needed
to heal and protect.
[*Go to a direct approach or trance
termination.*]

RAFT TRIPS

A metaphor script for high blood pressure.

When you take a raft trip,
or drift down a river in a canoe,
you begin to notice things
that otherwise would go overlooked,
especially those things
that change the flow of the river,
speed it up, or slow it down,
because when the river is wide and
        deep
the water flows gently along,
and you can lie back,
with your eyes closed,
listening to that quiet sound.
But when the walls of that canyon
begin to close in,
and get narrower and narrower,
the water rushes through faster
and creates dangerous rapids,
that you have to navigate carefully,
until you get back to that place,
where the river bed gets wide again
and deep peaceful quiet returns.
Because water is just like anything else,
the more you compress it,
the faster it goes,
as it flows along,
and the bigger the space it has to fill,
the calmer and quieter it becomes.
And every child knows this, too,
they know when something is too small
that they need to make it bigger
to hold everything they have,
so they get a bigger glass
or they get a bigger bowl
or they get a bigger pair of gloves
so their hands can feel relaxed and
        comfortable,
larger than they felt before,
and everywhere inside
expands to hold it all.

Such a wonderful feeling of relaxation,
like loosening a tight belt
after a huge meal,
and feeling that relief
the pleasure of letting go,
of letting things expand,
feeling the new space provided,
a new freedom to relax,
the kind of quiet calmness you hear
when those noisy children
leave the room and go outside,
and the teacher relaxes,
the pressure relieved.
Even those old riverboats,
with their paddlewheels and steam
        engines,
could relieve some pressure
by blowing their whistles
when things got too hot inside,
and everyone could relax on deck,
watching the river banks go by,
and the slow flow of the water
in the deep channels they followed,
taking their time
to get from here to there,
with nothing to do in the meantime
except relax from the inside out,
and feel the calm stillness
of a quiet pool
moving gently in the moonlight,
while the soft sounds of evening
drift by in an effortless flow,
a calm slowing down
to a gentle softness
as relaxation continues
and becomes a part
of *you.*
[*Go to a direct approach or trance
termination.*]

BREAKDOWNS

A metaphor script for cardiac anxieties following a heart attack.

When something is really valuable,
people get afraid of losing it,
like the man who bought
a new Cadillac car.
It was his life's dream,
he had wanted one his whole life
and so he put his life savings into it.
He felt proud to own such a beautiful
    machine
and he was excited when he drove it
    home.
All his life he had heard what great cars
    they were,
so reliable and well built,
so safe and dependable.
He loved the way it sounded when he
    closed the doors,
everything seemed to work so smoothly
    and well.
Even though it was used
it seemed to be in perfect condition,
so it never occurred to him
that something might go wrong
until one day that week he and his wife
went for a drive,
and when they were miles out into the
    country
a hose to the radiator broke,
the car overheated,
and there they were, stranded,
    frightened, angry,
waiting for a tow truck from the dealer
    to rescue them.
and when they finally got home
he parked that car in the garage
and he refused to go on any more long
    drives.
He drove it to work at times,
but he was always listening, waiting
for something else to go wrong.

His wife told him he was being silly,
but it didn't feel silly to him.
He felt betrayed and disappointed
and his dreams of driving on long
    vacations,
exploring places they never had been,
all turned into thoughts of being
    stranded again,
of being someplace where no one could
    fix it,
as if the local dealer
were the only one who knew anything
    about his car
so his wife took that car to a mechanic
and had him go over it with a fine-
    toothed comb.
He replaced everything worn or
    weathered,
he tuned the engine and changed the
    plugs,
he put extra belts and hoses in the
    trunk
and he test drove it over old back
    roads,
and then they went home and got her
    husband
and took him for a drive in the country,
and the mechanic told him
everything he had done,
and reassured him that his car
was in excellent shape for its age
but that it needed to be driven on long
    drives
to keep the engine cleaned out,
which gave his wife a perfect excuse
to plan a vacation for the next month.
Before they left
on their two thousand mile drive,
he bought a CB and a cellular phone,
so that no matter where they were

they could always get help if something went wrong,
and he still was very concerned at first,
but when some stranger told him
what a beautiful car he had
he started to relax and feel good again,
and began to enjoy the trip.
He still checks that car over carefully each day,
and washes and waxes it often,
and of course a few things have gone wrong
and it has had to be worked on a few times,
but now he is retired
and his life's dream belongs to him
and he can truly enjoy it comfortably,
feeling safe and secure and proud.
[*Go to a direct approach or trance termination.*]

WARMING TRENDS

A metaphorical and direct approach for migraines.
Pain management is a central issue for migraine sufferers. Thus, the approaches presented in Chapter 7 may be especially useful for them. On the other hand, by learning how to divert blood flow into the extremities to warm hands and feet, many individuals become able to alleviate or even prevent their migraines. Because the exact etiology of migraine headaches is not known, it is not clear to us why this works, but the simple fact that it frequently does work leads us to include the following script.

Now, while you relax
and allow yourself to experience
the variety of changes that occur
as you drift into a trance,
I would like to help you learn
how to change those things
that will allow you to be able
to prevent or reduce your headaches.
And the thing you need to learn is this,
that when you feel a headache coming
     on,
what you need to do
is to be able to allow your *hands* and *feet*
to become very warm or *hot* very
     quickly.
So as you pay attention to those hands
     and feet,
I would like you to realize
that you can imagine how it feels
to have those hands and feet
sitting in the hot rays of the sun . . .
or resting in the warm water of a
     bath . . .
or whatever other image comes to mind
when you begin to pay attention to that
     warmth there,
and begin to feel the warmth grow,
get warmer and warmer, almost hot,
comfortably swollen and warm,
a warmth that may seem to spread
into the arms and legs after a time,
And as that warmth grows
and becomes more clear in your
     awareness,

you can continue to relax and drift
     down
into a comfortable trance state
where your unconscious mind can find
its own way to let your mind
become aware of that warmth and
     heaviness,
a growing warmth and relaxation
in the fingers of that hand
and the other hand,
and the feet in your shoes
and your arms and legs too, perhaps,
heavy and warm, warm and heavy.
That's right,
and from now on
whenever you feel a headache coming
     on,
what you need to do and can do
is to relax in this way,
remembering the quiet heaviness
and allow that warm thought to return,
greater than before perhaps,
until you feel that warmth everywhere,
or just in those hands and feet,
because now you can buy
gloves and socks
that heat up by themselves,
powered by little batteries
that make those thick gloves warm
and make those soft socks hot,
almost as soon as you put them on,
they begin to get warmer and warmer
you can try them on in a store
and actually feel that heat increase,

as they give off their own heat,
a surprising feeling of warmth
that works so well
they use them in Alaska
where even the bitterest cold
is soon replaced by the pulsating warmth,
as those gloves heat up,
and those socks heat up,
and the hands and feet begin to thaw,
begin to feel soft and swollen and warm,
swollen with a comfortable feeling
that spreads up the arms
and it continues on with you
even after you drift upward to wakeful awareness,
and reach that point where the eyes open.
That's right,
drifting upward now,
as that warm feeling continues,
a nice warm feeling
that you can create anytime you need to,
anytime you want to.
That's right, a warm wakefulness now,
as the mind drifts up
and the eyes
are allowed to open.
[*Go to a direct approach or trance termination.*]

DRAWING ATTENTION

A metaphor script for insomnia.

Have you ever tried
to not think of a pink elephant,
to avoid thinking of a pink elephant at
    all costs?
There is a lesson there
but it is different from the lesson
    learned
when you try to do something
only your unconscious can do for you,
because no one can think a thought
that will add one inch to their height
or digest their food in a different way,
and if you ever go someplace with a
    child
who is very, very hungry,
you will very quickly learn
that telling a child to ignore that hunger
won't help matters at all.
They know they want something
and they want it now
and telling them to ignore it
won't help them to forget it
but distracting their attention
with something of great interest
may help them forget that hunger
    entirely.
So you can take them on a roller
    coaster
or you can do something that makes
    them laugh,
or you can have them close their eyes
and draw circles on their forehead
asking them to tell you
what color is this circle,
and what color is the next,
and what color is the line you trace
from one side to the other,
that looks a bit like the edge of a pond,
with cattails growing here and there,
and rabbits playing in the grass

while the sun shines warmly
and the breeze gently blows in the trees
as the water washes against the shore
and the turtles sleep in the light
with clouds drifting by above
in the clear blue sky,
changing form and shape
as the birds sing to each other.
And that drifting off occurs
without knowing where or when
even as the child tries
to open the eyes
and not drift away,
that pleasant scene quiets the mind
and helps it forget to try
to be aware or unaware
of anything at all,
and that's all there needs to be
and all you need to do.
[*Go to a direct approach or trance
termination.*]

TRUST

A metaphor script for relaxation prior to dental work, surgery,
chemotherapy, and other intrusive medical procedures.

Now I can remember
a story a man told me
about his father
who stood him on a chair
when he was five years old
and told him to fall backward,
to let him catch the boy,
and the boy did fall backward
but the father did not catch him,
just let him fall to the floor,
then told the crying child
to let that be a lesson to him
that he should never trust anyone,
which is a very different lesson
from the one learned in encounter
     groups
led by psychotherapists
back in the 1970s,
when the members of those groups
took turns falling backward
into the arms of the others,
learning how good it felt
to know they could trust those people
to catch them
and not let them get hurt,
to take care of them
and watch out for them
and if you have ever done that
then you already know how it feels
to cross that line inside,
to decide to trust someone else
and to just relax and let go,
to just fall backward,
but if you have never done that
then you will have to imagine it,
or remember another experience
you have had before
when you knew it was OK
to really trust that other person,
to just let them take care of you,
with no hesitation
and no second guessing,
not needing to pay any attention at all
to what is going on,
but some people have trouble
even riding in a car
if someone else is driving,
like the man I met years ago
who could not drive
but could not stay relaxed
when his wife did so,
was always questioning her every move,
not going fast enough
or going too slow,
be careful of that truck,
watch out for that car,
what was that noise,
there is a red light up ahead.
And he really found it difficult
to understand why she got so upset
when all he was doing
was making sure she did it right,
until one day she finally told him
if he did not trust her driving skills
she would not let him get in the car
or take him anywhere
and he could hire a driver he trusted
if he could find one,
or one who would not mind
if he did not,
but that she was tired
of him acting like he knew
how to drive better than she did
when he could not drive at all,
and she had never had an accident,
or even come close to one,
.so he agreed to read instead,
or just shut his eyes and relax,

which was difficult at first,
until he decided
to just trust her judgment and skill,
at which point he could relax
and just go along for the ride
without being a back seat driver
or worrying about something
he really knew nothing about,
like the old TV ad,
leave the driving to us,
let the experts do what they do,
so he could drift in dreams,
like you are now,
until the trip was through
and so can you,
can you not?
[*Go to a direct approach or trance termination.*]

15

PROBLEMS IN LIVING

This chapter deals with common life issues that often cause intense stress, fear, anger, perseverative thinking, overwhelming sadness, impulsivity, and confusion. Sometimes clients are already aware that a pending or recent divorce, demanding and dissatisfying job, or feeling of spiritual disconnection from life around them is the source of their discomfort. Sometimes they are not. Sometimes the underlying problem is blatantly obvious to the therapist, even if the client is not yet aware of it. Sometimes it is not.

The Diagnostic Trance process described in Chapter 2 is an effective way to identify such issues when their influence is not readily apparent. On the other hand, it is one thing to identify these problem areas and another to promote their resolution. Issues such as those dealt with in this chapter are problems because they keep people mired in the past or prevent them from seeing the future in a positive light. When people lose their sense of direction because they cannot imagine a better life or let go of old goals to pursue new ones, their vision must be redirected, turned toward an awareness of untapped potentials and possibilities.

Thus, the metaphorical anecdotes presented in the following are designed to encourage clients to examine their situation from a distance, consider alternative images of themselves and their roles in life, and start constructing positive orientations toward the future. Letting go of the familiarity of the past in favor of an uncertain, unknowable future is a difficult or frightening challenge, but when that familiar past becomes an ongoing source of pain, letting go and going in a different direction may be the only viable option.

ANTIQUES

A metaphor script for dealing with an unwanted divorce.

I don't know about you,
but for many people
collecting is a relaxing
and rewarding pastime,
one that is becoming more popular
with shows on TV,
like the Antiques Roadshow,
where people bring in things
they have inherited
or bought at auctions
or found at yard sales,
things somebody else
no longer wanted,
or no longer needed,
or could no longer use,
but are now prized possessions
of somebody new,
things made out of gold
and silver and wood,
finely crafted objects
from all over the world,
tables and chairs,
chests of drawers,
sculptures and paintings,
bracelets and rings,
and you have to wonder
at times,
what the people were thinking
who gave them away
or threw them away
or traded them in,
because it is quite clear
that some people
have no appreciation
for their increasing value,
like the silver Viking helmet,
over five hundred years old,
covered with decorative scenes,
a beautiful thing
that someone discarded

in the rafters of an attic
and just forgot about
when they sold the house
many years ago,
but when recently found
turned out to be worth
over 400,000 dollars.
Quite a find for the lucky one
who recognized its beauty,
quite a loss for the other one
who tossed it away,
who had no appreciation
for its inherent value,
much less its artistry,
but people toss away
wonderful things every day,
replace gorgeous furniture
with the latest plastic fads
and then get upset
when it breaks,
while their old furniture
gets a new home
with someone who appreciates
its solid construction,
the curves of the legs,
the carved beauty of its arms
and the warmth of its seat
and the way they just don't
make things like that any more,
with that quality and care,
and so just because some people
have no taste,
have no appreciation,
or simply think
that they will be happier
if only they get something new,
without realizing
that what they are letting go of
is much more valuable
than when they got it

or more desirable
than what they are getting,
is no reason to forget
that the people who collect
what others no longer want
are the really smart ones,
the ones who are willing,
and even enjoy,
looking for prized possessions,
things they love
that fit right in
and have value that
cannot be ignored
and cannot be diminished
by the failure of someone else
who could not see it,
and maybe never will,
but still, it is there
for everyone to see
and everyone to feel,
which is why
many people have become rich
beyond their wildest dreams,
because they knew that quality
never goes out of fashion
and will always bring
the highest price from someone
who has fine taste
and appreciates the best
in you.
[*Go to a direct approach or trance termination.*]

TRUE BELIEVERS

*A metaphor script for people who are obsessed by thoughts
and feelings about old lovers or ex-spouses.*

Now,
listening to you earlier
talking about that other person,
for some reason
I began thinking about a book
by Tom Robbins
called *Another Roadside Attraction*,
and in that book
there is a woman named Amanda
who at one point says,
"You can't argue someone out of
something they weren't argued into."
And I don't know if that is true
or not true,
but I do know
that many years ago
I got to know a man
who I thought was very nice,
seemed polite and considerate,
was funny at times
and witty at others,
and people seemed to like him
and so did I
so we became friends,
or so I thought,
although later on
I began to notice
that he did not leave tips
and did not always do
what he said he would,
and would cancel appointments
at the very last minute,
and would argue over nothing
or disagree for no reason,
but I tried to ignore those things,
made excuses for them
and got upset if others
said bad things about him,
because I believed

he was really a nice guy,
my friend,
and it is not nice
to say or think bad things
about your friends,
until one day
he did something so outrageous,
so inconsiderate and selfish,
that my whole view of him
suddenly changed,
and in that moment
I got a clear view of him
and I stopped believing
what I had wanted to believe,
and accepted what was true instead,
a difficult thing to do,
I just couldn't believe it,
but there it was,
the kind of thing that happens
when you drive clear across town
to buy something
you have always wanted,
and when you get it home
you realize it is just not right,
maybe doesn't even work,
or doesn't even fit,
and you just can't believe it,
won't give up on it,
keep trying to make it fit
or trying to make it work,
because it is hard to admit
you made a mistake
and it isn't what you thought it was
after all,
it just isn't
and so you force yourself
to take it back
or just get rid of it
and don't look back

when something or someone
is not what you believed
it was,
not what you wanted
it to be.
[*Go to a direct approach or trance termination.*]

BREAKING FREE

A metaphor script for mid-life crises.

And now,
just for a moment or two,
consider the lilies of the field,
or the flocks of birds flying by,
or the leaves falling from trees,
each dancing with the wind
across fields and front yards,
perfect in their beauty,
effortless in their grace,
not stopping to think
how to do what they do
because like you
they grow without knowing how,
they change without knowing when,
they do not think about what to do,
they just know how to follow
that urge and knowing within,
not following someone else's rules
or doing what is expected,
not thinking about how
to impress others,
or planning where to go,
they just flow
from one thing to another,
going where they are supposed to go,
where nature tells them to,
where their wisdom takes them,
in a glorious orchestration
of an opportunity
to be free,
free to just be
exactly what they are
unless they are trapped,
confined by their decisions,
caught in a web
of their own making,
where they go through their paces
and feel angry or scared,
cheated of a life
that should have been,
until they decide to break out,

to run and fly free again,
to start over again,
but often become confused
and even afraid
when they discover that the door,
the door to their cage,
is unlocked and open
and they are free to go,
but at first cannot go out,
and will not ever go
too far away,
because once captured and tamed,
they are changed,
have developed new patterns,
new expectations and anticipations,
new connections and new learnings
that make them different
from what might have been,
and so they begin to discover
how to make the best of where they
    are,
how to stay in the cage at times
and play around the cage at others,
how to enjoy the best of both worlds,
take advantage of the old and the new,
put the two together
to create something better
than either could be alone,
free to be and to enjoy,
to explore beyond the boundaries,
yet captivated by the pleasures
that old treasures provide,
the best of both worlds,
the best of themselves,
a wonderful opportunity
to finally grow up
to be more
than you have imagined
you can be.
[*Go to a direct approach or trance
termination.*]

MIGRATIONS

A metaphor script for uncertainties about career or life goals.

And so,
as you relax more and more,
your mind wanders at times,
the way gypsies wander,
from place to place,
never going anywhere special,
just drifting from here to there,
which sounds romantic and relaxing
unless there is someplace,
you really want to be,
something you really need,
because it is hard to be stuck
where you do not belong,
doing something that is just not you,
but it is even harder
to not know where to go
to get where you're going,
when you do not have a map,
but instead just turn here or there
or go wherever the road takes you
without planning ahead,
without knowing how to know
what is the right direction for you,
what you really want to do.
Consider the animals of the world,
how they migrate from place to place,
and you can wonder
how would it feel to wake up one day
and suddenly feel a feeling
that tells you as sure as sure
that it is time to do something different,
time to fly south or to swim north,
time to cross the tundra
or time to cross the ocean,
the feeling that whales feel,
that elk feel and birds feel,
that King salmon and monarch butter-
     flies feel,
a feeling inside
that directs Canada geese

in the right direction.
So how does it feel
to know something
without knowing why,
to know something
with every cell in the body,
something very quiet,
something unspoken,
the way a small child knows,
with absolute certainty,
when it wants a drink of water
and will cry until it gets it
but is still not old enough to know
what the word thirsty means,
like how you feel
when you want something to eat,
a craving, perhaps, a desire, a wanting,
somewhere deep inside,
the kind of feeling we feel
when we picture
the kind of meal we crave.
Watching people in a restaurant
looking over the menu,
trying out different foods
in their minds,
imagining the tastes and textures
until they find the one
that tastes perfect to them,
they just know that is it,
like trying on clothes to see if they fit,
or imagining possible futures
to discover one that is right,
imagining how you want to feel
and discovering the place and time
that just goes with that feeling,
that feels or tastes or looks or sounds
exactly right for you,
a place where you feel
just like you want to feel,
doing what lets you feel

the way you want to feel.
That's right,
imagining that future feeling
where everything is just fine,
and you've finally gotten what is needed,
finally moved where you belong,
know where you fit,
know where you are going,
and can enjoy going there
as sure as any animal
that somehow seems to know
which way to go to get there,
back where it belongs,
knows what direction to go,
you just go there,
right to where you need to be
to be comfortable and happy
and where you belonged
all along.
[*Go to a direct approach or trance termination.*]

MAGNETIC ATTRACTIONS

A metaphor script for spiritual longings.

At some point in their lives
most people have played
with magnets,
felt them pull toward
and push away from each other,
felt that invisible force,
invisible connections
between separate things,
that can only be seen
with iron filings on paper
that dance between them
and line up along curves
that connect one to the other,
to show us what we feel
but cannot touch or see,
like the unseen connections
between everything everywhere,
that are felt but not seen,
and really are there,
holding everything together
making everything work,
from atoms and quarks,
on up to the stars,
those invisible forces
that give things their form,
the sources of energy
that power the sun,
feed plants as they grow,
and light up the sky,
flows through our bodies
and powers our minds,
minds that reach out
as far as the stars,
minds that can wonder
at the wonder of it all,
and wonder at the power
that flows through it all,
that connects each to all
and attracts our attention,
makes us aware

that somewhere inside,
when that door opens up,
and the air flows through
you can feel something different,
a warm clear light
that shines from within,
filling the room
and the space beyond,
touching and becoming
one with it all,
feeling that force,
that source of attraction
that pulls all into one
and one into all,
letting yourself go,
going with that flow
and letting yourself know
that it really is OK
to go on that journey,
to visit those places,
to find what you need
deep down inside
that connects you to something,
something beautiful and true,
that lets you be there
where you want to be,
free to feel it,
free to hold it,
free to know
it all belongs to you.
[*Go to a direct approach or trance
termination.*]

16

IMPULSE CONTROL AND HABIT OR ADDICTION PROBLEMS

When people repeatedly misbehave in ways that give them pleasure or alleviate discomforts but also cause them problems, there is a tendency to label it an "addiction" or a "disease" and treat it as such. Although this model is effective at times, as indicated by the reported success of Gamblers Anonymous, our experience with such risk-taking, high pleasure behaviors is that they often are quite amenable to hypnotherapeutic interventions, even when they involve actual physiologic addictions.

Like Peele (1989), we have found that these behaviors frequently are indications of a lack of coping skills, a sense of entrapment in a life that feels empty or meaningless, and an overwhelming sense of distress. When deprived of an important ingredient to a healthy, happy life, like water or food, people experience distress and a deep craving for whatever it is that is missing. Unfortunately, cravings for a better life or a better sense of self are difficult to decipher and resolve. Instead, the underlying experience is something like, "I feel like I want or need something. I wonder what it is? It must be sex, food, some new clothes, a cigarette, excitement, something I can get right now to make this uncomfortable feeling go away."

The "rush" associated with shoplifting, gambling, or illicit sexual activity, the thrill of spending large sums of money on consumer goods, and the taste of various foods are all inherently pleasurable. Attention is highly concentrated, emotion is intensified, and the act itself culminates in a powerful sensation of release, relief, and satisfaction. It feels like that vague underlying need is finally being met. When an individual's life is dominated by uncomfortable feelings of insecurity, inadequacy, or dissatisfaction, one or more of these activities may serve as a temporary but effective respite from the resulting cravings. That activity then becomes the individual's primary source of pleasure and relief. Treatment, therefore, may involve the development of an awareness of what is actually wanted or needed but, more importantly, it involves activation of the motivation and determination required to stop using the problem behavior to alleviate those fundamental needs. The discovery of alternative sources of pleasure and relief is also a desirable goal.

Unfortunately, the people who consult a hypnotherapist for help with such problem behaviors usually do so because they believe that they lack the ability or willpower to deal with such issues by themselves. This is especially true when the problem is a long-standing habit problem such as smoking or overeating. Hypnosis often is a last resort in a long chain of efforts to alter such behaviors. Furthermore, many of these clients do not actually want to change their behavior. The behavior involved may provide much pleasure, a sense of security, relief from the nagging desire for something more, and various secondary gains. These people may be seeking help only because they believe they "should" or they have been told to do so by a physician, friend, family member, or judge. Thus, clients with impulse control or habit problems seek out hypnosis because either they or someone they know believes that hypnosis can or will somehow magically impose the desired behavior changes upon them.

The natural consequence of this belief is that most clients with habit or impulse control problems fully expect the hypnotist to use direct suggestions such as "Chocolate will no longer taste good to you," "Cigarettes will make you sick," or "You will no longer feel an urge to steal things." They are on the alert waiting for such directives and until they hear them they will not relax or feel like they have gotten what they expected or needed. After passive clients hear a direct suggestion they tend to relax, comforted by the belief that they now have received a powerful hypnotic suggestion that will take care of the problem for them. Resistant clients, on the other hand, tend to relax once they hear a direct suggestion because they are comforted by the feeling that there is no way that suggestion is going to work.

Whether the client believes such direct suggestions will work or not, as we noted in Chapter 5, they usually are completely ineffective. Hypnosis does not create obedient automatons, and direct suggestions do not produce automatic or uncontrollable compliance. Nonetheless, we typically insert a direct suggestion for specific behavior change just to satisfy client expectations.

Although clients usually enter the office believing hypnosis will be used to force them to change their behavior, the comments and metaphors we use with habit and impulse control problems are designed to shift the entire burden of responsibility for change back onto the client. To avoid giving in to what is experienced as an "irresistible impulse," the client must be motivated to change and have a specific understanding of the responses required to overcome that impulse. Erickson (1966) accomplished this in a very direct manner with a smoker by having the gentleman describe in great detail what he wished to have happen with regard to cigarettes as he entered into a trance. A script for this simple yet effective approach ("A Generic Direct Approach #1") is presented in Chapter 5 because it can be used with virtually any presenting problem, including those mentioned in this chapter.

The scripts presented in the current chapter shift the burden of responsibility for change onto the client by redirecting attention toward previous experiences, learnings, and abilities that can be used to implement the desired behavior change. They also encourage the unconscious to confront the client with an awareness of the needs underlying the behavior, the negative consequences of the undesirable behavior, and/or the positive consequences of change. Several scripts also indirectly encourage the unconscious to create experiences, such as alterations in sensation or perception, that will make it easier to alter the undesirable behavior. Meanwhile, direct suggestions for specific changes in perception or action are embedded within the metaphors. The goal is to appease the conscious expectation for direct suggestions while also generating experiences and understandings that will motivate the individual to make the changes needed and will provide alternative responses to any urges to engage in the undesirable behavior. This covers all the bases and frequently makes it possible to deal with these problems in one sitting.

Each of the scripts presented in this chapter is a response to the symptom patterns, interests, and motivations presented by a specific individual. As such, they contain metaphorical anecdotes designed to help that specific individual. These interventions are intended to foster a new perspective on the behavior, provide alternative sources of pleasure and satisfaction, and encourage changes in life circumstances. They may or may not be appropriate for other individuals engaging in similar self-destructive activities, but the principles and purposes they demonstrate are universally applicable.

A SMOKING ABSTINENCE SCRIPT

Now many people come to me
and ask for help in solving
some particular difficulty,
and they say to me
"I have no motivation,
I have no discipline!"
And I say to them,
"The unmotivated person
doesn't call for an appointment.
The undisciplined person
doesn't show up on time."
The unmotivated person
does not distinguish the place
they wish to be,
from the place where they are now.
The undisciplined person
stays home.
Now you have all the motivation
you need,
you have all the discipline
you need,
though there is one thing
you still need
which you don't have . . . yet,
and that's self-confidence,
the self-confidence it takes
to set out on a journey
completely prepared for the trip,
knowing you've read the map,
you've charted the course
reservations taken care of,
believing you can, will,
reach your destination
quickly, easily, effortlessly.
The self-confidence it takes
to recognize all the signs of success—
just as now, you recognize
those comfortable hypnotic sensations
in the hands, arms, legs . . .
those physical signs
that allow you to know
you've traveled from one state

to another state
in a calm, confident way.
And you can offer your self
large portions of self-confidence,
large portions of self-esteem,
you can breathe in self-confidence
and breathe out self-doubt
as you continue to enjoy
the journey toward your goal.
Throughout the years
that I have worked with people
I have had many clients come here
with a particularly interesting problem.
They have become obsessed
with the idea of making love
with someone they are attracted to,
and when they've raised the subject
with the object of their desire
they've been told,
in no uncertain terms,
that a physical relationship
was an impossibility.
And the reasons given
for the impossibility have been many:
It is too dangerous or risky,
unhealthy or even unethical.
And yet, faced with all these obstacles,
these clients became more and more
        obsessed,
convinced that their happiness de-
        pended
on the consummation of their desires,
to the neglect of all other aspects
of their lives.
Which reminds me of the man
who had just bought a brand new
        house,
an expensive house,
in the nicest part of town.
He had admired that house
for many, many years,
maybe since he was a teenager,

maybe from his twenties.
He couldn't remember exactly,
but he did know
he'd been wanting to buy that house
for a long, long time.
And now here it was—all his.
He lavished care and attention on it,
decorated it in tasteful colors
of _____ (*insert colors of client's*
        clothing)
He papered and painted
and hardly paid any attention at all
to that growing headache at first.
In fact, it was several years
before he noticed
that his head seemed to have
a continuous dull ache,
and his muscles were aching as well.
He felt tired a lot, too,
so he visited a doctor
who gave him a prescription,
but he just never felt much better
and everything failed to stop that
        headache,
or the irritation
and the insidious feeling
that his health was fading away.
But at least he had his house!
And it is easy to understand
how he might feel
if you've ever gone from house to house
real estate open houses perhaps,
or just going to someone else's home,
seeing how the other half lives
can be an educational experience.
But I can understand my client's obses-
        sion
with something that's not about to
        happen,
from the day I saw my dream house.
Of course the price was very beyond
what I could possibly afford,
and yet I couldn't get it
out of my mind.

I imagined myself in the living room,
in the kitchen and in the den
and was certain I must have it
to be happy.
Now everybody knows that no body
likes to be told what to do,
and if I could tell you what to do
you wouldn't have to be here today.
You'd call me on the phone,
you'd say "I'd like to quit smoking."
and I would say
"That's a wonderful idea,
quit smoking . . . now."
But everybody knows nobody likes
to be told what to do,
so I wouldn't say to you,
you already know all the reasons
for ending this smoking problem.
I wouldn't have to say to you that
smoking is dangerous and unhealthy.
I wouldn't have to tell you that you will
receive no pleasure from smoking.
I never need to say that
cigarettes are a poor substitute
for _____ (*insert client's rationale*
for smoking, i.e., controlling anxiety,
eating management, boredom, etc.).
But one thing I *will* say to you is,
"*Not smoking* is not a task
you won't find easy."
And when you leave here today
you'll no longer be
somebody who smokes.
You know you have the desire to
        smoke,
and you know you know it
and no one can talk you out of it.
But what you now know,
that you didn't know before,
is you also have a large amount
of *no desire*,
and you can get to know this place
of no desire
as it expands and grows

larger and larger.
And the feelings of no desire
can reach deeper and deeper,
the time of no desire continues to
    lengthen,
and no way is easier than this.
And I read once:
"When I was a child,
I thought like a child,
I acted like a child.
Now that I am grown
I put away the things of childhood."
What does that really mean?
I'm not sure,
but it certainly meant a lot
to my clients who were obsessed with
a sexual desire that could never be
    fulfilled.
Perhaps it was the thought of putting
old ways behind them
that finally allowed them to be free,
or perhaps they simply grew up
and took responsibility for their feelings
and their behavior.
Disappointment is something we all face
from time to time,
and you can imagine how disappointed
that man was to learn there was
    insecticide
in the floor and walls of that house.
He went on his dream vacation,
and was amazed to discover his head-
    aches
and sickness disappeared in just
a few days time.
When he got home
he contacted an expert in the field.
The expert gently broke the news,
his entire house was slowly being
    poisoned . . .
and so was he.
It took him only one day to pack his
    things,
he knew for certain

his health was worth more
than any house—
no matter how long
he'd wanted it.
And I guess I finally came to terms
with the fact that I couldn't buy
a $300,000 home,
no matter what I did.
It was a nice dream,
but the price is too high to pay,
especially since there was no
Jacuzzi!
And it is good
to finally resolve those feelings
and to just let go,
not needing to know
how the unconscious mind knows
what to do . . . for you,
thinking with an awareness
of things thought,
without needing to know
those things that will get done—
automatically,
you know what to do.
Now, I'd prefer
you stop smoking immediately,
but it's entirely up to you
to discover, today,
the best time and way for you.
Some clients wait an hour,
some wait until after dinner,
and some stop entirely right before bed.
Now, I'd prefer you stop immediately,
but it's completely up to you
to choose the time, a time today,
when you free yourself
from smoking, forever.
[Go to the trance termination procedure.]

A WEIGHT MANAGEMENT SCRIPT

Now you've been waiting
many years to say
the last word on this subject.
And your last word
is still there . . . in reserve,
spending a lifetime arming yourself
with final words,
like the forest animals who
store up nuts and berries
for a long winter, or collect
every form of twig, leaf, paper, string
to structure an elaborate nest
as shelter from the winter's cold
or a lurking predator,
real or imagined.
Perhaps a memory of the words
a mother sings to her sleeping child,
rocking, rocking, words
of a soothing lullaby,
full of safety, warmth.
And you can drift away on words,
recalling the word you really want to
         say
as soon as you get the chance.
And chances are, as you drift
you'll recognize some part of you
that's only just begun
to find a voice,
a voice of confidence and belief
in yourself and your ability
to solve this problem,
once and for all
to exercise your privilege,
your right to have
the body you desire,
and you can offer yourself
large portions of self-confidence,
large portions of self-absorption,
large helpings of self-esteem.
Voicing the part of you
that knows the words
to your body song,

and anyone who gets to know Vivian
knows she spent ten years
of her childhood
taking voice lessons
two or three times a week.
And it was difficult at times
to give up playing with the other kids,
after school to walk
the mile or two a day
to the huge white house
where her singing teacher lived,
until she discovered she could
make a game of it,
wondering as she walked
how persons in so many houses
lived their lives from day to day.
And soon she felt as if
she was not giving up a thing,
not playing with the other kids,
the game she played was so
stimulating and rewarding.
And so when she finally
reached her singing teacher's home
she was completely ready
to begin . . . and to work
on exercising her voice
and learning to manage and use it
exactly as the musical instrument
it was.
Not many people even realize
the multiple and various ways
there are to train a voice,
but she certainly discovered them,
exercising vocal cords
three times . . . five times a week,
carefully monitoring herself
to nurture herself,
to take care of herself in every way,
and gaining in confidence,
gaining in skill,
gaining in self-knowledge.
As she put every bit of energy

into shaping her voice
into its richest, sweetest tones.
and she sang, publicly
and privately for many years,
and never felt a bit of stage fright,
even when the audience
really couldn't appreciate
the operatic quality of her voice,
and would have preferred
a thinner, less resonant voice.
Of course, for her, it never seemed
a problem
that her voice
was so much bigger than others,
although she knew it sometimes was,
for her high school chorus teacher,
who kept giving Vivian a signal
to tone it down.
She really believed everyone should look
and sound the same,
so Vivian would struggle to fit in,
and sing along, not drawing attention
to herself.
And it wasn't until she went to college
and sang in choruses where everyone
was talented that she knew
it was okay to be more gifted
than the people singing with her.
And she learned that it doesn't matter
if you fit in—in fact,
it's much more fun to stand out,
be different, have a particular style
that's all your own.
Now about this business
of losing weight,
you can wait to begin,
but haven't you waited long enough.
When you reach that fork in the road
you know you're going to make a
        choice
to leave something before you
behind and continue on the journey,
remembering, something you've
        forgotten

that you know.
Now eating is for pleasure,
and you've forgotten how
to experience the pleasure
of feeling hungry,
the pleasure of feeling full,
the pleasure of feeling satisfied,
the pleasure of saying "No, thank you."
No, you eat a lot
but you don't get much pleasure.
You can eat less and get more . . .
pleasure.
You can want less and have more . . .
pleasure.
You can heighten your metabolism,
feel the warmth caressing your skin,
spreading through your arms, your legs,
as you feel the pleasure of
less is more,
as you experience the increased energy
warming you all over,
feeling the pleasure of having
the body you desire,
and you don't have to wait any longer
to exercise your ability, your right,
to gain the body you desire.
Remembering that time
in your life when you knew
how beautiful you are,
recognizing that corpus of knowledge
you have, and
speaking your mind
once and for all,
the reserve of last words
finally voiced,
hearing your voice
as it fills the emptiness with sound.
[Go to the trance termination procedure.]

A GENERIC HABIT PROBLEM SCRIPT

Application: For use with any of a variety of habit problems including nail biting, finger sucking, smoking, overeating, and so on.

So you've come to see me,
about fixing the problem,
getting rid of this habit
and I would like to tell you
that I am quite impressed
by your willingness to do so,
because it isn't easy
to admit you need help.
It isn't easy
to admit that you have failed
to correct the problem, yet.
But it is clear to me
that you have the ability to do so,
because the people who cannot
do not go to the trouble or expense
of making an appointment,
they just keep telling themselves
that it is silly to seek help
to do something they could do over-
      night
if they really put their mind to it,
which of course they never remember
      to do.
But you have come here today
because you really want to get help,
because you really want
to get rid of that habit,
and you've come none too soon,
and it's certainly not too late,
and I know you can change,
I know you can stop that behavior,
because I've seen what people can do.
Why there is even a program
that helps schizophrenics, psychotics,
and people who are brain damaged too,
to learn how to manage their behavior,
which is very difficult for them.
A simple program designed by a Dr. Zec,
it consists of nothing more

than writing down what they want to
      change,
then writing down the steps involved,
the specific things they need to do
to accomplish their goal.
And then they write down why,
they write down why they should,
the benefits of that change,
as many as they can think of.
They write them down
and then each day
they look at that thing they want to do,
they look at the specific steps involved
and they look at why they want to do it,
to remind themselves.
And all this writing down
is necessary for them, absolutely
      necessary,
because they can't remember
from one day to the next
what it is they meant to do
or why they wanted to do it,
or what they needed to do
to accomplish that goal,
they can't remember it,
because they are handicapped in some
      way,
which makes it a pleasure
to work with you,
because I know that you
will remember what you want to do,
and *why* to do it, and *how* to do it,
so I don't have to make you
write it all down in detail
or look at it every day,
except in your mind, your unconscious
      mind perhaps.
I can just ask you to think it through,
to define what you want to do, exactly,

to look at how to do it exactly,
what you need to do each moment of
      every day
and I know that you
will remember it thoroughly later on.
And I also know
that if Dr. Erickson were here today,
he would tell me
that I really don't need to tell you
that you won't do that anymore,
that you'll find it easier to not do it,
because now you know
what you're not going to do
and you know how to not do it
all by yourself, reminding yourself,
but he might say to you
in a way that would reach into your
      unconscious
and create an irresistible response
that no matter how hard you try
you'll never be able
to ———(insert undesirable habit) again,
in exactly the same way, or at all,
without noticing how unpleasant
it seems to make you feel,
which you had probably overlooked
      before,
or forgot all about,
but not as much forgetting
as the people I mentioned before,
who have a disability in that arena,
which is why they write it down
which reminds me of a man I saw on TV,
who forgot to live his life.
He went to work every day,
he stayed home every night,
he saved money for his retirement,
when he would finally do what he wanted.
But when he retired
he found out he had cancer,
only a few months left to live,
and he cried as he talked
and said he'd wasted his entire life
putting off what he wanted to do,

ruined it by forgetting
to pay attention to what he did each day,
and to give himself strict orders
to take care of himself now,
to be good to himself now,
which is not the same
as being forced to eat your spinach
or told never to give yourself a treat,
but some people have to write it down
before they get the point
that now is the time to do
what you can do or can not do
that you have decided to do for you.
So you can leave here today
with the full recognition
that you can remember what to do,
and that not remembering
is not something you'll find easy,
because now it belongs to you,
even after you leave here
it will be there with you,
the memory of an ability
to find a different way
to do those things for you
that *it* used to do
but can't do now, anymore,
because now if you do it
you'll be doing it on purpose,
and that's not the same, is it?
So I would rather you stop now,
and remember to keep on stopping,
but you may prefer to stop
tonight at bedtime,
or an hour from now,
just so you can remind yourself
what it is you can remember
that those other poor people
had to write down
before they did it,
successfully,
so of course
so can you,
will you not?
[*Go to a trance termination process.*]

CARRY ON

A metaphor script for compulsive gambling.

I don't know if you know,
I see many clients
who are in chronic pain
from different types of injuries,
but cannot get any help
from standard medications
or physical therapy,
and so as a last resort
their physicians refer them to me
to see if hypnosis can help them,
and so I use hypnosis with them,
not to eliminate their pain,
but only to point out to them
that it would be a good idea,
in their own best interests,
a smart thing to do,
to stop making matters worse
by doing whatever they want to do
no matter how much it hurts,
no matter how much movement
they lose as a result,
no matter how much pain
or loss of time
they experience when they do,
they keep doing it,
because they won't quit,
won't give in,
they get on their hands and knees
to wax the floor,
they lift heavy furniture
to rearrange the room,
they do not want to give up,
to be seen as a sore loser,
to feel like a chicken
or a wimp,
so they just keep doing it,
over and over again,
hurting no one but themselves,
and so they fool themselves
but really they are a big pain

for everyone they know
who do not understand the thrill
of such silly victories,
the payoff for stupidity,
when all they really have to do,
is stop trying to prove
how tough or smart they are,
no matter how lucky they feel.
And so I simply tell them
in no uncertain terms,
that if they want to get over it,
to feel better,
to behave better,
all they have to do
is admit what they already know,
face the facts of their own experience,
accept that they are no better
than anyone else
and have no better chance
of winning a race
if they lose every possibility
of healing
by dealing themselves
blow after blow
in an effort to demonstrate
how special they are,
instead of accepting
how lucky they are
to simply be alive,
because by risking everything
they amplify the pain,
the losses,
and make it harder
to do anything,
and anyone can see
how that makes them look,
and that the really special thing,
the hardest thing to do,
is to just take it easy,
to pay attention to what you know,

be smart and wise
and find other ways
to enjoy yourself
or prove yourself,
because it is so obvious to others,
and to you too I suspect,
that continuing to do things
that end up hurting you,
that can break your back,
or rip a cord,
and paralyze forever
on the false belief
that it doesn't hurt,
that it might pay off,
is the kind of thinking
reserved for the kind of people
you really do not want to be
and really do not respect,
so take your time
to think it through
what you would,
if you knew
you can quit now,
take charge of you
and be fine.
And each and every one
of those clients
eventually learned
to stay away from
what hurt them,
and accept the realities
of everyday life,
difficult though it is
to give up those fantasies,
to become ordinary,
to break free of those ideas,
but they did it,
felt something change inside,
and that was that,
and this is too,
for you,
when you think about it,
is it not?
[*Go to a trance termination.*]

OUTLAWS

A metaphor script for kleptomania.

Now,
while you continue to wonder
when I am going to tell you
in no uncertain terms,
what you need to hear
to stop taking things that way,
and to relax,
I will take the chance
to mention to you
that I know a man,
let's call him Billy,
he is just a kid really,
who got caught not long ago
tearing pages out of books
in a university library,
not pages he wanted to use
for studying or writing a paper,
not pages about anything
he wanted to know more about,
just pages of whatever book
he pulled off the shelf
when he thought no one was looking.
And when I asked him
what he thought he was doing,
he said he was just being bad,
not because he was mad,
but it gave him great pleasure
to destroy books and things
when he thought no one was looking,
just to get away with it,
to show them what he could do,
to show them he could do
whatever he wanted to,
and not get caught
in spite of the risk,
the risk of getting caught
doing something that made him bad,
like an outlaw,
a bad guy bandit,
a person who could break the rules

and not get caught,
made him feel important,
better about himself,
less messed up in some way,
a big shot
like Jesse James,
or Billy the Kid,
or all those other outlaws
he had read about,
even Robin Hood.
That is what excited him,
turned him on,
made him feel smarter
than all those eggheads,
smarter than those librarians,
just like a gangster,
or a bank robber,
or little bored kids throwing rocks
through school windows,
who took the risk,
and got the rush,
the physical excitement,
the challenge
of destroying something,
getting away with something,
like playing a game of chicken,
and not getting caught.
But it only worked
as long as he was scared,
scared of getting caught,
scared of being found out,
excited by the possibility,
so he could feel better
when he got away with it,
thrilled by the relief
of not getting caught.
So I told him
that he had come to me for help
and I was willing to help him,
if he would agree to one thing,

without knowing what it would be,
just something he had to agree to,
just like you,
if he really wanted to put an end
to his book tearing days,
and never have to worry again
about getting caught,
and he said OK,
so I told him that he all he had to do
was read two books every week
for the next two months,
books I would pick out for him
and he would buy,
but after he read each page,
he had to tear it out
and throw it away immediately,
no hesitations or cheating allowed
and he agreed that he would
and he did,
he read books about psychology,
philosophy, and religion,
self-help books and autobiographies,
and by the time he returned
two months later
he was mad as he could be,
because he had called
the month before and begged
to stop tearing out those pages
of books he bought
and wanted to keep
but I told him he had promised,
and so he kept his promise
but now he had to go back
and buy the books again
that he wanted to read again
because they seemed important
and useful
and he was mad,
but his days of being scared
about getting caught
were completely over,
because why be scared
if you are not going to do it
and you are not going to do it

if you are not scared
of getting caught,
and are mad instead
about having to do it
because no one who does not do it
is ever scared of being caught,
and now you won't do it either
because what you already know
is that whenever you do,
or even think about doing it,
you will remember
you have to buy something
you really do want,
and take it outside
and throw it away,
not even give it away,
not something
you can be proud of,
it is just something
to want to not have to do,
because there are much better,
much happier ways of being,
and the way of being
that best works for you
is learning that you already know
what you need to do
to take better care of you,
to make your life better,
to feel better,
and you do now,
do you not?
[*Go to a trance termination.*]

17

TRANCE TERMINATION
PROCEDURES

It is quite possible to end a hypnotherapy session by saying simply, "Okay, it is time to quit now, so go ahead and wake up completely and open your eyes." Such an approach acknowledges that the subject is in control of the experience and can reorient or wake up at any time. The primary drawback of such an abrupt ending is that it provides no time for review or rehearsal of new learnings, ratification of the trance experience, or distraction of the conscious mind. It also may leave the client feeling a bit disoriented or dazed.

The comments presented in the following are designed to lead the subject gradually back to wakeful alertness, provide an opportunity for reviewing and integrating new learnings, and create an experience that validates the trance as an atypical state of mind. Instructions also are given for procedures designed to distract conscious attention and "seal off" the trance as a separate phenomenon before follow-up questions are asked. It is best to follow each of these steps in the trance termination process when ending a hypnotherapy session, even if that session involved only a light trance.

STEP I: REVIEWING TRANCE LEARNINGS

And so,
before you allow yourself
to drift up completely
into conscious, wakeful alertness,
it may be useful for you
to utilize the opportunity now,
to think about what you've experienced,
the thoughts, images, understandings,
and how you might use these things later on
from one day to the next.
Because you have an unconscious mind
and you have a conscious mind,
and those two minds can learn,
from your experiences here today,
some things that you can utilize
to deal more effectively with those things
that have been problems for you before.
And so before you continue to drift up
into conscious awareness,
normal wakeful awareness,
it is your privilege
to use this comfortable self-awareness
to become more aware of those things
you can use later on,
those learnings,
abilities, and skills
you may have overlooked before,
to give you a new view
of the possibilities for a new way
of thinking and feeling and doing things.
That's right, take some time now,
a brief time that seems to be a long time,
to review and plan,
at some level of awareness,
those things you will do later on,
those things you may change later on,
as you begin to use more and more of *you.*
[*Pause for several seconds, then continue with
the ratification suggestions.*]

STEP II: RATIFICATION SUGGESTIONS

You can use that time now,
because in a few moments from now,
when you drift up and awaken,
it may be interesting for you to know
that in that drifting, relaxed state of mind,
where thoughts drift by like dreams,
that enter awareness for a time
and drift through the mind,
while some are left behind,
to be utilized later on,
and others are remembered,
or seem to be remembered at first
but then become more and more distant,
forgotten over time,
and the entire experience
can seem so far away,
as your unconscious mind
protects the conscious mind
and leaves those things, behind,
forgotten but remembered too.
And time changes too,
so you can know
what a trance it's been
when you begin to know
that what seemed to take a short time,
turns out to have been a long time,
or what seemed a long time,
was really no time at all.

STEP III: REORIENTATION TO WAKEFUL AWARENESS

So for now,
as the unconscious mind
allows the conscious mind
to become more aware of sounds,
sounds in the room, the sound of my voice,
[*Voice volume and tempo*
of speech should be increased
a bit at this point.]
the sensations in an arm, a leg,
the variety of thoughts and feelings
as the conscious mind drifts up
and conscious wakeful awareness
returns quite completely *now*.
Up to the surface of wakeful awareness,
restfully refreshed, comfortably awake,
even as the mind drifts up completely
and the eyes . . .
are allowed to open *now* . . .
That's right, eyes open,
and wakeful awareness returns
quite completely *now* . . .
[*Pause briefly to allow the client to finish opening*
his or her eyes. Many people begin moving and
stretching at this point, whereas others simply open
their eyes and remain motionless. In either case,
move on to the distracting comments shortly after
they have opened their eyes. All post-trance
comments, including distractions, should be offered
in a normal conversational tone of voice.]

STEP IV: DISTRACTIONS

There are innumerable possible distracting comments. What follows is a brief description of several types. Use your own creativity to generate a new one for each session.

A. *Back to the beginning*—This type of distracting comment continues a previous conversation or refers back to an incident that occurred prior to the trance induction process. As the client focuses upon the threads of this pretrance memory, he or she tends to lose track of the memories about the intervening trance process.

Examples:

— "Now you say that ———"[*insert any topic the client mentioned prior to the induction*].
— "But I do think it might be important for you to examine your feelings about ——— [*again, insert a previously discussed topic*]."
— "It also occurs to me that ———" [*insert a follow-up observation regarding a previous topic*].

B. *Non sequiturs*—These comments are so irrelevant to the current situation that they take the client by surprise. The resulting confusion prevents undo cognitive processing of the preceding trance experience.

Examples:

— "I really like your [*shoes, shirt, tie, dress, or any article of clothing the client is wearing*]! Where did you buy it?"
— "What do you think about that [*lamp, rug, chair or any object in the office*]? I've been thinking about replacing it."
— "Do you know what the weather forecast is for tomorrow?"

C. *Future plans*—These comments encourage the client to review his or her plans for the future and thus discourage reviews of the immediate past. Again, a partial amnesia for the trance is the usual result.

Examples:

— "So, what are you planning to do this weekend?"
— "Good, let's discuss a time for our next appointment. How would it be if we met on _____ [*specify a time and day*]?"

D. *Ratifications*—Some comments or questions not only serve to distract the client from reviewing trance events, but also tend to ratify the trance at the same time.

Examples:

— "Hello! Welcome back. How was your trip?"
— "Do you really think you are completely awake yet or should I give you a few more seconds to pull yourself back together more completely?"
— "Are your hands and legs still feeling a bit strange?"
— "Now, how long to you think you were in that trance? How long has it been since we started?"

STEP V: FOLLOW-UP QUESTIONS

Once the client has been distracted from an immediate analysis of the trance, it is safe to probe for feedback regarding the experience. Insights and decisions that should remain in the protective realm of the unconscious for the time being will have receded. The remaining conscious memories can be used to determine which internal events captured the attention of the conscious mind most dramatically and which external events seemed to disrupt the process. This information, in turn, can be used to improve the effectiveness of future hypnotherapy sessions.

Examples:

— "Is there anything in particular that you would like to mention about that experience?"
— "What do you remember most clearly about that experience?"
— "I would like to find out a bit about what happened to you, such as what was most interesting or pleasant to you and what, if anything, seemed to disrupt the process."

Some clients find it difficult to put their experiences into words at first and others seem reluctant to discuss the process at all. These post-trance responses should be respected and no effort made to probe for additional information. Similarly, clients who wish to discuss the hypnotherapy experience at length should be allowed to do so.

As mentioned in Chapter 3, assessments of the therapeutic impact of a hypnotherapy session cannot be based upon these post-trance reports. Clients may report that nothing of significance happened to them while at the same time they are saying things that clearly reflect a significant change in attitude or perspective. Furthermore, the effects of a hypnotherapeutic intervention may not become apparent until several days or weeks after the session. The purpose of post-trance questioning is merely to determine what facilitated or inhibited the trance experience for the client, not to determine therapeutic effect. Therapeutic effects will be reflected by subsequent changes in affect, cognition, or behavior, not necessarily by the client's post-trance reports.

After you have completed the steps involved in trance termination, you may conduct the remainder of the session in whatever way you choose. The hypnotherapeutic approach described in these pages is an adjunct to your other psychotherapy techniques, not a replacement for them. Use hypnotherapy when it seems appropriate to do so, but do not be misled into thinking you can rely exclusively upon it. In order to be effective, it must be used within the context of a positive psychotherapeutic relationship.

18

WRITING YOUR OWN HYPNOTHERAPY SCRIPTS

Although the scripts presented in this book offer an opportunity to practice the skills and procedures involved in hypnotherapy, ultimate responsibility for the content of a hypnotherapy session rests with the individual therapist. Ideally every hypnotherapy session is developed in response to the unique needs, interests, personality, and ongoing responses of the client. In other words, effective hypnotherapy depends on an ability to develop on-the-spot ideas for induction procedures, metaphorical anecdotes, and suggestions and to modify the procedures used as the client reacts to what is being said.

As mentioned in Chapter 3, Erickson wrote out and then edited many of his hypnosis sessions early in his career and recommended this strategy to his students. Erickson's genius as a hypnotherapist did not appear overnight. He spent years studying

the multiple meanings of words and revising his approach. Like any skill, his hypnotherapeutic abilities were the product of a great deal of study and practice.

Writing out what you intend to say during a hypnotherapy session will give you
an opportunity to edit and condense your message, and it will sensitize you to the
multiple implications of every word or phrase. Recording and listening to what you
have written, in turn, will amplify your awareness of the effects of each word, voice
inflection, and pause. This personal feedback will enable you to further simplify and
intensify your communications and will enhance your appreciation for the delicately
powerful influence words can have on what people think, feel, imagine, experience,
and learn. Whether or not you ever use hypnosis during a therapy session, the insights and awareness gained by the exercise of writing, listening to, and editing at
least one hypnotherapy script will help you select and deliver your basic therapeutic
messages more effectively.

Using a script you personally have written makes it much easier to conduct a
hypnotherapy session. Instead of being distracted by a self-conscious internal search
for what to say next, a script you are personally familiar with allows you to relax and
carefully observe the subject as you read, watching for signs of relaxation in the
muscles of the face and arms, observing eye movements underneath the eyelids,
noticing changes in pulse rate and blood pressure in the neck, seeing changes in skin
tone, and being alert for any signs of restlessness or negative reactions to what is
being said and experienced. Such observations will tell you immediately what parts of
your script are working and what parts are not. This, in turn, will enable you to
further refine your approach.

Constructing your own hypnotherapy script is relatively easy once you understand
the basic structure and format of a trance induction and learn how to select appropriate metaphors and construct engaging anecdotes. The following instructions are
offered as a supportive guide in your efforts to begin writing your own hypnotic
messages.

WRITING TRANCE INDUCTION SCRIPTS

Contrary to popular opinion, even among many experts in the field of hypnosis,
there are no secret words, phrases, or rituals required to help a person enter a trance
state. Anything that captures attention and, at the same time, turns attention inward
toward a person's own sensations, thoughts, and memories is an effective trance
induction process.

People who demonstrate an ability to become highly immersed in their own imagined images or sensations typically require virtually no induction at all. You can test
this by asking clients to stand with their feet together, close their eyes, and imagine
that they are falling backward. Stand behind them as you give these instructions and

if they almost immediately begin to sway or fall backward, you can be fairly certain that you will not need to use a lengthy induction process with them. Or ask them to hold an arm out in front of them and imagine they are holding a heavy bucket of water. Watch to see if their arm begins moving down or they seem to be putting forth a lot of effort to keep holding it up. Or simply ask them to imagine biting into a slice of lemon and notice any swallowing or puckering in response to the imagined sour taste. The point is to quickly assess their tendency to become so absorbed in an imagined event that they begin to experience it as real. If they do, then you probably do not have to worry too much about inducing, or helping them experience, a trance state.

Most people, however, require some assistance entering into and staying in a trance. Directing them to do it by saying things like, "You are going into a deep trance, deeper and deeper . . ." is not helpful because they do not know how to accomplish this state voluntarily. If they are going to enter such a state of mind you must say things that will help them do so. You must be hypnotic.

The easiest way to decide what to say to help people experience a trance is to keep in mind that you want them to do two things: (a) pay full attention to what you are saying and, at the same time, (b) carefully *observe* (not control, just observe) their own thoughts and sensations. The easiest way to create such responses is to only say things that the person can agree with and to only say things about what that person is currently doing or experiencing.

The first few comments in your induction script, therefore, should be simple statements describing things that the person can notice and accept as true.

Examples:

You are sitting in that chair.
You are breathing in and breathing out.
You are hearing my voice speaking to you.
You are aware of many different things.

Such comments are sometimes referred to as "pacing" statements (cf. Bandler & Grinder, 1975) because they are in step with what the person is experiencing or doing at that moment. They are undeniably true and give the impression that you are now entering into that person's inner world, walking along beside him or her. This captures attention and begins to hold it steady.

Write down as many of these types of statements as you can. You do not have to use them all in each of your induction scripts, but the more of them you develop now and become familiar with the more flexible you can be in the future.

After you have written down as many pacing statements as you can, select four or five and list them one after the other on separate lines. Begin the first statement with the word "Now," and each line thereafter with the word "and."

Example:

Now, you are sitting in that chair,
and you are breathing in and breathing out,
and you are hearing my voice talking to you,
and you are aware of many things.

Beginning with the word "Now" focuses attention on the present and conveys the idea that past considerations are now irrelevant. What is important begins now. Writing three to six or seven words per line establishes a slow and regular rhythm of presentation that can be timed with the subject's breathing. This connection with the client's rhythm helps the person relax and just go along with what is happening. Connecting each phrase or idea with connective words such as "and," "or," and "but" creates an uninterrupted flow of thought from one thing to another that has a similarly relaxing effect.

After pacing the person's ongoing experiences for a while you can start inserting comments that begin to lead very gradually in the direction you want to go; that is, toward a passive observation of internal events that are themselves responses to the ideas or suggestions you provide. This is similar to walking next to someone and gradually changing the pace or direction in which you are headed until you are no longer following them but, instead, they are following you.

This gentle taking control of what the person is experiencing is accomplished by making vague or general speculations about what that person might experience next.

Examples:

And you may be able to notice many different sensations in your arms or hands.
And you can wonder what will enter your awareness next.
One of your legs may begin to feel heavier and more relaxed than the other.
Or one hand may begin feeling warmer or cooler than before.
You may begin to notice your entire body relaxing at times.
There may be a slight tingling sensation here or there.

Such statements are so conditional, ambiguous, and permissively worded that they are essentially truisms. Even if a person's hands feel exactly the same as before, they still "may begin feeling warmer or cooler" eventually. And it is invariably the case that anyone sitting quietly can "notice many different sensations" or a "slight tingling sensation here or there." Thus, the person cannot disagree with what you are saying, is almost literally forced to check internal thoughts or sensations to determine whether or not what you are saying is true, and cannot help but verify that it is true. This approach not only directs attention inward, which is the direction you are heading, but also it creates the impression that your words are directly affecting or controlling that person's experiences.

Make a list of as many of these ambiguous but mildly directive statements as you can and insert a few into the script you are working on, gradually reducing the number of pacing statements you make and increasing the number of these more leading comments. Again, use "and" or some other connective word at the beginning of most statements because this simple verbal stratagem imparts a sense of continuity and coherence to the ongoing experience.

At this point most subjects will be under the impression that something unusual is happening and will begin wondering what is going to happen next. This attitude increases the focus of attention on both your voice and on their internal experiences. It also encourages a passive observation of subsequent events, rather like the expectant open-mindedness of the audience of a good magician. As you continue to offer leading statements and suggestions, the person will continue developing a hypnotic trance.

Eventually, as the client adjusts to being in a trance state and that state becomes more stable, you can begin to offer more direct suggestions to deepen the trance and stimulate specific hypnotic effects if you wish. Even at this point, however, it is good to avoid being too directive. For example, saying something straightforwardly directive such as, "Your right arm is now heavy, too heavy to lift," presents an immediate challenge to the subject. In general, people do not like to be told what to do and are perfectly happy to prove the experts wrong. The typical response to such a statement, therefore, is something like, "No, it is not heavy, and I can too lift it, see?" Consequently, to avoid creating resistance it is preferable to carefully word even direct suggestions for specific hypnotic responses with permissive, yet directive, terms such as "may" and "might."

Examples:

*And that tingling sensation may continue to develop, becoming more and more intense, like a kind of
    numbness.*
You may become aware that the heaviness in your right arm is starting to grow.
Or you might begin to feel like you are floating, a kind of drifting feeling.
And as you breathe out, it would be OK for you to feel yourself drifting deeper and deeper.

Noticing such mild alterations in sensation tends to ratify the idea that a trance is developing and provides reassurance that things are going as expected. On the other hand, because you are primarily interested in using the trance state of mind to facilitate therapeutic change, rather than demonstrate a variety of hypnotic phenomena, you need only promote a vague awareness of such changes. Once the person has become entranced by these internal events, it is time to move on to the use of a therapeutic metaphorical anecdote to stimulate new ways of thinking and behaving.

WRITING METAPHORICAL ANECDOTES

A therapeutic metaphorical anecdote is a story that can be interpreted as a story about the client, a situation the client is experiencing, something the client is doing, or something the client should consider doing, even though it is ostensibly a story or series of comments about something other than the client. Metaphorical anecdotes are a way of saying something to a client in an indirect way that the client probably would reject or ignore if it were said directly. When used effectively, metaphorical anecdotes can precipitate therapeutic change in attitude or behavior with no conscious awareness of the source of that change. The underlying message slips past the conscious mind's filters and censors and becomes transformed into unconscious tendencies and responses.

On the other hand, all metaphorical anecdotes are inherently ambiguous. They seem to be about one thing, but everyone knows that they are really supposed to be about something else (i.e., the client). When faced with this ambiguity, clients try to figure out exactly why the therapist is telling this story and what it is supposed to mean. Some metaphorical anecdotes do turn out to be so perfectly relevant for a specific individual that they almost literally demand an unrestrained compliance with specific therapeutically beneficial understandings or responses, but this seems to be a rare occurrence. In most cases, the inner search for meaning that the anecdote stimulates produces unpredictable and unique therapeutic understandings, ideas, and responses. What any given client gets out of a metaphorical anecdote usually turns out to have nothing at all to do with what you thought you were communicating because people invent or impose meanings that are personally relevant to them.

Actually, this greatly simplifies the task of selecting and constructing metaphors. Instead of worrying too much about finding exactly the right metaphor for each person, your task is simply to construct metaphorical anecdotes that people will listen to and wonder about. You can then rely on their inherent curiosity and self-healing capacities to accomplish the desired goals.

The basic problem, therefore, is how to select and present metaphorical anecdotes that will capture and hold attention and stimulate the desired search for personal relevance without creating resistance. It should be obvious that metaphorical anecdotes are not useful if they are so boring, irrelevant, or confusing that the patient pays no attention to them or if the underlying message is so blatant that it leads to critical questioning or disagreement. People have to pay attention to and accept what you are saying before it can have any effect. Only when they think there is something there worth finding will they find something worthwhile.

Before introducing metaphorical anecdotes, the Neo-Ericksonian approach uses trance induction to capture and redirect attention so that patients subsequently will sit still and calmly pay attention to ideas and issues relevant to their well-being. But that quietly focused attention quickly wanders if the therapist starts talking about things that are meaningless or irrelevant or starts saying things in ways that are uninteresting and boring. An engaging and effectively delivered metaphorical anecdote, as Erickson often demonstrated, can even replace the need for a trance induction. The anecdote itself generates a trance state of focused attention and a comfortable self-awareness while also promoting a search for meaning. On the other hand, an irrelevant or a poorly presented anecdote may quickly replace a trance with a wandering mind or even a disapproving reaction.

Luckily, selecting a topic for a metaphorical anecdote that will capture the interest or imagination of a patient is not particularly difficult. The first step in this process is the identification of nonpsychological and nondiagnostic words or terms directly or indirectly relevant to that person. These can be nouns, adjectives, or phrases that come to mind as you consider the patient's physical characteristics, mannerisms, style, and interests. One client may remind you of Mickey Mouse, the mannerisms of another may bring the image of a caged lion to mind, whereas another's speech pattern may sound to you like a jackhammer. Some people remind you of relatives or friends, or even previous clients. Write all of these down as well.

The terms your clients use to describe their problems and current status also may be worth considering. If a client begins a session by saying that he feels like he has been "run over by a truck," then truck, crushed cans, or highways could be added to the list of possible topics. If another mentions feeling "trapped," then prison, jail, cages, and animal traps are obvious possibilities for a story. Your clients' dreams offer yet another source of potential topics. The idea is to develop a collection of settings and/or topics that are associated with, reminiscent of, or directly related to the particular client for whom you are writing this script. Just write down whatever topics come to mind as you allow yourself to consider that individual's various quirks, comments, complaints, and characteristics, no matter how weird the associations might seem to be at the time.

After you have developed a list of potential topics, read through them again and pick one of them to use as the basis for your anecdote. Two considerations guide this selection. The topic you choose ought to be one that reminds you quite strongly of that person or that person's situation. In addition, however, the topic you choose needs to be one that immediately brings to mind one or more experiences you personally have had, such as an event in your childhood, a program you saw on TV, an article you read about a natural event or animal, a story you know about a friend, or even a story about another client. For example, if the item on your list that reminds you most strongly of your client is a teddy bear, the thought of a teddy bear may also remind you of your own beloved teddy bear from childhood and how hard it was to give it up. You might also be reminded of a program you saw about bears in Yellowstone Park learning from their mothers how to break into campers and cars for food. And you might think about the bear cubs you saw when you took your children to the zoo. Whether it is obvious to you or not at this point, each of those incidents contains the basic ingredients of an effective metaphorical anecdote. Furthermore, because these different experiences are related in some way to each other (they all contain bears), you eventually could weave each of them into your presentation.

We prefer to use real events and true information as the basis for our metaphorical anecdotes rather than inventing fictional events or even fairy tales. In our experience, stories about real events are inherently easier to present, more believable, and easier for people to enter into imaginatively. Consequently, they are more likely to be therapeutically effective.

Next, review the personal experiences that came to you as you thought about that key word or phrase and pick the specific incident or story you want to use as the basis for your metaphorical anecdote. Although it should go without saying, pick an incident or area of information that culminates in a positive outcome or insight into how to respond to the realities of everyday life, such as success in some endeavor, a pleasurable emotion or sensation, learning a new skill, or developing a new appreciation for one's own abilities.

After you have selected the anecdote you want to use, take a few minutes to write down all of the words you can think of that are relevant to that story. For example, let us say that the client reminds you most strongly of a chugging train working hard to go up a hill and this, in turn, reminds you of a train trip you took through the mountains in Alaska. Your list, therefore, might include the following: *engineer, conductor, car, whistle, steam, track, tunnel, train, scenery, eagles, bears, forests, mountain peaks, snow, river,* and *locomotive.*

Now, for each of these associated words or phrases, write down all of the possible alternative uses or meanings of each word as you can. Include homonyms as well. "Train," for example, might be used to refer to a *"train of thought," "training a dog,"* or *"the train of a wedding dress."* "Track" might lead you to *"one-track mind," "keeping track of details,"* or *"staying on track."* "Bear" could be used in the phrases *"bear hug," "hungry as a bear," "bare facts," "barely old enough to walk,"* or *"baring it all."* Let your mind go off in a lot of different directions; be creative as you collect possible puns, rhymes, and loose associations.

You now have the topic for your story and a collection of interrelated, somewhat poetic and captivating words or phrases to use as you tell that story. The central topic of that story, a hard working train in our example, will automatically capture the interest or attention of the client because it is metaphorically or associatively related to that individual in some way. What are still required, however, are a beginning, middle, and end to the story that lead the person toward the idea of therapeutic change of a general or particular nature.

As you begin writing your story, it is appropriate to use terms or phrases that relate in some way to the client's current situation. Continuing with the train trip anecdote, for example, the story could begin in the following manner.

Now, as I think about
what you have told me
about your situation
and about what you
have tried to do about it,
I am reminded of a time
many years ago
when I took a trip
on an old steam-powered train
through the mountains of Alaska.
That train worked very hard at first

to pull us up that first steep slope,
and I wondered if it really had the strength,
the power, to keep going,
because the wheels slipped a bit at first,
and ground on the track
and the engine strained
and seemed to be getting nowhere,
but it stayed on track,
like people need to,
and kept pulling us up,
with lots of noise and huffing and puffing.

The initial content or action of the story captures the feeling of being stuck and unable to get anyplace that the client expressed during his first therapy session. This captures attention. Repeating certain words, such as "about" and "first" in the preceding example, tends to lull the listener into a passively receptive state of mind. We also like to insert puns and plays on words that both amuse and stimulate automatic therapeutic associations. For example, the phrase "it stayed on track, like people need to," can be taken as a playful aside but also as a direct message to the listener.

We find that people become more immersed in a story when terms that stimulate visual, auditory, and kinesthetic involvement are used. The idea is to help people enter into the experience as fully as possible by encouraging them to fill in the details regarding what is being seen, heard, or felt. On the other hand, it is best to avoid specific descriptions that might conflict with the images or perceptions that each person has already conjured up. For example, we might refer to a "noise," but not necessarily try to describe the exact nature of that noise. When you allow or encourage the client to fill in the details, the details become much more compelling.

The middle of this train story, and yours, should describe events that lead from a difficult beginning toward a therapeutically useful ending. In this particular case, the story could progress by describing how the train gradually overcomes the difficult terrain and it could end with a description of the incredible natural beauty that eventually surrounds the passengers as the train slowly but surely winds its way through the tunnels and over the bridges built to make its journey not only possible, but eventually rather easy.

Along the way, you may find a transition point where you can weave in a story about something else entirely before you finish your original anecdote. Embedding one story within another adds interest to the presentation and also is a bit confusing. This confusion further stimulates the search for meaning and increases the likelihood that the individual will discover (i.e., impose or invent) something of great personal significance. Continuing with the train example presented in the preceding, the simple process of transitioning into a new story might be accomplished in the following way.

And the people there
conducted themselves well,
enjoyed the views
as they looked out the windows
that seemed quite clear
until they moved into a tunnel
and in that darkness
those windows became mirrors
that reflected each person
back at themselves,
and gave them an opportunity
to reflect on what they saw
like Carrie did one day,

while looking in a mirror,
wondering who she was
and who she wanted to be,
because what she saw there
reflected back at her
was someone she barely knew
but seemed to like a lot more
than she had imagined before,
just like those people on the train
had never imagined
that such beauty could exist
in each new scene
around each new corner . . .

Now, keeping all of these instructions and suggestions in mind, relax, drift into a light trance yourself if you wish, and begin to write your own metaphorical anecdote using the basic metaphorical topic, story, and various related words and phrases you have developed thus far. At first, this may seem to be a difficult or confusing assignment. But if you allow yourself to think of it as writing song lyrics or poetry and let your mind flow in creative directions, you soon will discover that enchanting phrases and associations effortlessly spring to mind.

RECORDING, LISTENING, AND EDITING

After you have written your anecdote, get out a tape recorder and record yourself reading both the trance induction you created and your anecdote. Then close your eyes, relax, and listen to yourself. Take note of anything that tends to jar you, seems to interrupt the easy flow of thought as you follow along with the words, or just does not sound right. If you find that you read the script too fast, stop and record it again.

You may find that certain words or phrases in your script are too complicated or judgmental or require too much thinking to allow for relaxed listening. In general, we tend to stick to a fairly simple vocabulary and try to avoid ideas that are controversial or debatable. You may also find that at times your mind starts to wander to irrelevancies, like what to have for dinner, because what is being said is not engaging enough. When your mind is stimulated by the script to ponder personal issues or issues that merit attention, that is good. But when you find yourself wandering off into trivia, then you know that that part of the script needs to be edited.

Following this experiential review, go back over your script and edit it. Take out anything that did not sound right to you or that led you astray. Reword anything that seemed awkward, irrelevant, or difficult to follow. Smooth out any abrupt transitions and fill in any gaps in the ongoing flow of events.

Once you are reasonably satisfied, go over the script again and try to shorten it by one-third at least. Words are packed with meaning and implications and, thus, one carefully chosen word often can take the place of five or six. Eventually, you will find that you can give an explanation for the presence of every word in your script.

Record and listen to your "final" product again. This may lead to additional changes or you may be pleased to discover that it seems fine just as it is. Add a short version of the trance termination procedures presented in Chapter 17 and you are done— with this script at least. The next chance you get, write, record, and edit a second script, then a third, and so on until the entire process begins to seem easy and even fun.

Eventually, after some practice and experience, the basic assessment and decision-making processes involved in creating your own hypnotherapy sessions will become so automatic that the scripts and instructions in this book will be superfluous. You will know intuitively how to say things in a way that encourages clients to examine themselves and their situations from a new, less restrained, point of view. At that point you can relax and trust your own unconscious knowledge and understandings to guide you because you will have become a hypnotherapist.

POSTSCRIPT

New clients often ask if we ever get tired of listening to the same problems day after day. Evidently it is difficult for them to believe that therapy can be a constant source of fascination and satisfaction. But within the framework of the approach described here, each new client is a new and completely unique opportunity to re-experience the wondrous complexity, perfect harmony, and vast potentials of every human being on this planet.

When we conduct a Diagnostic Trance our clients give us the privilege of entering into that previously unseen inner world with them. They take us where their pain takes them, and we are allowed to share their amazement as understanding replaces confusion. Some clients prefer to keep that inner world private, a secret even from themselves, perhaps, and with these clients we are taught a reverence for the Self and an acknowledgment that not all knowledge needs to be conscious.

Above all, however, our clients consistently demonstrate to us the self-healing, growth-seeking potentials within us all. Hypnotherapy merely sets the stage and provides an opportunity for change. Like masters of improvisation, clients seize the opportunity and utilize it in their own creative ways to relieve their pain, find pleasure, and foster change. Each client is different, each situation is different, and what each client needs in each situation is different. The marvel is that almost all of them can find and use what they need when given the right opportunity and encouragement to do so.

When you incorporate hypnotherapy into your practice you will enter into a new relationship with your clients. Like an orchestra conductor or a master playright, the hypnotherapist creates an atmosphere that often evokes transcendent thoughts, intense emotions, and powerful insights. Primarily, however, hypnotherapy involves a mutual recognition and celebration of the client's inherent potentials and abilities. By agreeing to rely upon these unconscious capacities for understanding and relief, both you and your client agree to trust that client's resources completely. As a result, the respect and admiration you demonstrate for each client by using these hypnotherapeutic procedures establishes a strong precedent for that individual's personal sense of competence and self-reliance.

This brings us to our concluding observation. Although we have endeavored to provide hypnotherapy scripts that we have found to be useful with many different types of clients, it must be emphasized again that these scripts were designed to serve as templates or examples. To the extent that they are relevant to the needs and dynamics of any given individual, they may prove to be therapeutically useful. On the other hand, we strongly encourage you to begin as soon as possible devising metaphors and phrasings for each of your clients that are specifically selected to express the unique problems and personality of that client and your own unique style as well.

Our initial injunction to workshop participants to trust their unconscious probably did not work very well because their unconscious minds had not yet had an opportunity to learn what was needed. Thus, if you practice creating hypnotherapy scripts using the instructions and examples presented here until you have developed a familiarity with the basic concepts and processes, you can then trust your unconscious. Its powers of observation, comprehension, and creativity may surprise you and your clients as well.

APPENDIX A

*Results of the Research
Project to Study the
Effectiveness of Scripts*

The subjects for this study were thirteen graduate students in psychology and related fields who volunteered to participate in a free one-day workshop and research project on hypnotherapy. Following a didactic training session the participants were randomly divided into a script condition (n = 7) and a no-script condition (n = 6) and were instructed to pair up and take turns inducing hypnotic trance with arm levitation. The subjects in the script group simply read the script. The subjects in the no-script condition made it up as they went.

Each of the thirteen participants completed a five-item questionnaire prior to the workshop and immediately following his or her practice session. The questionnaire asked the participants to use a four-point scale (1 = poor, 4 = excellent) to rate: (a) their skills in hypnotic induction, (b) their ability to elicit an arm levitation, (c) their self-confidence in their ability to induce a trance, (d) their comfort with using hypnosis in an actual clinical setting, and (e) the odds that they actually would attempt to use hypnosis in a clinical setting. In addition, after a participant had served as a practice subject he or she was asked to complete a questionnaire regarding the depth of trance experienced (1 = none, 4 = very deep), the degree of lightness or lifting experienced in the arm (1 = none, 4 = very strong), and any increase in understanding of trance as a result of that trance experience (1 = none, 4 = very great).

The results are presented in Tables 1 and 2. Briefly stated, the preworkshop self-ratings of the participants eventually assigned to the script condition did not differ

Table 1
Self-Ratings as Hypnotists

Variable Rated		Script N = 7		No Script N = 6	
		$\bar{X}$	S.D.	$\bar{X}$	S.D.
I. Skills in hypnotic induction	Pre	1.714	.488	1.667	.816 (N. S.)
	Post	2.857 (p<.01)	.377	2.333 (N.S.)	.516 (p<.05)
II. Ability to elicit an arm levitation	Pre	1.429	.534	1.167	.408 (N. S.)
	Post	3.143 (p<.01)	.690	1.833 (N.S.)	1.329 (p<.05)
III. Self-confidence in ability to induce trance	Pre	1.714	.756	1.667	.816 (N. S.)
	Post	3.143 (p<.01)	.690	2.166 (N.S.)	.752 (p<.05)
IV. Comfort with ability to use hypnosis in a clinical setting	Pre	1.714	.488	1.500	.548 (N. S.)
	Post	3.000 (p<.01)	.577	2.000 (N.S.)	.894 (p<.05)
V. Odds of attempting to use hypnosis in a clinical setting	Pre	1.714	.756	2.167	.983 (N. S.)
	Post	3.429 (p<.01)	.787	2.500 (N.S.)	.837 (p<.05)

Table 2
Self-Ratings of Hypnosis Subjects

Variable Rated	Script N = 7		No Script N = 6	
	$\bar{X}$	S.D.	$\bar{X}$	S.D.
I. Depth of trance	3.000	.577	2.333	.516 (p<.05)
II. Degree of arm levitation experienced	3.714	.488	2.000	1.095 (p<.05)
III. Learning from the trance experience	3.429	.534	2.667	.516 (p<.05)

significantly from the preworkshop self-ratings of the participants eventually assigned to the no-script practice condition. By the end of the workshop, however, the self-ratings of the participants who used a script had increased significantly on each item (p's < .01), whereas the ratings of the participants in the no-script practice condition had not changed significantly. Along the same lines, the post-practice ratings obtained in the script condition are significantly higher than the post-practice ratings of the no-script participants (p's < .05).

These increases in self-confidence may be attributable to the simple fact that the script worked and the unstructured practice did not. This is reflected by the ratings obtained from the hypnotic subjects during these practice conditions. Ratings of trance depth, arm levitation, and learning from the experience all were significantly higher in the script condition than in the no-script condition (p's < .01).

The results of this simple study confirmed our hypotheses regarding the potential value of hypnosis scripts as a means of increasing skills and self-confidence. They also confirmed our decision to provide scripts for every step in the hypnotherapeutic process. This book is the product of that decision.

REFERENCES

Bandler, R. & Grinder, J. (1975). *Patterns of the hypnotic techniques of Milton H. Erickson, M.D.: Volume I*. Cupertino, CA: Meta Publications.

Bargh, J. A., & Chartrand, T. L. (1999). The unbearable automaticity of being. *American Psychologist, 54*(7), 462–479.

Bownds, M. D. (1999). *The biology of mind: Origins and structures of mind, brain, and consciousness*. Bethesda, MD: Fitzgerald Science Press.

Brickman, H. (2000). *The thin book: Hypnotherapy trance scripts for weight management*. Phoenix, AZ: Zeig, Tucker & Co.

Corsini, R. J. (1978). *Readings in current personality theories*. Itasca, IL: F. E. Peacock.

Cousins, N. (1976). *Anatomy of an illness*. New York: Norton.

Csikszentmihalyi, M. (1990). *Flow: The psychology of optimal experience*. New York: Harper & Row.

Csikszentmihalyi, M. (1993). *The evolving self: A psychology for the third millennium.* New York: HarperCollins.

Csikszentmihalyi, M. (1997). *Finding flow: The psychology of engagement in everyday life.* New York: Basic Books.

Erickson, M. H. (1954a). Pseudo-orientation in time as a hypnotherapeutic procedure. *The Journal of Clinical and Experimental Hypnosis, 2,* 261–283.

Erickson, M. H. (1954b). Special techniques of brief hypnotherapy. *The Journal of Clinical and Experimental Hypnosis, 2,* 109–129.

Erickson, M. H. (1966). The burden of responsibility in effective psychotherapy. *The American Journal of Clinical Hypnosis, 6,* 269–271.

Erickson, M. H. (1980). *The collected papers of Milton H. Erickson on hypnosis. Vol. III: Hypnotic Investigation of psychodynamic processes.* (Edited by Ernest L. Rossi). New York: Irvington Publishers.

Erickson, M. H. (1983). *Healing in hypnosis: The seminars, workshops, and lectures of Milton H. Erickson.* (Edited by E. L. Rossi, M. O. Ryan, & F. A. Sharp) New York: Irvington Publishers.

Erickson, M. H. (1985). *Life reframing in hypnosis: The seminars, workshops, and lectures of Milton H. Erickson.* (Edited by Rossi, E. L. & Ryan, M. O.) New York: Irvington Publishers.

Erickson, M. H. (2001). *The seminars of Milton H. Erickson: Number 1.* Phoenix, AZ: Milton H. Erickson Foundation Press.

Erickson, M. H., & Rossi, E. (1977). Autohypnotic experiences of Milton H. Erickson. *American Journal of Clinical Hypnosis, 20*(1), 36–54.

Erickson, M. H., Rossi, E. L., & Rossi, S. I. (1976). *Hypnotic realities: The induction of clinical hypnosis and forms of indirect suggestion.* New York: Irvington Publishers.

Ewin, D. M. (2001). Letter to the editor: What suggestion is best for pain? *American Journal of Clinical Hypnosis, 43*(3 & 4), 329.

Faymonville, M. E., Meurisse, M., & Fissette, J. (1999). Hypnosedation: A valuable alternative to traditional anesthetic techniques. *Acta Chirurgica Belgica, 99,* 141–146.

Fisch, R., Weakland, J. H., & Segal, L. (1982). *The tactics of change.* San Francisco: Jossey-Bass Publishers.

Fisher, S. (1991). *Discovering the power of self-hypnosis: A new approach for enabling change and promoting healing.* New York: HarperCollins.

Fodor, J. A. (1983). *The modularity of the mind.* Cambridge, MA: The MIT Press.

Fromm, E. (1975). Self hypnosis: A new area of research. *Psychotherapy: Research, Theory, and Practice, 12,* 295–301.

Gallwey, W. T. (1974). *The inner game of tennis.* New York: Random House.

Gardener, H. (1993). *Multiple intelligences: The theory in practice.* New York: Basic Books.

Gazzaniga, M. S. (1983). Right hemisphere language following brain bisection: A 20-year perspective. *American Psychologist, 38*(5), 525–537.

Gazzaniga, M. S., Bogen, J. E., & Sperry, R. W. (1967). Dyspraxia following division of the cerebral commissures. *Archives of Neurology, 16,* 606–612.

Gendlin, E. T. (1981). *Focusing.* New York: Bantam Books.

Gerrig, R. J., & Pillow, B. H. (1998). A developmental perspective on the construction of disbelief. In J. de Rivera & T. R. Sarbin (Eds.), *Believed-in imaginings* (pp. 101–119). Washington, DC: American Psychological Association.

Gilligan, S. (1987). *Therapeutic trances: The cooperation principle in Ericksonian hypnotherapy.* New York: Brunner/Mazel.

Hafen, B. Q., Karren, K. J., Frandsen, K. J., & Smith, N. L. (1996). *Mind/body health: The effects of attitudes, emotions and relationships.* Needham Heights, MA: Allyn & Bacon.

Haley, J. (1973). *Uncommon therapy: The psychiatric techniques of Milton H. Erickson, M.D.* New York: W. W. Norton.

Haley, J. (1985). *Conversations with Milton H. Erickson, M.D. Vol. 1: Changing individuals.* New York: Triangle Press.

Haley, J. (1993). *Jay Haley on Milton H. Erickson.* New York: Brunner/Mazel.

Hammond, D. C. (Ed.) (1990). *Handbook of hypnotic suggestions and metaphors.* New York: W.W. Norton.

Havens, R. A. (1985). *The wisdom of Milton H. Erickson.* New York: Irvington Publishers.

Havens, R. A. (1986). Posthypnotic predetermination of therapeutic progress. *American Journal of Clinical Hypnosis, 28,* 258–262.

Havens, R. A. (1991). *Trance and "flow": Results of an Ericksonian attempt to teach subjects how to attain the state of focused attention Csikszentmihalyi has identified as the basis for optimal performance and tranquility.* Paper presented at the annual meeting of the American Society of Clinical Hypnosis, St. Louis, MO.

Hunter, M. E. (1994). *Creative scripts for hypnotherapy.* New York: Brunner/Mazel.

Kirsch, I., & Lynn, S. J. (1997). Hypnotic involuntariness and the automacity of everyday life. *American Journal of Clinical Hypnosis, 40*(1), 329–348.

Kirsch, I., & Lynn, S. J. (1999). Automaticity in clinical psychology. *American Psychologist, 54,* 504–515.

Koestler, A. (1967). *The ghost in the machine.* Chicago: Henry Regnery Company.

Libet, B. (1985). Unconscious cerebral initiative and the role of conscious will in voluntary action. *Behavioral and Brain Sciences, 8,* 529–566.

Martinez-Tendro, J., Capafons, A., & Cardena, E. (2001). Rapid self-hypnosis: A new self-hypnosis method and its comparison with the Hypnotic Induction Profile (HIP). *American Journal of Clinical Hypnosis, 44*(1), 3–11.

Olness, K., & Libbey, P. (1987). Unrecognized biologic bases of behavioral symptoms in patients referred for hypnotherapy. *American Journal of Clinical Hypnosis, 30*(1), 1–8.

Ornstein, R. (1991). *The evolution of consciousness.* New York: Prentice Hall.

Ornstein, R., & Sobel, D. (1989). *Healthy pleasures.* New York: Addison-Wesley.

Peele, S. (1989). *Diseasing of America: Addiction treatment out of control.* Lexington, MA: Lexington Books.

Rosen, S. (1982). *My voice will go with you.* New York: W. W. Norton.

Rossi, E. L. (Ed.). (1980). *The collected papers of Milton H. Erickson on hypnosis.* New York: Irvington.

Rossi, E. L. (1986). *The psychobiology of mind-body healing: New concepts of therapeutic hypnosis.* New York: W. W. Norton.

Rossi, E. L., & Cheek, D. B. (1988). *Mind-body therapy: Methods of ideodynamic healing in hypnosis.* New York: W. W. Norton.

Seaward, B. L. (1999). *Managing stress.* Sudbury, MA: Jones and Bartlett.

Seligman, M. P., & Csikszentmihalyi, M. (2000). Positive psychology: An introduction. *American Psychologist, 55*(1), 5–14.

Stanton, H. E. (1991). Diagnostic trance: Its value in the school environment. *Journal of the Society for Accelerative Learning and Teaching, 16*(3), 267–285.

Walters, C. & Havens, R. A. (1993). *Hypnotherapy for health, harmony, and peak performance: Expanding the goals of psychotherapy.* New York: Brunner/Mazel.

Wegner, D. M., & Wheatley, T. (1999). Apparent mental causation: Sources of the experience of will. *American Psychologist, 54*(7), 480–492.

Zeig, J. (1980). *A teaching seminar with Milton H. Erickson.* New York: Brunner/Mazel.

Zeig, J. K. (1985). *Experiencing Erickson: An introduction to the man and his work.* New York: Brunner/Mazel.

Printed in Great Britain
by Amazon